COURT OF APPEAL

COURT OF APPEAL

THE BLACK COMMUNITY SPEAKS OUT ON THE RACIAL AND SEXUAL POLITICS OF CLARENCE THOMAS VS. ANITA HILL

Edited by
Robert Chrisman and Robert L. Allen

Ballantine Books New York

To Thurgood Marshall and the many generations of Black Americans who have struggled for our freedom and equality.

Published in the United States by Ballantine Books, a division of Random House, Inc., New York, and simultaneously in Canada by Random House of Canada Limited, Toronto.

Most of the contents of this work originally appeared in the Winter 1991–Spring 1992 issue of *The Black Scholar: Journal of Black Studies and Research.*

"Becoming the Third Wave" originally appeared in *Ms.* Magazine.

Grateful acknowledgment is made to The New York Times Magazine for permission to reprint "Taking Sides Against Ourselves" by Rosemary L. Bray. Copyright © 1991 by Rosemary L. Bray. Reprinted with permission from The New York Times Magazine.

Library of Congress Catalog Card Number: 92-73580

ISBN: 0-345-38136-X

Cover design by Kristine V. Mills

Text design by Holly Johnson

Manufactured in the United States of America

First Ballantine Books Edition: September 1992

10 9 8 7 6 5 4 3 2 1

Acknowledgments

The Black Scholar gives special thanks to its dedicated staff, Marsha Carter, Betty Brundage-Turk, and Camille Spencer and to Editorial Consultant Delores M. Mortimer. Special thanks to the Center for Afroamerican and African Studies at the University of Michigan, Ann Arbor, for the award of a faculty research grant to Robert Christman, which assisted him in his work on this book.

Robert Christman
Robert L. Allen

Editors' Note

To preserve the flavor and intent of these essays, we have retained the style of each author, with reference to the terms, black, Black, and African American. These essays draw from a number of disciplines with different conventions for documentation, endnotes, and text citation, and we have preserved that variety.

CONTENTS

INTRODUCTION

Few recent events in the United States have generated such a level of controversy and debate as the Senate Judiciary Committee's confirmation hearings on Judge Clarence Thomas's fitness to serve as the 106th Justice of the U.S. Supreme Court.

The process was charged with suspense from the moment President George Bush nominated Judge Thomas to fill the vacancy created by the retirement of Justice Thurgood Marshall, the only African-American ever to sit on the High Court. At the heart of the problem is the fact that, in all of U.S. history, there have been but this one black Justice and three black senators—Hiram R. Revels (R-MS, 1870–1871), who was appointed to serve out Confederate president Jefferson Davis's term; Blanche K. Bruce (R-MS, 1875–1881); and Edward W. Brooke (R-MA, 1966–1978)—an insufficient presence to establish a black tradition of jurisprudence, inquiry, and method at the national level. The absence of such a tradition, and the question of how to represent a powerful minority that is systematically disenfranchised from government bodies, has resulted in total public confusion—both black and white—in all aspects of the political process.

The very composition of the U.S. Senate and the Judiciary Committee—overwhelmingly white and male—could only inflame the tinderbox situation that finally exploded with the testimony of Professor

Anita Hill charging Judge Thomas with sexual harassment in the workplace. The testimony of Professor Hill did two things. First, it brought a substantive charge against Clarence Thomas's fitness to serve on the Supreme Court. And, secondly, it catalyzed the fundamental issues around both black American rights and women's rights that the Senate had been so carefully trying to skirt. In however spontaneous a fashion, this intervention brought the popular voices of blacks and women of all colors into the Senate chambers with a powerful presence and immediacy.

Over the few short weeks of the Clarence Thomas confirmation hearings—from September 10 to October 14, 1991—the entire spectrum of the histories, realities, metaphors, and mythologies of black-white relations, as well as the various relationships within the African-American community itself, was played out again via television in the nation's living rooms.

The confrontation between the United States Senate, Clarence Thomas, and Anita Hill also underscored white America's continuing obsession with the unresolved business of racial justice in this country. The evidence for this distinctively American preoccupation can be seen in the long-lasting impression created in the national psyche by such ideologically charged works of fiction and film as *Uncle Tom's Cabin* (1852), *Birth of a Nation* (1915), and *Roots* (novel, 1976; television, 1977). These race-based sagas present the major icons, myths, and metaphors that continue to haunt and shape the American imagination and that helped determine the powerful national response to an actual historical event of major magnitude—the Clarence Thomas confirmation hearings.

Two days after the hearings concluded, the Senate voted 52 to 48 to confirm Clarence Thomas as the newest Associate Justice of the Supreme Court. And yet, the deeper meaning and true impact of the hearings remained cloudy and unresolved. A vote for Clarence Thomas could be seen as either a liberal or a conservative gesture; as a pro-black or anti-black statement; or as an absolution of Thomas from the charges of sexual harassment.

What did all this mean to the black community? In order to provide a national forum for dialogue and debate, *The Black Scholar* decided to issue a call to more than eighty of the leading black intellectuals, scholars, artists, and activists for papers analyzing the meaning and impact of the drama that had unfolded in Washington.

Since 1969, *The Black Scholar: Journal of Black Studies and Research* has devoted itself to a critique of the black condition and an analysis of the African-American perspective in both historical and contemporary movements. Its mission is rooted in the philosophy of reciprocity of thought and action, and the belief that intellectuals are also individuals who assume the responsibility for acting upon their ideas.

Over the years, *The Black Scholar* has provided an outstanding forum for research, scholarship, and criticism on such important issues as the black prisoner's movement; the black sexism debate; the anti-apartheid struggle in South Africa; events in Nicaragua, Grenada, and Cuba; and the recent social crises of the black family and the black underclass. These vital subjects have been examined by black intellectuals, scholars, artists, and activists representing a wide variety of ideological persuasions.

The response to our call on the Clarence Thomas–Anita Hill controversy was enthusiastic and swift. Within two months we had received over thirty-five essays presenting commentaries spanning the full sociopolitical spectrum—from ultraconservative to liberal to radical, and from both women and men. This collection became *The Black Scholar*'s special Spring 1992 issue: "The Clarence Thomas Confirmation." It offered the black community its first opportunity to explore such vital issues as:

• How do African-Americans perceive their interests? Is there a contradiction between Clarence Thomas's hostility toward the traditional black agenda of strong governmental support for civil rights and social and economic justice, and the support he received from blacks?

• The disturbing sexist backlash against Professor Hill and what it says about the position of black women—and by extension all women—in the U.S.;

• The inability of some members of the Judiciary Committee to comprehend the very existence and nature of sexual harassment;

• White America's continuing confusion and fixation on black sexuality;

• The character, goals, and values of the new generation of post–civil rights blacks;

• The media's skilled reformulation and manipulation of race-based images and stereotypes.

INTEGRATION AND THE SUPREME COURT

To fully appreciate the events of the Thomas confirmation, it is necessary to understand the historical and political context in which it took place. The issue at hand in the politically charged national arena was the filling of a vacancy created by the retirement of the first black justice in U.S. history, Thurgood Marshall, whose tenure ran from 1967 to 1991.

However, the composition of the Supreme Court had long been a political issue. With its monumental decision of *Brown* v. *Board of Education* in 1954, the Court dissolved the legal, ideological, and cultural bases for the segregation of African-Americans. From that moment on the Court became a target of racist and conservative wrath.

Before the Brown decision, race relations in the U.S. had been determined by the Supreme Court ruling of *Plessy* v. *Ferguson,* 1896, which had upheld "separate but equal" facilities for blacks and whites. The practical effect of *Plessy* v. *Ferguson* was the legalization of segregation and the disenfranchisement of blacks in all social, economic, and political sectors. With the Brown ruling of 1954, and a supplemental decision—*Brown* v. *the Board of Education of Topeka* in 1955, which delegated to the Federal courts the task of evaluating desegregation activity—the deconstruction of Jim Crow society had begun.

The architect of the Brown case was Thurgood Marshall, then chief counsel for the National Association for the Advancement of Colored People (NAACP), who argued it before the Supreme Court. Under Marshall's direction, the legal strategy of the NAACP from 1948 on had become the total dissolution of segregation itself—not the correction of its abuses on a case-by-case basis.

Even with the Supreme Court's remarkable initiative in 1954, the struggle to dismantle Jim Crow structures had already made impressive gains during World War II. The push for desegregation had come from pressure groups, black demonstrations, spontaneous protests, and the growing liberalism in establishment circles. Franklin Delano Roosevelt's Executive Order 8802 of June 25, 1941, integrated the wartime labor force by barring discrimination in government and in the defense industry. Roosevelt's action came in direct response to national black pressure, notably the planned March on Washington of July 1, 1941, spearheaded by labor leader A. Phillip Randolph, with the cooperation of the NAACP.

At the conclusion of World War II, most of the realistic thinkers in this country understood that the U.S. could not present itself to the world as a model democracy as long as blacks continued to be segregated and deprived of full participation in American society. There may have been an Iron Curtain in Europe, but there was also a Cotton Curtain in the United States.

Direct action was also taken by Presidents Harry S. Truman (1945–1952) and Dwight D. Eisenhower (1952–1960). On July 26, 1948, Truman issued Executive Orders 9980 and 9981, which began the integration of the U.S. armed forces, a process that was finally completed in 1954. Truman's orders created the Fair Employment Board to eliminate discrimination in the Civil Service, and established the President's Committee on Equality of Opportunity in the Armed Services. As it had in the Civil War, battlefield necessity also established a basis for equality.

In World War II only 30 percent of black troops overseas were in combat units, among them the 99th Pursuit Squadron, the first black unit in the Air Force, and the 761st Tank Battalion, the first black armored unit in combat in the war. The 761st was attached to General George S. Patton's 3rd Army. In his welcoming address, Patton said: "Men, you're the first Negro tankers ever to fight in the American Army. I would never have asked for you if you weren't good. I don't care what color you are, so long as you go up there and kill those Kraut sons-a-bitches."

In his 1948 platform, President Truman insisted upon a civil rights plank, despite the Dixiecrat rebellion of Southern segregationists led by Strom Thurmond, then Governor of South Carolina. Truman also became the first President to address the NAACP.

Parallels were also occurring in popular culture. In sports, the Brooklyn Dodgers integrated professional baseball in 1947 with the hiring of Jackie Robinson. Soon after, black athletes were integrating other formerly all-white professional sports.

In the entertainment field, blacks began to appear as fully

rounded characters in such films as *Lifeboat* (1944) and *Home of the Brave* (1949). Increasingly, a number of post-war films explored the problem of human relations in a society plagued by racism. Hollywood's first black superstar, Sidney Poitier, appeared in a number of such films, debuting in *No Way Out* (1950), and continuing with *Blackboard Jungle* (1955), *Edge of the City* (1957), *The Defiant Ones* (1958), and *A Raisin in the Sun* (1961).

From the late 1950s through the 1980s, Congress and the Presidency established the basic legislative foundation of contemporary civil rights. Racist resistance occurred in the form of Ku Klux Klan activity, the creation of White Citizens Councils by segregationists in 1954, and the blockage of integration initiatives in the House and Senate.

In one such instance, on September 2, 1957, Arkansas Governor Orval Faubus deployed the state National Guard to take control of Central High School where nine black children were to be integrated. On September 29, 1957, President Eisenhower mobilized the National Guard and sent in the 327th Battle Group of the 101st Airborne Division to assure the integration of Central High School. Thus, he became the first president since the Reconstruction period to employ Federal police power to protect black rights.

President John F. Kennedy continued this policy with the use of Federal marshals to ensure James Meredith's enrollment in the University of Mississippi in September of 1962. President Kennedy also coined the phrase, "affirmative action," in his Executive Order 10025 of 1961, establishing the precedent of aggressive hiring of Afro-Americans to overcome the legacy of biased hiring practices with agencies and institutions operating with federal funds.

Over fifteen major pieces of legislation were passed in this period, among them the Civil Rights Act of 1957, the comprehensive Civil Rights Act of 1964, the Voting Rights Act of 1965, and the Equal Employment Opportunity Act of 1972. In 1957 the U.S. Commission on Civil Rights, and in 1964 the Equal Employment Opportunity Commission (EEOC) were also established through this legislation. On their own initiative, black Congress members created the Congressional Black Caucus in 1971, which addresses itself to national black social, economic, and political issues.

The Supreme Court was, of course, the final arbiter of such

executive and legislative actions. Because of its high visibility and its power to crystallize ideological issues, as well as its political malleability—nine individuals appointed by the Executive Branch and approved by the Senate—the Court became the target of conservative forces who opposed this liberal trend.

In the late 1950s and 1960s, a campaign to impeach liberal Justice William O. Douglas was launched by the John Birch Society. Among the advocates for impeachment were Republican Senator Barry Goldwater of Arizona and former President Gerald Ford. All through the 70s, the conservatives continued their demand for a restructuring of the Supreme Court. Finally, by 1980, the right wing of the Republican party was in power, and Ronald Reagan had become President. Boosted by Nixon's appointment of William Rehnquist, Reagan went ahead with the restructuring of the Supreme Court full steam, appointing Justices Sandra Day O'Connor, Anthony M. Kennedy, and Antonin Scalia.

With George Bush's incumbency, the high drama centered on the issue of how a conservative president would respond to the upcoming vacancy of Thurgood Marshall's seat on the Supreme Court. Justice Marshall had come to represent not only the black community but also the most liberal thought on the Court. Would Bush appoint another black or a member of another minority to the Court? Or, a conservative white?

President Bush's answer was Clarence Thomas. He was a black and a jurist, but he was also a conservative with a long record of opposition to existing civil rights legislation and affirmative action programs. Thomas, a graduate of Yale Law School, had also publicly upbraided Thurgood Marshall and civil rights leaders.

Bush's nomination flaunted both mainstream black and liberal preferences, and offered a difficult proposition. If one endorsed the idea of black representation and supported Clarence Thomas, one opposed the black agenda. On the other hand, if one opposed Clarence Thomas for his record, it might very well mean sacrificing black representation on the Supreme Court for years to come. Furthermore, a white liberal would feel impelled to vote for a black person, as would vigorous black advocates of representative interests.

Like a skillful chess player, President Bush had forked white liberals and African-Americans with Clarence Thomas, his black knight, and established the politics of racial representation as the venue through which the nomination would be debated on national television. Once on television, the process would follow standard marketing procedure. As historian Earl Lewis observes in his essay, "Race as Commodity: Hill and Thomas as Consumer Products:"

> The selling of Clarence Thomas has many antecedents in American history. If one thinks of the history of advertising in this country, you realize that the techniques were perfected by selling people of African descent. . . . After the abolition of slavery, the selling of blacks continued—although in different form. The commodifiers no longer sold people, they sold images of groups. The message always had dual themes and minstrelsy and vaudeville expanded its audience. We gleaned from the cultural lesson plan that blacks were docile, simple-minded, child-like creatures and sophisticated dandies and no-goods.

The wide-ranging essays compiled here represent the power, the wit, and the passion of black intellectuals responding to a moment of crisis. The Clarence Thomas confirmation hearings marked a defining moment for this era, and these essays rise to that challenge, with all the strength, engagement, and intelligence that distinguishes the African-American intellectual community as a national and international force of magnitude.

TELEVISION: STEREOTYPE AND SPECTACLE

Since the 1960s, television has become more than a medium through which we are informed about reality. It is the vehicle through which a great many of us interpret our lives and the events of our world. In fact, the images television has given us have come to define much of recent history: gray aircraft carriers on shrouded seas; the chatter of helicopters; water cannons and police dogs tearing black flesh; napalm burning Vietnamese children; the shrill fury of a Nixon aide; or the avuncular drone of a Southern white senator; panic and the assassins—Oswald, Ruby, Sirhan, and the failed Hinckley. Increasingly we have come to experience all the major rituals and celebrations of life through the TV screens in our homes.

While television's wide-ranging coverage may be seen as a natural outcome of democratic government, it may also be viewed as a subversion of the very democratic processes it seems to enhance. This is because television's powers of sensual saturation inflame the continuing tensions between reason and emotion, judgment and prejudice, reflection and impulse. On television, image becomes reality, symbol becomes substance, sound becomes sense, and shock becomes cognition. This produces an intimate compatibility between television and ideology, between visual images and the evocation of unconscious and profound hopes and fears, yearnings and anxieties.

Ideology exists primarily at the unconscious level, and any skilled producer or performer in the television medium—actor, president, athlete, lawyer, executive, victim, or defendant—pitches to the ideological as well as the cognitive dimensions of the audience and courts the irrational in the guise of fact. Modern democracy's premises of reason, education, detachment, rational judgment, and careful deliberation are regularly challenged and increasingly scorned by those who make clever use of the medium for their own purposes.

For example, George Bush's 1988 presidential campaign, headed by Lee Atwater, produced anti-Dukakis ads in which the lurid images of black rapist Willie Horton, a polluted Boston harbor, and a meandering Sherman tank were juxtaposed with images of a relaxed, patriarchal George Bush swathed in the flag, playing with children, and caring for the elderly, in a setting of mythical Midwestern small-town nostalgia.

Since antiquity public spectacle has been used as a powerful medium for molding public opinion, and today, television is its most convenient vehicle. The special capacity of spectacle to engage all the senses, its power to evoke and intensify simple and primordial emotions, and the exaggerated sense of group solidarity that it creates are especially appealing to so many of us today who have become increasingly alienated from the basic textures of life. Ironically, however, the isolated circumstances under which we watch television preclude any real participation by the audience. Since 1960, public crises, continuing alienation, and the temporary catharsis of the buildup of tensions through televised spectacle have become a staple of American politics. And, in fact, it has increasingly become a kind of government.

THE COURT OF APPEAL

Thus when the Clarence Thomas confirmation hearings reached their climax in October 1991, television became an electronic arbiter for the nation, its amphitheater for reviewing—or as some might say, venting—the unresolved issues of racial and gender justice. In the words of literary and cultural critic David Lionel Smith in "The Thomas Spectacle: Power, Impotence, and Melodrama":

> [The process] also incited the emotional engagement of the public, thus giving the illusion of democratic participation, while at the same time revealing the impotence and confusion of the public as spectators empowered to make noise but not to make change. This is the paradox of television; It appears to offer immediate participation, but in fact, it perpetuates alienation.

Racial images and stereotypes held toward black Americans were evoked the moment George Bush nominated Clarence Thomas on the eve of July 4. Clarence Thomas—young, vigorous, affable, smiling—was extolled by his sponsors George Bush and Senator John Danforth as a self-made black man in the Horatio Alger tradition, who had succeeded despite childhood poverty and racial prejudice. Thus purified in the American crucible of poverty, hard work, and duty, Thomas's race did not matter. President Bush assured the American public that this was an appointment of pure merit, that Thomas was "the best man for the job." Thomas's conservative philosophy of black self-help, his eschewal of affirmative action, economic and educational endowment, and all social-enrichment programs for minorities were hailed as a continuation of Booker T. Washington's philosophy of black self-reliance. All of this suggested to white America that this black man had earned the nomination on his own.

Within the persona presented to the public there were individual touches: Thomas was independent enough as an undergraduate to have smoked reefer, read Malcolm X, and protested campus racism. Later he would marry, divorce, remarry, change his religion, and be enough of a "man's man" to enjoy earthy movies and be a Dallas Cowboy fan in Washington Redskin territory. Thomas also claimed to have had no prior thoughts on *Roe* v. *Wade,* the liberal cornerstone decision for current abortion policy, and while he had discussed natural law, it was in terms of its use as a rebuttal to pro-slavery arguments, not in any anti-abortion context.

The obvious complexity of this man was shunted aside in preference for a simplistic image of an honest, hard-working black man who accepts his lot in white America, much like the faithful slave, or the contented servant of minstrelsy, vaudeville, film, and television. In the theater of ethnic politics, Clarence Thomas was viewed as a trustworthy, compliant black man by his supporters, and an "Uncle Tom" by his detractors—that is, a black man deliberately catering to the racist expectations of white America from motives of fear, profit, or self-hatred. America was reassured.

And yet, within ninety days, another Clarence Thomas emerged—A sensual black man who extorted sexual favors from black women, spoke with vulgarity, and relished pornographic films. In testimony, Thomas dropped his smiling demeanor, rocked back and forth in his chair, his face pulsing with fury. He spoke with anger and disdain of the nomination process, which he dismissed as a "high-tech lynching of an uppity black man," and challenged the Senate committee to make short work of him. Ironically, this final transformation secured the nomination for Clarence Thomas.

If one regards the Thomas hearings as theater, this rapid role change, from contented slave to primitive black to angry militant, was not inconsistent. Blacks have always been forced to play roles in this society, both to accommodate and to thwart white America's obsession with racial stereotypes. The existential circumstances of black life itself require constant improvisation and manipulation, simply to survive. Ralph Ellison's novel *Invisible Man* affords us such a figure in Bliss Proteus Rinehart, a black trickster who moves easily through a dazzling array of black personae, ranging from storefront preacher to street hustler, numbers runner to reefer man.

Thus, Clarence Thomas's switch from smiling obsequiousness to chair-rocking anger was credible because the American populace had already been schooled in a theater that freely interchanges these symbolic characters, much as the heroine of *Swan Lake* moves easily from Odette, the good white swan, to Odile, the demonic black swan, with no burden upon the Russian imagination, or as the commedia del l'arte manipulates masks and types. The cultural roots of the Clarence Thomas hearings lie in the minstrel show, an art form originated by white actors in the South during the 1830s and 1840s. Fuelled by increasing Northern criticism of plantation slavery, Southerners defended their treatment of blacks through the theater of propaganda, presenting blacks as primitive, animalistic creatures bound to the basic impulses of lust, anger, and sensualism.

Blacks, they maintained, were incapable of abstract thought or reasonable behavior. Whenever blacks did venture into the realm of reason, culture, and imagination, the results were either comical, because misapplied, as in Zep Coon or the Kingfish of the "Amos 'n' Andy" radio show; or they were seen as sinister, because they reflected self-realization and resistance against slavery, as in the character of the "bad nigger." Blacks were thus happiest under the guidance of the benign Southerner, not the abolitionist Yankee.

Performed by whites in blackface, the minstrel show was a complete mockery of the humanity of the African-American, for the imposition of a homogeneous mask of blackness on a white face denied all variety and heterogeneity to the black American. Uniformity of features was matched by uniformity of clothing—the billowing aprons and mammy dresses, head wraps, serving jackets, or various cuts of rough and tasteless clothing.

During Reconstruction the stereotypes were reformulated to demonstrate the dangers of freed blacks and their incapacity for political leadership and self-government. In her essay, "Tom, Buck, and Sambo, or How Clarence Thomas Got to the Supreme Court," Llenda Jackson-Leslie marks three progressions in the Thomas persona, from Uncle Tom, "he will hear not one word against old massa," to Sambo, "that colorful, comic minstrel character who can remember nothing without his master's help," on to " 'Buck,' a virile, insatiably sexual black man who satisfies his casual lusts with black women but whose heartfelt desire is for white women . . . [and who] also had a reputation for being bad and uncontrollable."

When Thomas came up against the testimony of Anita Hill, all the stereotypical roles assigned to the black woman came into play once again. These images were intended to rationalize the sexual vulnerability and abuse the black woman suffered from white men and women under slavery, not only through rape and sexual extortion, but through severance from her family, the torture of her husband, and the sale of her children. Like the black male, she was thought to be lacking civilized graces, as promiscuous, and as yielding easily to her animal impulses. Most importantly, the black was seen as having no sexual integrity that any white man, or woman, was bound to respect.

Jackson-Leslie notes that:

> Although Hill's behavior and demeanor did not conform, she was portrayed as a black woman bringing a "good" black man down. Like Lena Horne's sultry temptress in "Cabin in the Sky"; Dorothy Dandridge's amoral gold digger in "Carmen Jones"; or Fredi Washington's tragic mulatta in "Imitation of Life," Hill just didn't know her "place." Hill bore the brunt of intraracial hatred: the resentment of black men toward upwardly mobile black women; the contempt of black men who view all black women as bitches, skeezers, and 'ho's; the envy of black women who are less talented and less attractive.

According to these old stereotypes, because of their sexual appetites, black males and females cannot have a steadfast relationship. When Anita Hill presented her testimony of alleged sexual harassment by Clarence Thomas before an all-white male Senate committee, she asserted her dignity in the face of such prejudice. In response, she suffered the full fury of male racism and sexism, particularly from senators Specter, Hatch, and Simpson, who impugned her motives, her integrity, and even her sanity.

The fact that she was a tenured law professor at the University of Oklahoma, a graduate of Yale Law School, and a citizen testifying reluctantly in response to an FBI investigation and a Senate subpoena carried little weight with this committee. Clearly a compelling witness, Hill spoke with clarity, poise, and intelligence, but more effort was put into discrediting her than into pondering her testimony. That testimony had already been dismissed twice, once by the FBI evaluation that it was "not significant," and then by the Senate committee's decision not to consider it. Only public protest brought Anita Hill's testimony to national attention.

The fact that Anita Hill and Clarence Thomas were placed in conflict with each other intensified the impact of racial stereotype. As professor and film critic Clyde Taylor observes in "Clarence Thomas and the Question of Fitness":

> We were being asked to choose between two venomous myths. One, that black women, not being angels, must be whores, with no feelings about their sexuality that men need respect (a variation on the Dred Scott decision). . . . Or two, that black men of whatever training were oversexed, animalistic rapists unable to control their impulses. . . .

For Maulana Karenga in "Under the Camouflage of Color and Gender: The Dread and Drama of Thomas-Hill," the televised confrontation was a variation upon those "battles royal" depicted in Ralph Ellison's *Invisible Man* and Richard Wright's *Black Boy* in which two blacks fight for the amusement of a white crowd:

> One could not help but remember the Holocaust of Enslavement and the "buck fights" and "nigger fights" which whites staged for their own perverse entertainment. It is this spectacle of mutual degradation that made Black people reject Hill's eleventh-hour appearance and all it stereotypically represented.

For Trellie Jeffers, "We Have Heard: We Have Seen: Do We Believe? The Clarence Thomas–Anita Hill Hearing," the final outcome was pathetic:

> For Black America, nothing positive came from the Clarence Thomas-Anita Hill hearings. Personally, I felt that black women were raped on national television, and black men were doused with gasoline and burned in front of one million viewers.

CRISIS IN THE BLACK COMMUNITY: "SELECTIVE BLACKNESS"

In addition to these political and ideological concerns, the Clarence Thomas confirmation hearings raised a number of other questions for African-Americans. How do African-Americans perceive their interests in view of the seeming contradiction between Thomas's hostility toward the traditional black agenda of strong governmental support for civil rights, social and economic justice, and the support he received from blacks? While blacks criticize sexist treatment of black females, how did this position square with the disturbing sexist backlash against Anita Hill? Many African-Americans who supported Thomas acknowledged misgivings about his qualifications and experience, yet insisted upon his nomination. Why? Many of the essays in *Court of Appeal* address exactly these questions.

The failure of blacks to achieve any general accord in such basic areas in the Clarence Thomas issue suggests a crisis of ideology within the black community. The black power ideology developed during the 1960s emphasized unity, pride, self-determination, economic empowerment, community control of black institutions, and the accountability of black leaders to the black community.

But the strategy and tactics for achieving such admirable goals were never clearly defined. The black community exists within the hegemony of Euro-American capitalism, whose development was based upon the exploitation of black labor and the denigration of black humanity. While black activists explored the contradiction between black power and white dominance and control in the broadest terms in the sixties, what that conflict meant within the black community, the block, the home, was not examined in analytical terms.

Today, coming to terms with how white racism operates as a cultural system within the black community and within black men and women, is essential even though it means facing some naked and unpleasant truths. As political scientist Charles P. Henry notes in "Clarence Thomas and the National Black Identity":

> . . . the hearings have led to unprecedented soul-searching in the black community. Issues of class and gender that have been simmering below the surface since the sixties have now burst into the open. The parade of black Yale law school

graduates before an all-white male panel of Senators should tell us a number of things about our contemporary situation.

Henry's comments raise questions about the vaunted new black middle class and its relationship to African-American political processes. Mainstream Americans—conservatives and liberals alike—have assumed that since the 1960s the key to the elevation of the black community lay in the development of a black middle class. In 1966, Stokely Carmichael (now Kwame Ture) proclaimed "Black Power" in the teeth of Mississippi racists. In 1972, Richard Nixon would say, "Black power is green power," and coined the slogan "Black capitalism" to enlist middle-class black support for his 1972 presidential bid.

The dream of a black middle class that would elevate all of black America is not unique to whites. Both Booker T. Washington and W. E. B. Du Bois developed such a model—Washington in economic terms, Du Bois with a social and political emphasis upon the talented tenth of the black population. Although theorists have often viewed these approaches as antagonistic, they are fundamentally complementary, as W. H. McClendon observes in his essay, "Dismal to Abysmal": "It is critical for civil rights struggles and self-help structures to be perceived as complementary and not as contradictory doctrines."

However, Du Bois discovered that too often this black elite absorbed the values of white America and became assimilated into the larger society, acting as collaborators rather than performing an oppositional role. This tendency calls into question the premise of a homogeneous, even monolithic, black society upon which much of the political theory of the 1960s was based. On the other hand, the recognition of different class interests offers the black community a timely opportunity for thorough class analysis and the creation of common accords.

The Clarence Thomas confirmation hearings brought many of these unresolved issues to a head, none more controversial than the emergence of the black conservatives.

BLACK CONSERVATIVES

Many commentators on the black condition have balked at the term "black conservative." Historically, conservative connotes an elite capitalist class that aggressively protects and advances its interests, that generates and sequesters wealth, and that is color-keyed "white."

Black Americans, in contrast, do not have a national bourgeoisie with wealth and political power comparable to the Fords, Rockefellers, Mellons, Vanderbilts, Carnegies, or Du Ponts. The largest single enterprise in Black America is the Johnson Publishing Company, which produces *Ebony, Jet, Sepia,* and other magazines, and grosses over $250 million a year.

The institution of slavery itself barred blacks from accumulating the vast wealth that the white elite of America garnered during that period in our nation's history. Since slavery, blacks have been locked into work and service modes. In the absence of the correlative power, wealth, and class standing of the white conservative establishment, what, then, is a "black conservative," and what do blacks have to conserve?

We find black conservatives such as Thomas Sowell and Shelby Steele highly critical of the social welfare programs constructed in the 1930s by President Franklin Roosevelt's programs to pull the nation out of the Great Depression, with concommitant social philosophy of liberalism. By establishing social security, unemployment insurance, health and nutrition programs, welfare and educational enrichment, liberal policies improved much of America's lot. But the black agenda was not completely fulfilled. Much of the discourse of black conservatives centers around the idea that liberal policies are designed to restrict black self-empowerment and possibilities. In their view, affirmative action, welfare, designated government contracts ("setasides"), and any other measures that treat blacks as a disadvantaged people restrict them from open competition and achievement of the American dream.

Black conservatism thus appears to be more of an ideological and attitudinal creed than it is a specific economic and political doctrine. It serves to rebut the perceived paternalism and racism of the current liberal posture toward blacks—that all blacks are ghetto dwellers, products of broken families, fugitives from the underclass, and deficient in mainstream cultural achievement.

But the very practice of this philosophy distances black conservatives from the black community as a whole, and, with it leads to a lack of social commitment to the general black community, under the rubric "I made it on my own." The black conservative vision might more reflect the attitudes and aspirations of a middle class that chafes at its frustrations than it does the ideology of a grand, national bourgeoisie. The liberal welfare state—the designated instrument for black advancement for the past sixty years—becomes the logical target of criticism because of its shortcomings and its visibility. Black conservatives are not unique in this regard. Similar critiques of the white American welfare state have been made by black radical groups with quite different agendas, such as the Marxist-Leninist Black Panthers and black nationalist Nation of Islam.

But despite the special nature of its origins, the black conservative orientation draws it into the orbit of those economic and political forces that are the most explicitly racist and that have benefited most from black exploitation. This contradiction lies at the base of the debate over black conservatism within the African-American community.

Clarence Thomas's conservatism derives from such sources. Since the era of Richard Nixon, Republicans have actively courted blacks in an effort to break the Democratic party's stronghold on that voter block. Thomas's chief supporters, Republican senators Strom Thurmond and John Danforth, are rooted in the Southern establishment, but they argue that their fresh approach to black empowerment might well succeed where several generations of liberalism have failed.

Many blacks, whatever their political orientation, partially concur in the criticism of liberalism and welfare programs. They have argued that Clarence Thomas, despite his deviation from liberal orthodoxy, should have the freedom to advance in his career, including a chance to serve on the Supreme Court.

Commenting on the hearings from this perspective, sociologist Orlando Patterson asserts in his essay "Race, Gender, and Liberal Fallacies" that:

> . . . superficial liberal stereotypes of blacks as victims or bootstrap heroes are seen for what they are, a new form of racism that finds it hard to imagine African-Americans not as a monolithic group but, as several of the African-American panelists on TV correctly informed the nation, a diverse aggregate of perhaps 30 million individuals with all the class

differences, subcultural and regional resources, strength, flaws, and ideologies we find in other large populations.

In "Testimony," anthropologist and president of Lincoln University Niara Sudarkasa reviews the African-American political tradition from this perspective. Within it she discerns several tendencies, notably a political and economic black nationalism framed by the views of Martin Delany, Booker T. Washington, and Marcus Garvey. For Sudarkasa, who supported his nomination, Clarence Thomas legitimately belongs within that tradition.

Poet Maya Angelou, well known for her liberal views, supported Clarence Thomas on this basis in "I Dare to Hope":

> Because Clarence Thomas has been poor, has been nearly suffocated by the acrid odor of racial discrimination, is intelligent, well trained, black, and young enough to be won over again, I support him.
>
> The prophet in "Lamentations" cried, "Although he put his mouth in the dust . . . there is still hope."

In a similar dismissal of the liberal vs. conservative dichotomy, sociologist Jacquelyne J. Jackson states, in "Them Against Us: *Anita Hill* v. *Clarence Thomas,*" ". . . I unabashedly pulled 'all the way' for now Associate Justice Clarence Thomas, just as once during my bachelor's and master's years back in the early 1950s at the University of Wisconsin I zealously cheered for any black football player on our team *and* on any opponent's team." Espousing the primacy of blackness, Dr. Jackson condemns Anita Hill's behavior as divisive, yet concludes, "We must forgive and forget Hill, but not the continued fight for racial *and* sexual liberation including, for black women, freedom from and ample monetary compensation for racial and/or sexual harassment."

Perhaps nothing more clearly illustrates the complexity of the Clarence Thomas confirmation than the very misgivings his supporters have about him. Ms. Angelou, Dr. Sudarkasa, and Reverend Joseph Lowery, Executive Director of the Southern Christian Leadership Conference, endorsed Thomas, yet abjure a number of his political positions and hope that, during his tenure on the court, he will change his views. Some supporters felt that "better any black than no black at all," and were willing to overlook questions of fitness and qualifications. The immediate availability and the continuation of a black Supreme Court seat was of prime importance, despite the possibility that another black or a non-black might be better. Once Thomas declared that he was being racially attacked, he gathered further support.

THOMAS'S CONSERVATIVE ROOTS

Clarence Thomas's life has been atomized and magnified in every detail, yet the general public overlooked some obvious aspects of this man. The assumption is that he is in some way an aberration because of his conservative position on civil rights and on human rights, generally. Or that, because he has drawn his political succor from white conservatives, he is unusual. Thus, the fantasy that, "once he gets to the Supreme Court Clarence Thomas will change and be a black advocate" assumes that what Thomas did during the first forty three years of his life to succeed, he'd done against his will and deeper desires. That as the archetypal self-made American man, he was ennobled by his humble origins and thus specially endowed with sympathy for the downtrodden.

To pursue this line of thinking is to ignore the obvious complexity of Clarence Thomas's personality and to avoid the recognition that Thomas represents a prototypical development within the black community. Once he entered the household of his maternal grandfather, Myers Anderson, at the age of seven, Thomas was subjected to stern but effective discipline from both his grandfather and the Catholic schools he attended. Hard work and discipline at school were complemented by long, hard hours of work in the family fuel business. Anderson's insistence upon proper conduct and respect were enforced through a variety of punishments—beatings, tongue lashings, and isolation.

Anderson's businesses were also successful enough for him to afford private education for his grandson. Thomas's enrollment in private Catholic schools in 1960 was an upwardly mobile move, but once enrolled, he was subject to scorn and derision from his white racist classmates. He was also separated from the black classmates he would have had if he'd attended a black public school. He then attended Holy Cross College in Massachusetts, and then Yale Law School.

Despite being handled in the confirmation hearings as a distinctly "black" candidate, Thomas was socialized by elite white Catholic boarding schools from first grade through high school. He was nurtured in authoritarian familial and academic environments in which he was expected to model his conduct in all ways upon white American models of success and dominance, and he was successful in this emulation.

Once graduated from Yale, Thomas continued the same pattern of affiliation with powerful white figures and institutions. He worked with Missouri State Attorney General John Danforth, and then after several years with the Monsanto corporation, rejoined newly elected Senator Danforth in Washington. Thomas's rise continued with the U.S. Office on Civil Rights, the EEOC, the Federal Appeals Court and, finally, his appointment to the Supreme Court.

Despite the impact of Myers Anderson on his life, Thomas's deviation from his grandfather's political activism as a Democrat and NAACP member is so significant that it suggests basic rebellion, and it is possible that the scalding experiences of white racism made him eschew his black heritage.

Whatever his politics and personal ethics, Clarence Thomas is an aggressive, strong-willed, and defiant black man who had the audacity to confront fourteen white U.S. Senators on television and intimidate them. There is thus a suggestion of the anti-hero in Clarence Thomas's persona. As his 100 days of testimony concluded, one sensed in Thomas a double alienation, both from the traditional black values and mores he inherited and from the hegemonous values he acquired when he lashed out at the Senate: "The Supreme Court is not worth it . . . This [hearing] is a circus. It's a national disgrace. And from my standpoint as a black American, it is a high-tech lynching for uppity blacks who in any way deign to think for themselves. . . ."

While Clarence Thomas reached the pinnacle of American success in gaining the Supreme Court, his life suggests a process of existential creation. In its alienation and daring, it evokes the apostasies of folk-heroes Stackolee or *Native Son*'s Bigger Thomas, who defied all norms. The contradiction between Clarence Thomas's heritage and his Luciferian rebellion has perhaps touched a similar chord in other blacks of his generation and generated a secret empathy.

The relationship between the creed of black conservatism and the welfare of black people as a whole raised considerable comment in *Court of Appeal.* In his essay, "Clarence Thomas and the Meaning of Blackness," political scientist Ronald W. Walters refutes the idea "that the civil rights movement and other movements for social change were launched in order to make possible the elevation of *any* black person, espousing *any*—presumably credible—set of values." Walters continues:

> . . . to be black also has a political content that emerges out of the way in which the group has sought to pursue its interests, often in conflict with other groups in society. Perhaps the issue here is what it means to be *politically black* and to share the goals and methods of the black mainstream both in their historical importance and in their current application to problems facing the black community. I would argue that Clarence Thomas and his supporters are not politically black.

Historian Henry Vance Davis expands on this idea in his essay, "The High-tech Lynching and the High-tech Overseer: Thoughts from the Anita Hill/Clarence Thomas Affair" in critiquing Thomas's "selective blackness":

> This selective blackness is troubling because it is a symptom of a greater malaise that is sweeping higher education, politics, and business. . . . Like the person who worked the slave for the master during slavery, in the twentieth century the high-tech overseer has become a person with black skin who will stand between oppressive policies and the majority of African-Americans. . . . She/he can be anything from "yo' bro' what's happenin'?" to Warrington Mostuphigh III, Esq., if the price is right.

William W. Sales, Jr., in his "Comments on the Controversy Surrounding the Nomination and Confirmation of Judge Clarence Thomas to the Supreme Court," establishes the continuing African-

American struggle for equality and freedom as the basic political tradition of black America, from which its legitimate leaders develop. For Sales, "in every respect Thurgood Marshall represented the kind of 'talented tenth' leadership that has historically emerged out of the African-American protest tradition." As chief counsel for the NAACP for many years, Marshall "was further trained and tested for leadership within the indigenous protest tradition of twentieth-century African-American history—the Civil Rights Movement."

Contrary to this tradition, Sales asserts, "Black neo-conservatism is mounting an attack against Malcolm's doctrine of 'by any means necessary' because it is attempting to inject into an essentially political protest tradition an essentially economist doctrine."

GENDER POLITICS

Besides dealing with issues of black consciousness and black politics, the essays in *Court of Appeal* also trace the complex issues of gender raised by the confirmation. Much of this complexity results from the way the U.S. Presidents, Congress, state officials, and regulatory agencies have chosen to define the African-American struggle for equality and thereby determine policy.

The general practice has been to de-racialize the African-American protest, eschewing terms such as "black," "racism," "exploitation," and "oppression" in favor of "minority," "ethnicity," "underprivileged," "disadvantaged," or "diversity." These words create frameworks that remove African-American protest and criticism from its specific historical and political contexts, and this, in turn, confuses the issues and confounds solutions. Despite being the numerical majority within U.S. society, all women of whatever ethnicity have traditionally been viewed as a "minority." However, while there are many similarities, the specific causality that oppresses all women is not the same causality that deprives African-Americans, Native Americans, and Chicanos, each of whom have a unique historical, economic, and political identity as well as a unique set of grievances. There are, of course, sufficient common concerns among these groups to provide a basis for unified action.

However, a well-to-do middle-class white woman may very well get an affirmative action hire over a racially diverse field of candidates because she is a victim of sexism, despite the structured economic and social power her race gives her. On the other hand, black women who protest sexist treatment from black men are often reminded that they are black first, female second. As black studies scholar Melba Boyd points out in "Collard Greens, Clarence Thomas, and the High-tech Rape of Anita Hill":

> The periphery of comments made by many women and men, even when they believed Anita Hill was harassed, is a reflexive of a cultural code that dictates: "As a black woman, she should have checked him and got him straight from the get go, but she should have never exposed him in front of white America."

As the Thomas hearings demonstrated, a black woman suffers double jeopardy: racial discrimination from white America, and sexual discrimination from both black men and white men. One may or may not agree with Anita Hill's version of events, but the general public's response to her indicated there were serious problems with sexism in American society, black and white.

Many of these selections display open support and admiration for the example of Anita Hill, and they support her difficult travail during the hearings. There are, however, numerous shadings of opinion in the evaluation of Professor Hill. Attorney Karen Wanza, in "The Three Ring Circus of Clarence Thomas: Race, Class, and Gender," finally finds Hill's conduct noble but problematic, and observes:

> But in reality Anita Hill unwittingly occupied one ring in Bush's three ring circus (the other two rings being occupied by the Senate and Thomas) and much of the content of her testimony has become a national joke (e.g., Long Dong Silver jokes and comments about hairs in a soda can). . . . There are many who ask why Anita chose to wait so long to speak. A better question is, How did she risk so much so calmly in the first place?

Novelist Sarah E. Wright expresses specific reservations in "The Anti-Black Agenda":

> However, one can hardly refrain from noting, painful though it may be, that Anita F. Hill was more than willing to hug up to (figuratively speaking) the worst oppressors of her people. . . . Perhaps naiveté might appear too generous, but it is the best we can allow. And for that she was amply rewarded. She even supported that man with the notoriously racist and sexist reputation, Judge Robert Bork, in his unsuccessful campaign for a seat on the Supreme Court.

Women's studies scholar Joy James has a similar criticism of Hill in "Anita Hill: Martyr Heroism and Gender Abstractions," and cautions against reductionism:

> Supporting Anita Hill's right to a fair hearing on sexual harassment reveals compassion and outrage concerning sexual abuse. Placing Anita Hill (who implemented Reagan policies, taught at Oral Roberts University Law School, and maintains that Robert Bork was unjustly denied a seat on the Supreme Court) on a pedestal reveals how analyses surrounding sexual-racial abuse and democratic policies have become inane.

To a lesser extent, Anita Hill suffered the same credibility problems with the black community that Clarence Thomas did. But their very similar career trajectories and political affinities suggest that we are viewing a sociological phenomenon, as well as two highly complex and interesting personalities who have assumed mythic proportions in the American imagination.

Closely related to reductionism is the problem of tokenism, as noted by Melba Boyd in her essay:

> The stratification of race, gender, and class can no longer be assessed by token representation. The New World Order is the Old World Order constructed to the benefit of global corporations. Representation in the hierarchy by people of color, women, and even homosexuals too often reflects a careful selection of well-trained, articulate functionaries who facilitate the expectations and directives of that ruling order.

Still another aspect of this problem is presented by publisher and activist Barbara Smith in this passage from "Ain't Gonna Let Nobody Turn Me Around":

> Some black women have so thoroughly internalized the message that blackness and femaleness are inherently worthless that they think the only way to cancel out these "negatives" is to embrace the political agendas and values of whites and males. The black feminist movement has worked very hard to offer black women a more accurate perception of ourselves. Confronting our self-hatred has been a necessary prerequisite to organizing on our own behalf. . . . If white women really want to support the struggles of women of color, the best thing they can do is to clean the racism out of their own house, and they can only accomplish this when they participate in political organizing that directly challenges the multiple oppressions that women of color face, oppressions which undermine their lives as well.

Other black women, such as novelist Sarah E. Wright, have been more circumspect concerning Anita Hill herself, recognizing her dilemma as a female but remaining critical of her conservative alignment with right-wing Republicans. Black social theorists Nathan and Julia Hare, in "The Clarence Thomas Hearings," critique the many oxymorons and ironies of the alliances operating during the hearing.

However diverse their viewpoints, these essays assert the need for change, criticism, and renewal within the black community, in both the politics of black America as well as gender politics within the black community. Robert L. Allen, in "Time to Heal the Wounds of Pornography," finds the tolerance of any instrument degrading humanity a social issue: "Pornography corrupts our sexuality, our most intimate relations with other human beings."

Suggesting that post–World War II civil rights groups endorsed anti-communism in exchange for integration, Gerald Horne cautions in "The Thomas Hearings and the Nexus of Race, Gender, and Nationalism" that "the erosion of left influence within the African-American community set the stage not only for the hegemonic influence of various forms of nationalism, it also led directly to the devaluation of the gender question." Sociologist Robert Staples urges a reevaluation of the gender question in his essay "Hand Me the Rope: I Will Hang Myself." Clyde Taylor perhaps best summed up the mood in his essay, stating, "Black America badly needs new political energy, new ideas, goals, and agendas, new personalities, a new political posture—and black women as leaders in a new campaign for social justice is one place, out of a narrow field, we might find them."

THE CLARENCE THOMAS LEGACY IN LAW AND POLITICS

Since his appointment to the Supreme Court, Clarence Thomas has continued to be a controversial jurist. With his first year as an associate justice concluded, his record indicates a clear alliance with the thought of Justice Antonin Scalia, his apparent mentor. And, in fact, once he was confirmed, Thomas hired a former law clerk of Scalia's. With Justice Scalia and Chief Justice William Rehnquist, Thomas has formed the "hard core" of conservative thought on the court.

As an African-American filling the vacancy of Thurgood Marshall, Thomas drew special attention regarding his attitudes toward minorities and the impoverished. During his confirmation hearings, Thomas informed Senator Herb Kohl (D-WI) that he felt he " 'could bring something different to the court,' an understanding of how the court's decisions affect the underprivileged," according to *The New York Times* of February 26, 1992.

Nevertheless, several of Thomas's decisions regarding prisoners, capital punishment, the mentally ill and civil rights have raised the eyebrows of many, including his court colleagues. In the case of *Hudson* v. *McMillan* (no. 90-6531), Louisiana prison inmate Keith J. Hudson had been handcuffed and beaten by two prison guards while a third looked on. Successfully suing for $800 damages, Hudson had his verdict overturned by the Fifth Circuit Court, then upheld by the Supreme Court, 7–2, on February 26, 1992. Justice Thomas dissented, with Justice Scalia, arguing that such treatment was not cruel and unusual punishment as proscribed by the Eighth Amendment. Justice O'Connor's majority opinion made particularly pointed reference to Thomas's opinion: "To deny, as the dissent does, the difference between punching a prisoner in the face and serving him unappetizing food is to ignore the concepts of dignity, civilized standards, humanity, and decency that animate the Eighth Amendment."

Thomas attracted controversy in another case, *Dawson* v. *Delaware* (no. 90-6704), ruled upon by the court on March 9, 1992. The plaintiff, David Dawson, a convicted felon and a member of the white racist prison gang the Aryan Brotherhood, escaped from a Delaware state penitentiary and while at large murdered a white woman.

During the sentencing phase of the trial, the prosecution introduced Dawson's membership in the Aryan Brotherhood as evidence. This prompted the Supreme Court to overturn his death sentence on the grounds that Dawson's First Amendment right to freedom of association had been violated. Writing the majority opinion, Judge Rehnquist stated: "On the present record one is left with the feeling that the Aryan Brotherhood evidence was employed simply because the jury would find these beliefs morally reprehensible."

Judge Thomas cast the lone dissenting vote against this opinion. He argued that, "In my judgment, a jury reasonably could conclude from Dawson's membership in a prison gang that he had engaged in some sort of forbidden activities while in prison," and added that he had "difficulty seeing what the First Amendment adds to the analysis."

In yet another case, *Riggins* v. *Nevada* (no. 90-8466), David Riggins, a paranoid schizophrenic, was forced to take large doses of medication months before his trial, producing a behavior that was seemingly sane. In his appeal, Riggins argued that the drugging concealed his condition, thus denying him due process and leading to his conviction. On May 19, 1992, the court found for the prisoner, 7–2, with Justices Thomas and Scalia dissenting.

In a related case, *Foucha* v. *Louisiana* (no. 90-5844), the court overturned, 5–4, a Louisiana law that required people found not guilty by reason of insanity to remain in a mental institution, even though no longer insane, until proven to be no longer dangerous. In the process of writing the majority opinion, Justice Byron White addressed "a particularly scathing [footnote], consuming two full pages of text, to Justice Thomas. He accused Justice Thomas of providing a partial and misleading account of the current state of the law of criminal insanity." (*The New York Times,* May 19, 1991.)

The current controversy over conservative dominance of the Supreme Court has brought into sharper focus the differences between the "traditional" school of conservative thought, which supports individual liberty and expression, with a minimum of government regulation, and "ideological" conservatism, which favors strong state and Federal regulation of individual action, particularly in the areas of crime, morality, and national interest.

Classic conservatism is often buttressed by the first ten amendments to the Constitution that assure freedom of speech and assembly, the right to bear arms, freedom of belief, and all due processes of law, as well as the Thirteenth, Fourteenth, and Fifteenth Amendments to the Constitution, which prohibit slavery, establish voting rights, and assure equal citizenship. However, through the interpretation of these amendments, more subtle concepts have emerged and become points of dispute for ideological conservatives. These issues include the right to counsel, the admissability of evidence, courtroom procedure, writs of habeas corpus, and the right to privacy—the cornerstone of the thinking that legalized abortion.

In the case of *Keeney* v. *Tamayo-Reyes* (no. 90-1859), the Supreme Court voted 5–4 that "Federal courts are no longer obliged to grant a hearing on a state prisoner's challenge to his conviction, even if the prisoner can show that his lawyer had not properly presented crucial facts of the case in a state-court appeal." (*The New York Times,* May 4, 1992.) Justice Thomas concurred in this decision, which essentially curtails habeas corpus procedures.

The avowed mission of the Reagan-Bush presidencies to pack the Supreme Court with ideological conservatives has raised concern over the court's continued receptivity to these various amendments since they assure individual liberties. In criminal matters, Clarence Thomas's opinions reflect the conservative preference for powerful state regulation of individual conduct, as seen through his impatience with the First and Eighth Amendments. Thomas's orientation carries special import for blacks, who form a disproportionate percentage of prison populations. This has prompted *The New York Times* to call Thomas, editorially, "the youngest and the cruellest justice."

Several important cases affecting voter rights and desegregation were decided during Thomas's first year. In *Presley* v. *Etowah County Commission,* Thomas concurred in a Supreme Court decision limiting the scope of the 1965 Voting Rights Act, after counties in Alabama restricted the right of supervisors to individually authorize road repairs once blacks had begun to be elected as county supervisors, a position that holds the power to grant contracts. The Supreme Court upheld Etowah County's decision to shift such responsibilities elsewhere.

In the area of segregation in higher education, the Court ruled 8–1 in the case of the *United States* v. *Fordice,* that Mississippi must take further measures to eliminate the residue of segregation in its eight public colleges. The court's ruling applied this standard to Mississippi's historically black public colleges, rejecting the argument that these colleges should be funded equally with white colleges yet still be maintained as predominately black institutions.

The elimination of duplicate programs was recommended by Justice White in his majority decision. However, ominously, the elimination of a dual college system carries with it the possibility of eliminating one of the few avenues of higher education for blacks, since the ninety-four black colleges in the United States today provide nearly 50 percent of all black college graduates. Many educators foresee the dissolution of the black college system as a result of such rulings. Although Thomas voted with the majority, in his own opinion he demonstrated an understanding of the value of the historically black colleges:

> We do not foreclose the possibility that there exists "sound educational justification" for maintaining historically black colleges as such. Despite the shameful history of state-enforced segregation, these institutions have survived and flourished. . . .
>
> Although I agree that a state is not constitutionally required to maintain its historically black institutions as such, I do not understand our opinion to hold that a state is forbidden from doing so. It would be ironic, to say the least, if the institutions that sustained blacks during segregation were themselves destroyed in an effort to combat its vestiges."

Interestingly, Justice Scalia, the lone dissenter, wrote:

> There is nothing unconstitutional about a "black" school in the sense, not of a school that blacks must attend and that whites *cannot,* but of a school that, as a consequence of private choice in residence or in school selection, contains, and has long contained a large black majority.

Judge Thomas's first year of decisions has already cost him the support of the Southern Christian Leadership Conference, which was the only major civil rights organization to endorse him during the hearings. At its semiannual meeting in Baltimore, April 16, 1992, SCLC unanimously voted "no confidence" in Clarence Thomas, citing Thomas's rulings in *Presley* v. *Etowah County Commission, Hudson* v. *McMillan,* and *Dawson* v. *Delaware.* The SCLC resolution stated that: "Thomas has declined to be an independent voice, instead voting in an identical manner as Associate Antonin Scalia, except in two instances; . . . . and Justice Clarence Thomas has failed to demonstrate the compassion, sensitivity, independence, and intellectual courage in his first five months on the Court that was the prayer of the SCLC."

The climax of this Supreme Court term was its carefully constructed ruling on *Planned Parenthood* v. *Casey,* (no. 91-744). The Court decided, by a vote of 5–4, to sustain a woman's right to have an abortion, as established in *Roe* v. *Wade.* But in the Pennsylvania ruling, it permitted states to restrain and qualify that choice through mandatory counseling, a waiting period of twenty-four hours, a restriction upon minors to get approval from one parent or a judge, a modification of the trimester guidelines, and the introduction of the vaguely defined concept that restrictions should cause no "undue hardship upon a woman."

The dialectic of the decision lay between a newly emerging moderate center of Justices Sandra Day O'Connor, David Souter, and Anthony M. Kennedy, and the clearly ideological conservatives of Rehnquist, Scalia, and Thomas, who are often joined by Justice White. The latter four Justices, Rehnquist, Scalia, Thomas, and White, were in the minority, and all explicitly favored the overthrow of *Roe* v. *Wade,* the 1972 ruling that permits abortion "on demand" throughout the United States. Justice Thomas did not write a separate opinion, but he signed the two dissenting opinions of Justices Rehnquist and Scalia.

Despite the ambiguities surrounding Clarence Thomas's positions on black advocacy, reproductive rights, and criminal justice, his first year on the Supreme Court has established him as an ideological conservative, patterned upon the model of Antonin Scalia.

THE MOBILIZATION OF THE WOMEN'S MOVEMENT

The controversy concerning the confirmation hearings, especially the treatment of Anita Hill by the Senate Judiciary Committee, and the abortion controversy, have helped inspire a renaissance in women's politics. According to *The New York Times,* May 24, 1992, "There are 150 women candidates—94 Democrats, 54 Republicans, and two independents—for the House of Representatives, including 35 in California alone. Never before has there been anything close to that number."

At least two candidates for the Senate, African-American Carol Moseley Braun in Illinois and Lynn H. Yeakel in Pennsylvania, won the Democratic party primaries in their states. Both have expressed disgust with the Senate's treatment of Anita Hill, while acknowledging the inspiration of her courage. Yeakel is in fact running against Senator Arlen Specter, who led the Republican interrogation of Hill. In California, Democrats Dianne Feinstein and Barbara Boxer each won the primaries for senator. And each candidate ran specifically on gender issues. Allegations of sexual abuse have forced incumbent Brock Adams (D-WA) to retire from the Senate with the expiration of his term in 1993. A woman, Patty Murray, is running as a Democrat in his stead.

In addition to political will and sentiment, financial support for women candidates is running high. According to *The New York Times,* the Women's Campaign Fund, a bipartisan group, had doubled its donor list since the Hill–Thomas confrontation, and Emily's List, a Democratic fund-raising group, "expects to raise $3 million this year, compared to $1.5 million two years ago."

Many have credited Anita Hill's testimony and her treatment by the Senate Judiciary Committee as the catalyst for the surge in women's political activism. On Saturday, April 25, 1992, Anita Hill spoke at Hunter College before a cheering crowd of 2,100 New York women who, in the words of the *Detroit Free Press* on April 27, "seemed to hold her responsible for revitalizing feminism." Earlier, Hill had drawn over 2,000 people to her speech at the University of Pennsylvania.

During the New York address, Hill linked the necessity for her testimony to the necessity of the slave narrative, that the oppressed woman must find a voice, must speak out, that sexual harassment is not about sexual gratification but about the imposition of power upon the weak.

At the conference's conclusion, former Congresswoman Bella Abzug launched a petition drive, with the text, "We call upon all political parties to nominate and support only women for all open seats until women achieve parity in our government."

The ultimate ramifications of the Clarence Thomas Confirmation Hearings, as they have affected the black community, women in the United States, and the general body of citizens, will be more clearly revealed in years to come. It is our hope that the forty-one essays presented in this collection will stimulate dialogue and reaffirm that the black community is the final COURT OF APPEAL in this great debate.

Robert Chrisman
Ann Arbor, Michigan
May 28, 1992

PRIMARY DOCUMENTS

A chronology of events and the opening statements of Judge Clarence Thomas and Professor Anita Hill appear in this section.

THE CHRONOLOGY OF THE CLARENCE THOMAS CONFIRMATION*

Compiled by Camille Spencer

June 27: Thurgood Marshall, the first African American ever to serve on the Supreme Court, announces his retirement.

July 1: President Bush nominates Clarence Thomas, 43, a black conservative federal appeals court judge, to replace Marshall. Thomas is soon opposed by many civil rights and women's groups.

August: A former Yale classmate of Anita Hill, a University of Oklahoma law professor and former assistant at the Education Department and the Equal Employment Opportunity Commission, calls Nan Aron, a Thomas opponent, and suggests that Thomas sexually harassed Hill. Aron relays the tip to the staff of Senator Howard Metzenbaum (D-OH) a Democrat on the Judiciary Committee.

September 3–4: A Metzenbaum aide telephones Hill and mentions rumors of sexual harassment, but Hill makes no allegations.

September 5: Hill is approached by Ricki Seidman, an investigator from Senator Ted Kennedy's (D-MA) Labor and Human Resources Committee. Hill asks for more time to decide whether to talk further about sexual harassment at the EEOC.

*Prepared from *Newsweek*, October 21, 1991; *San Francisco Chronicle*, Tuesday, October 15, 1991; *Time*, October 21, 1991

September 9: Hill calls Seidman, saying she is ready to talk. She is referred to James Brudney (a Metzenbaum aide who attended Yale Law School with Hill). Hill leaves a message for Brudney.

September 10–20: The Senate Judiciary Committee holds eight days of public hearings on Thomas. He testifies for five days, followed by three days of outside witnesses.

September 12: *Morning:* Hill speaks to the staff of the Judiciary Committee. The discussion is short because Hill has to teach a class. She asks to be called back that evening.

Evening: Hill is called and assured that her name will be kept confidential, but is told that, under such conditions, the committee's hands would be tied because the nominee must be given an opportunity to respond. Hill confirms with Judiciary Committee staff that only the committee should know her identity. She supplies the name of Judge Susan Hoerchner, a friend in whom she has confided.

September 12: Hill contacts committee staff to discuss making allegations about sexual misconduct by Thomas. Discussion continues September 19–21.

September 18: Judge Hoerchner calls the committee staff, corroborating at least part of Hill's story.

September 19: Hill calls the committee staff and asks what her options would be if her name was revealed to Thomas.

September 20: Hill is told that committee members could not be told her story unless the nominee is told of her identity and has a chance to respond. If she wants to proceed, her name would be given to the FBI, which would interview both her and Thomas. Hill says she wants to think about it. Thomas's confirmation appears likely as the hearings end.

September 21: Hill says she is still not ready to give an answer.

September 23: Hill says her name can be used in the FBI investigation. She says she wants to send "a personal statement" to the committee. She is told that as soon as the staff receives the FBI report, members will be informed of her charges. Hill faxes statement with allegations to the committee.

September 25: The FBI completes its report. Hill says she wants her statement distributed to all committee members. Senator Joseph Biden (D-DE) begins briefing Democratic members about the allegations. Thomas is informed about the charges and interviewed by the FBI. Thomas denies the allegations.

September 25–26: Biden and his aides brief the committee's seven other Democrats, but at least one isn't told about the FBI report. Senator Strom Thurmond (R-SC) fails to brief some of his five Republican colleagues, GOP sources say.

September 27: Shortly before the committee votes, several copies of Hill's statement are made available to committee members. Two copies of the FBI report are left with Biden and Thurmond, but none are distributed to the other members. To help ensure confidentiality, the staff retrieves Hill's statement after the vote. It appears that not all members read all the materials, and some Republicans were not even briefed. Chairman Biden and other committee members dismiss the charges and decide not to make them public.

The Judiciary Committee splits 7 to 7 on whether to confirm Thomas. Six Republicans and one Democrat vote for Thomas. No mention is made of Hill's charges at the public meeting; opponents say Thomas is too conservative and not qualified enough to get a life term on the high court. The Thomas nomination goes to the Senate without recommendation.

September 28: Thomas files a sworn denial of Hill's allegations.

October 1: Senate Majority Leader George Mitchell (D-ME), who has been told by Biden about Hill's allegations, gets unanimous agreement to begin debate on the confirmation on October 3 and to vote on the nomination at 6 P.M. on October 8.

October 3–4: Senate debate begins, with both supporters and opponents agreeing he will be confirmed.

October 5: Hill's name and at least a portion of the FBI report are leaked to *Newsday* and National Public Radio.

October 6: National Public Radio and New York *Newsday* break the story of Hill's allegations.

October 7: Hill gives a televised news conference in Oklahoma about her charges; some senators and women's groups call for a delay in the vote, but Mitchell says it will be held and Biden defends his handling of allegations; the nine-member Supreme Court opens its term with one vacancy.

October 8: Thomas requests a delay in the Senate vote. His denial of the allegations is made public. Pressure mounts throughout the day for a delay as several Democrats say they will withhold their votes unless the charges are investigated. Thomas releases an affidavit denying the charges. At 6 P.M., the vote is put on hold and at 8:15 P.M., Mitchell gets agreement to postpone the vote one week so that the committee can investigate Hill's charges.

October 10: Angela Wright, who also worked at EEOC, says Thomas asked her out on dates and made annoying comments to her. Wright, an assistant metropolitan editor at the *Charlotte* (NC) *Observer,* offers to testify as committee members argue about hearing procedures.

October 11: The hearings re-open, carried live on ABC, CBS, NBC and C SPAN networks. Thomas appears first, denies the charges and says his reputation has been ruined by unfair proceedings; Hill then gives graphic testimony about sexual comments that she says Thomas made to her about pornographic films and his own sexual prowess. Thomas returns in the evening to call the hearing "a high-tech lynching for uppity blacks."

October 12: Thomas testifies for more than six hours, again denies all the charges and says his life has been "hell" since September 25. Asked if he would withdraw his nomination before the vote, he says, "I would rather die than withdraw."

October 13: The committee hears several witnesses for Thomas and Hill. Four people who know Hill says she told them several years ago about Thomas's alleged actions. Her lawyer releases a lie detector test she took and passed.

October 14: The committee finishes its hearing at 2 A.M., without reaching a conclusion about whether Hill's charges are true. Biden says Thomas should get the benefit of the doubt.

October 16: The Senate votes, 52–48, to confirm Clarence Thomas as Associate Justice of the Supreme Court.

CAMILLE SPENCER is an editorial assistant at The Black Scholar.

STATEMENT OF JUDGE CLARENCE THOMAS TO THE SENATE JUDICIARY COMMITTEE OCTOBER 11, 1991

Following is the text of the opening statement by Judge Clarence Thomas at the Senate Judiciary Committee hearing on his nomination to be an Associate Justice of the Supreme Court.

Mr. Chairman, Senator Thurmond, members of the committee.

As excruciatingly difficult as the last two weeks have been, I welcome the opportunity to clear my name today. No one other than my wife and Senator Danforth, to whom I read this statement at 6:30 A.M., has seen or heard the statement. No handlers, no advisers.

The first I learned of the allegations by Professor Anita Hill was on Sept. 25, 1991, when the FBI came to my home to investigate her allegations. When informed by the FBI agent of the nature of the allegations, and the person making them, I was shocked, surprised, hurt, and enormously saddened. I have not been the same since that day.

For almost a decade, my responsibilities included enforcing the rights of victims of sexual harassment. As a boss, as a friend, and as a human being I was proud that I have never had such an allegation leveled against me, even as I sought to promote women and minorities into nontraditional jobs.

In addition, several of my friends who are women have confided in me about the horror of harassment, on the job or elsewhere. I thought I really understood the anguish, the fears, the doubts, the seriousness of the matter. But since September 25, I have suffered immensely as these very serious charges were leveled against me. I have been racking my brains and eating my insides out trying to think of what I could have said or done to Anita Hill to lead her to allege that I was interested in her in more than a professional way, and that I talked with her about pornographic or X-rated films.

Contrary to some press reports, I categorically denied all of the allegations, and denied that I ever attempted to date Anita Hill when first interviewed by the FBI. I strongly reaffirm that denial.

Let me describe my relationship with Anita Hill. In 1981, after I went to the Department of Education as an assistant secretary in the Office of Civil Rights, one of my closest friends from both college and law schools, Gil Hardy, brought Anita Hill to my attention. As I remember, he indicated that she was dissatisfied with her law firm, and wanted to work in government. Based primarily, if not solely, on Gil's recommendation, I hired Anita Hill.

During my tenure at the Department of Education, Anita Hill was an attorney-adviser who worked directly with me. She worked on special projects as well as day-to-day matters. As I recall, she was one of two professionals working directly with me at the time. As a result, we worked closely on numerous matters.

I recalled being pleased with her work product, and the professional but cordial relationship which we enjoyed at work. I also recall engaging in discussions about politics and current events.

Upon my nomination to become chairman of the Equal Employment Opportunity Commission, Anita Hill, to the best of my recollection, assisted me in the nomination and confirmation process. After my confirmation she and Diane Holt, then my secretary, joined me at EEOC.

I do not recall that there was any question or doubt that she would become a special assistant to me at EEOC, although as a career employee, she retained the option of remaining at the Department of Education.

At EEOC our relationship was more distant, and our contacts less frequent, as a result of the increased size of my personal staff, and the dramatic increase and diversity of my day-to-day responsibilities.

Upon reflection, I recall that she seemed to have had some difficulty adjusting to this change in her role. In any case, our relationship remained both cordial and professional. At no time did I become aware, either directly or indirectly, that she felt I had said or done anything to change the cordial nature of our relationship.

I detected nothing from her, or from my staff, or from Gil Hardy, our mutual friend, with whom I maintained regular contact.

I am certain that had any statement or conduct on my part been brought to my attention, I would remember it clearly because of the nature and seriousness of such conduct, as well as my adamant opposition to sex discrimination and sexual harassment.

But there were no such statements.

In the spring of 1983, Mr. Charles Coffey contacted me to speak at the law school at Oral Roberts University in Tulsa, Oklahoma. Anita Hill, who is from Oklahoma, accompanied me on that trip. It was not unusual that individuals on my staff would travel with me occasionally.

Anita Hill accompanied me on that trip, primarily because this was an opportunity to combine business and a visit to her home.

As I recall, during our visit at Oral Roberts University, Mr. Coffey mentioned to me the possibility of approaching Anita Hill to join the faculty at Oral Roberts University Law School.

I encouraged him to do so, and noted to him, as I recall, that Anita would do well in teaching. I recommended her highly, and she eventually was offered a teaching position.

Although I did not see Anita Hill often after she left EEOC, I did see her on one or two subsequent visits to Tulsa, Oklahoma, and on one visit, I believe she drove me to the airport.

I also occasionally received telephone calls from her. She would speak directly with me, or with my secretary, Diane Holt. Since Anita Hill and Diane Holt had been with me at the Department of Education, they were fairly close personally, and I believe they occasionally socialized together.

I would also hear about her through Linda Jackson, then Linda Lambert, whom both Anita Hill and I met at the Department of Education, and I would hear of her from my friend Gil.

Throughout the time that Anita Hill worked with me, I treated her as I treated my other special assistants. I tried to treat them all cordially, professionally, and respectfully. And I tried to support them in their endeavors and be interested in and supportive of their success. I had no reason or basis to believe my relationship with Anita Hill was anything but this way until the FBI visited me a little more than two weeks ago.

I find it particularly troubling that she never raised any hint that she was uncomfortable with me. She did not raise or mention it when considering moving with me to EEOC from the Department of Education. And she never raised it with me when she left EEOC and was moving on in her life. And to my fullest knowledge, she did not speak to any other women working with or around me, who would feel comfortable enough to raise it with me, especially Diane Holt, to whom she seemed closest on my personal staff. Nor did she raise it with mutual friends such as Linda Jackson and Gil Hardy.

This is a person I have helped at every turn in the road since we met. She seemed to appreciate the continued cordial relationship we had since day one. She sought my advice and counsel, as did virtually all of the members of my personal staff.

During my tenure in the executive branch, as a manager, as a policy maker and as a person, I have adamantly condemned sex harassment. There is no member of this committee or this Senate who feels stronger about sex harassment than I do. As a manager, I made every effort to take swift and decisive action when sex harassment raised or reared its ugly head.

The fact that I feel so very strongly about sex harassment and spoke loudly about it at EEOC has made these allegations doubly hard on me. I cannot imagine anything that I said or did to Anita Hill that could have been mistaken for sexual harassment. But with that said, if there is anything that I have said that has been misconstrued by Anita Hill or anyone else to be sexual harassment, then I can say that I am so very sorry and I wish I had known. If I did know, I would have stopped immediately and I would not, as I've done over the past two weeks, had to tear away at myself trying to think of what I could possibly have done.

But I have not said or done the things that Anita Hill has alleged.

God has gotten me through the days since September 25 and He is my judge.

Mr. Chairman, something has happened to me in the dark days that have followed since the FBI agents informed me about these allegations. And the days have grown darker as this very serious, very explosive, and very sensitive allegation, or these sensitive allegations were selectively leaked in a distorted way to the media over the past weekend.

As if the confidential allegations themselves were not enough, this apparently calculated public disclosure has caused me, my family, and my friends enormous pain and great harm.

I have never, in all my life, felt such hurt, such pain, such agony.

My family and I have been done a grave and irreparable injustice. During the past two weeks, I lost the belief that if I did my best all would work out. I called upon the strength that helped me get here from Pin Point. And it was all sapped out of me.

It was sapped out of me because Anita Hill was a person I considered a friend, whom I admired and thought I had treated fairly and with the utmost respect.

Perhaps I could have been—better weathered this if it was from someone else. But here was someone I truly felt I had done my best with.

Though I am, by no means, a perfect—no means—I have not done what she has alleged. And I still don't know what I could possibly have done to cause her to make these allegations.

When I stood next to the President in Kennebunkport, being nominated to the Supreme Court of the United States, that was a high honor. But as I sit here before you, 103 days later, that honor has been crushed.

From the very beginning, charges were levelled against me from the shadows—charges of drug abuse, anti-Semitism, wife beating, drug use by family members, that I was a quota appointment, confirmation conversion, and much, much more. And now, this.

I have complied with the rules. I responded to a document request that produced over 30,000 pages of documents. And I have testified for five full days under oath.

I have endured this ordeal for 103 days. Reporters sneaking into my garage to examine books that I read. Reporters and interest groups swarming over divorce papers, looking for dirt. Unnamed people starting preposterous and damaging rumors. Calls all over the country specifically requesting dirt.

This is not American. This is Kafkaesque. It has got to stop. It must stop for the benefit of future nominees and our country. Enough is enough.

I am not going to allow myself to be further humiliated in order to be confirmed. I am here specifically to respond to allegations of sex harassment in the workplace. I am not here to be further humiliated by this committee or anyone else, or to put my private life on display for prurient interests or other reasons.

I will not allow this committee or anyone else to probe into my private life.

This is not what America is all about. To ask me to do that would be to ask me to go beyond fundamental fairness.

Yesterday, I called my mother. She was confined to her bed, unable to work, and unable to stop crying. Enough is enough.

Mr. Chairman, in my forty-three years on this earth, I have been able with the help of others and with help of God to defy poverty, avoid prison, overcome segregation, bigotry, racism, and obtain one of the finest educations available in this country.

But I have not been able to overcome this process. This is worse than any obstacle or anything that I have ever faced. Throughout my life I have been energized by the expectation and the hope that in this country I would be treated fairly in all endeavors. When there was segregation, I hoped there would be fairness one day, or someday. When there was bigotry and prejudice, I hoped that there would be tolerance and understanding—someday.

Mr. Chairman, I am proud of my life. Proud of what I have done, and what I've accomplished, proud of my family. And this process, this process, is trying to destroy it all.

No job is worth what I've been through—no job. No horror in my life has been so debilitating. Confirm me if you want. Don't confirm me if you are so led. But let this process end. Let me and my family regain our lives.

I never asked to be nominated. It was an honor. Little did I know the price, but it is too high.

I enjoy and appreciate my current position, and I am comfortable with the prospect of returning to my work as a judge on the U.S. Court of Appeals for the D.C. Circuit, and to my friends there. Each of these positions is public service, and I have given at the office.

I want my life and my family's life back, and I want them returned expeditiously.

I have experienced the exhilaration of new heights from the moment I was called to Kennebunkport by the President to have lunch and he nominated me. That was the high point. At that time I was told, eye to eye, that, Clarence, you made it this far on merit; the rest is going to be politics. And it surely has been.

There have been other highs. The outpouring of support from my friends of longstanding, a bonding like I have never experienced with my old boss, Senator Danforth. The wonderful support of those who have worked with me. There have been prayers said for my family and me by people I know and people I will never meet, prayers that were heard, and that sustained not only me but also my wife and my entire family.

Instead of understanding and appreciating the great honor bestowed upon me, I find myself here today defending my name, my integrity, because somehow select portions of confidential documents dealing with this matter were leaked to the public.

Mr. Chairman, I am a victim of this process. My name has been harmed. My integrity has been harmed. My character has been harmed. My family has been harmed. My friends have been harmed. There is nothing this committee, this body, or this country can do to give me my good name back. Nothing.

I will not provide the rope for my own lynching, or for further humiliation. I am not going to engage in discussions, nor will I submit to roving questions, of what goes on in the most intimate parts of my private life, or the sanctity of my bedroom. These are the most intimate parts of my privacy, and they will remain just that: private.

STATEMENT OF PROFESSOR ANITA F. HILL TO THE SENATE JUDICIARY COMMITTEE OCTOBER 11, 1991

Following is the text of the opening statement by Prof. Anita F. Hill at the Senate Judiciary Committee hearing on the nomination of Clarence Thomas to be an Associate Justice of the Supreme Court.

Mr. Chairman, Senator Thurmond, members of the committee:

My name is Anita F. Hill, and I am a professor of law at the University of Oklahoma. I was born on a farm in Okmulgee County, Oklahoma, in 1956. I am the youngest of thirteen children.

I had my early education in Okmulgee County. My mother's name is Irma Hill. She is also a farmer and a housewife.

My childhood was one of a lot of hard work and not much money, but it was one of solid family affection as represented by my parents. I was reared in a religious atmosphere in the Baptist faith, and I have been a member of the Antioch Baptist church in Tulsa, Oklahoma, since 1983. It is a very warm part of my life at the present time.

For my undergraduate work, I went to Oklahoma State University and graduated from there in 1977. I am attaching to this statement a copy of my resume for further details of my education.

Senator Joseph R. Biden, Jr.: It will be included in the record.

Professor Hill: Thank you.

I graduated from the university with academic honors, and proceeded to the Yale Law School, where I received my J.D. degree in 1980.

Upon graduation from law school, I became a practicing lawyer with the Washington, D.C., firm of Wald, Hardraker & Ross. In 1981 I was introduced to now Judge Thomas by a mutual friend.

Judge Thomas told me that he was anticipating a political appointment, and he asked if I would be interested in working with him.

He was in fact appointed as assistant secretary of education for civil rights. After he was—after he had taken that post, he asked if I would become his assistant, and I accepted that position.

In my early period there, I had two major projects. The first was an article I wrote for Judge Thomas's signature on the education of minority students. The second was the organization of a seminar on high-risk students, which was abandoned because Judge Thomas transferred to the E.E.O.C., where he became the chairman of that office.

During this period at the Department of Education my working relationship with Judge Thomas was positive. I had a good deal of responsibility and independence. I thought he respected my work, and that he trusted my judgment.

After approximately three months of working there, he asked me to go out socially with him. What happened next, and telling the world about it, are the two most difficult things—experiences of my life.

It is only after a great deal of agonizing consideration, and sleepless—number of—great number of sleepless nights, that I am able to talk of these unpleasant matters to anyone but my close friends.

I declined the invitation to go out socially with him, and explained to him that I thought it would jeopardize at—what at the time I considered to be a very good working relationship. I had a normal social life with other men outside the office. I believe then, as now, that having a social relationship with a person who was supervising my work would be ill advised. I was very uncomfortable with the idea and told him so.

I thought that by saying no and explaining my reasons, my employer would abandon his social suggestions. However, to my regret, in the following few weeks, he continued to ask me out on several occasions.

He pressed me to justify my reasons for saying no to him. These incidents took place in his office, or mine. They were in the form of private conversations, which not—would not have been overheard by anyone else.

My working relationship became even more strained when Judge Thomas began to use work situations to discuss sex. On these occasions he would call me into his office for a course on education issues and projects, or he might suggest that because of the time pressures of his schedule we go to lunch to a government cafeteria.

After a brief discussion of work, he would turn the conversation to a discussion of sexual matters. His conversations were very vivid. He spoke about acts that he had seen in pornographic films involving such matters as women having sex with animals, and films showing group sex or rape scenes.

He talked about pornographic materials depicting individuals with large penises or large breasts involving various sex acts.

On several occasions, Thomas told me graphically of his own sexual prowess.

Because I was extremely uncomfortable talking about sex with him at all, and particularly in such a graphic way, I told him that I did not want to talk about this subject. I would also try to change the subject to education matters or to nonsexual personal matters, such as his background or his beliefs.

My efforts to change the subject were rarely successful.

Throughout the period of these conversations, he also from time to time asked me for social engagements. My reaction to these conversations was to avoid them by eliminating opportunities for us to engage in extended conversations.

This was difficult because, at the time, I was his only assistant at the office of education—or office for civil rights. During the latter part of my time at the Department of Education, the social pressures, and any conversation of his offensive behavior, ended. I began both to believe and hope that our working relationship could be a proper, cordial, and professional one.

When Judge Thomas was made chair of the EEOC, I needed to face the question of whether to go with him. I was asked to do so, and I did.

The work itself was interesting, and at that time it appeared that the sexual overtures which had so troubled me had ended.

I also faced the realistic fact that I had no alternative job. While I might have gone back to private practice, perhaps in my old firm or at another, I was dedicated to civil rights work and my first choice was to be in that field. Moreover, at that time, the Department of Education itself was a dubious venture. President Reagan was seeking to abolish the entire department.

For my first months at the EEOC where I continued to be an assistant to Judge Thomas, there were no sexual conversations or overtures. However, during the fall and winter of 1982 these began again. The comments were random and ranged from pressing me about why I didn't go out with him to remarks about my personal appearance. I remember his saying that some day I would have to tell him the real reason that I wouldn't go out with him.

He began to show displeasure in his tone and voice and his demeanor and his continued pressure for an explanation. He commented on what I was wearing in terms of whether it made me more or less sexually attractive. The incidents occurred in his inner office at the EEOC.

One of the oddest episodes I remember was an occasion in which Thomas was drinking a Coke in his office. He got up from the table at which we were working, went over to his desk to get the Coke, looked at the can and asked, "Who has put pubic hair on my Coke?"

On other occasions, he referred to the size of his own penis as being larger than normal and he also spoke on some occasions of the pleasures he had given to women with oral sex. At this point, late 1982, I began to be concerned that Clarence Thomas might take out his anger with me by degrading me or not giving me important assignments. I also thought that he might find an excuse for dismissing me.

In January of 1983, I began looking for another job. I was handicapped because I feared that if he found out, he might make it difficult for me to find other employment and I might be dismissed from the job I had. Another factor that made my search more difficult was that there was a period—this was during a period—of a hiring freeze in the government.

In February 1983 I was hospitalized for five days on an emergency basis for acute stomach pain, which I attributed to stress on the job. Once out of the hospital I became more committed to find other employment and sought further to minimize my contact with Thomas. This became easier when Allison Duncan became office director because most of my work was then funneled through her and I had contact with Clarence Thomas mostly in staff meetings.

In the spring of 1983, an opportunity to teach at Oral Roberts University opened up. I participated in a seminar, taught an afternoon session in a seminar at Oral Roberts University. The dean of the university saw me teaching and inquired as to whether I would be interested in further pursuing a career in teaching beginning at Oral Roberts University.

I agreed to take the job, in large part because of my desire to escape the pressures I felt at the EEOC due to Judge Thomas.

When I informed him that I was leaving in July, I recall that his response was that now I would no longer have an excuse for not going out with him. I told him that I still preferred not to do so. At some time after that meeting, he asked if he could take me to dinner at the end of the term. When I declined, he assured me that the dinner was a professional courtesy only and not a social invitation. I reluctantly agreed to accept that invitation but only if it was at the very end of a working day.

On, as I recall, the last day of my employment at the EEOC in the summer of 1983, I did have dinner with Clarence Thomas. We went directly from work to a restaurant near the office. We talked about the work I had done, both at Education and at the EEOC. He told me that he was pleased with all of it except for an article and speech that I had done for him while we were at the Office for Civil Rights. Finally he made a comment that I will vividly remember. He said that if I ever told anyone of his behavior that it would ruin his career. This was not an apology; nor was it an explanation. That was his last remark about the possibility of our going out or reference to his behavior.

In July of 1983 I left the Washington, D.C., area and I've had minimal contacts with Judge Clarence Thomas since. I am of course aware from the press that some questions have been raised about conversations I had with Judge Clarence Thomas after I left the EEOC. From 1983 until today, I have seen Judge Thomas only twice. On one occasion, I needed to get a reference from him and on another he made a public appearance in Tulsa. On one occasion he called me at home and we had an inconsequential conversation. On one occasion he called me without reaching me and I returned the call without reaching him and nothing came of it.

I have, on at least three occasions, been asked to act as a conduit to him for others. I knew his secretary Diane Holt. We had worked together at both EEOC and Education. There were occasions on which I spoke to her and on some of these occasions undoubtedly I passed on some casual comment to then Chairman Thomas.

There were a series of calls in the first three months of 1985 occasioned by a group in Tulsa which wished to have a civil rights conference. They wanted Judge Thomas to be the speaker and enlisted my assistance for this purpose. I did call in January and February, to no effect, and finally suggested to the person directly involved, Susan Cahall, that she put the matter into her own hands and call directly. She did so in March of 1985.

In connection with that March invitation, Miss Cahall wanted conference materials for the seminar and some research was needed. I was asked to try to get the information and did attempt to do so. There was another call about a possible conference in July of 1985.

In August of 1987 I was in Washington, D.C., and I did call Diane Holt. In the course of this conversation, she asked me how long I was going to be in town and I told her. It is recorded in the message as August 15. It was in fact August 20. She told me about Judge Thomas's marriage and I did say, "Congratulate him."

It is only after a great deal of agonizing consideration that I am able to talk of these unpleasant matters to anyone except my closest friends. As I've said before, these last few days have been very trying and very hard for me and it hasn't just been the last few days this week.

It has actually been over a month now that I have been under the strain of this issue.

Telling the world is the most difficult experience of my life, but it is very close to having to live through the experience that occasioned this meeting.

I may have used poor judgment early on in my relationship with this issue. I was aware, however, that telling at any point in my career could adversely affect my future career, and I did not want, early on, to burn all the bridges to the EEOC.

As I said, I may have used poor judgment. Perhaps I should have taken angry or even militant steps, both when I was in the agency or after I left it. But I must confess to the world that the course that I took seemed the better as well as the easier approach.

I declined any comment to newspapers, but later, when Senate staff asked me about these matters, I felt I had a duty to report.

I have no personal vendetta against Clarence Thomas. I seek only to provide the committee with information which it may regard as relevant.

It would have been more comfortable to remain silent. It took no initiative to inform anyone. But when I was asked by a representative of this committee to report my experience, I felt that I had to tell the truth. I could not keep silent.

Second Statement from Judge Clarence Thomas October 11, 1991

Senator, I would like to start by saying unequivocally, uncategorically, that I deny each and every single allegation against me today that suggested in any way that I had conversations of a sexual nature or about pornographic material with Anita Hill, that I ever attempted to date her, that I ever had any personal sexual interest in her, or that I in any way ever harassed her.

The second and I think more important point, I think that this today is a travesty. I think that it is disgusting. I think that this hearing should never occur in America. This is a case in which this sleaze, this dirt was searched for by staffers of members of this committee, was then leaked to the media, and this committee and this body validated it and displayed it at prime time, over our entire nation.

How would any member on this committee, any person in this room, or any person in this country like sleaze said about him or her in this fashion? Or this dirt dredged up and this gossip and these lies displayed in this manner, how would any person like it?

The Supreme Court is not worth it. No job is worth it. I am not here for that. I am here for my name, my family, my life, and my integrity. I think something is dreadfully wrong with this country when any person, any person in this free country would be subjected to this.

This is not a closed room. There was an FBI investigation. This is not an opportunity to talk about difficult matters privately or in a closed environment. This is a circus. It's a national disgrace.

And from my standpoint, as a black American, it is a high-tech lynching for uppity blacks who in any way deign to think for themselves, to do for themselves, to have different ideas, and it is a message that unless you kowtow to an old order, this is what will happen to you. You will be lynched, destroyed, caricatured by a committee of the U.S. Senate rather than hung from a tree.

INDIVIDUAL COMMENTARY

Here follows, in alphabetical sequence, a cross-section of opinion by African-American scholars, intellectuals, and activists on the Clarence Thomas confirmation. A number of conferences and debates were held in the wake of the hearings, among them African American Faculty Speak Out on the Clarence Thomas Confirmation Hearings at the University of Massachusetts, Amherst on November 13, 1991, sponsored by the W. E. B. Du Bois Department of Afro-American Studies. Three papers from this conference appear here.

Race and Gender Stereotyping in the Thomas Confirmation Hearings

Ernest Allen, Jr.

Much has been said both during and after Judge Clarence Thomas's recent confirmation hearings concerning the use of racial and gender stereotypes in American society. On the one hand, Thomas's supporters generously employed gender stereotypes to discredit the testimony of law professor Anita Hill; on the other, Judge Thomas himself was quite willing to invoke racial stereotypes of the African American male in order to lend greater credibility to his own testimony.

What were these stereotypes, and how were they used? First of all, let's take the one of gender, which is simply this: Males constitute the repository of analytical thought and action, while the ideas and behavior of females are governed by emotion and fancy. In such polarized light, the charges of sexual harassment brought by Anita Hill against Clarence Thomas could be dismissed as the fantasy of a woman who, deep down, desired Thomas sexually. Indeed, this was the gist of one of several of Senator Arlen Specter's discrediting (and now discredited) tactics. This line of attack was reinforced by the egomaniacal testimony of attorney John Doggett III, who testified that, on one occasion, Hill had "fantasized" about his own sexual interest in her—an interest which, he assures us, could not possibly have existed. This bit of stereotyping was dealt with quite adequately this past Sunday by *New York Times* columnist Alessandra Stanley. Clarence Thomas's defenders, she wrote, wished us to believe that Anita Hill was suffering from the characteristically female delusion of erotomania, "a rare mental disorder in which people . . . suffer from the delusion that they are having an affair with someone above their station." But Stanley hypothesizes that, rather than erotomania being at work in this instance, it was more probably an outbreak of the disorder erotomonomania, or the "male delusion that attractive young women are harboring fantasies about them." Erotomonomania, Stanley informs us, is also known as Doggett's Disease, a formulation which has a special poignancy for those of us who suffered through the final evening of the televised hearings.[1]

A second stereotype which surfaced during the hearings was the racial one which holds that, in contrast to the "normal" sexuality of Euro-Americans, peoples of African descent are possessed of an animal, that is to say a more primitive, a more fecundate sexuality; and that black male genitalia, in particular, are supposedly much larger than those of their white counterparts. This early myth fed into a third and more complex set of stereotypes which developed in the nineteenth-century antebellum South, and which crystallized in the post-Reconstruction era: On the one hand there was the chivalrous white male, whose duty it was to protect the purity of the white female. Because the female was assumed to be the bearer of civilization, and given the danger posed to her by the hypersexual black man, her protection from her own sexuality also meant the safeguarding of the purity of whites as a race—that is, protection from miscegenation. From this conjecture in American culture the lynching of African American males—a genuinely American form of popular entertainment which peaked in the 1890s but which also has continued until very recently—became synonymous with the stereotype of the black male as a rapist of white females. And this despite the fact that, statistically speaking, less than one-third of the thousands of African American males lynched from the 1880s through the 1950s were even *charged* with rape. This complex stereotype, then, harbored numerous dimensions. First, it served to justify the ritual murders of African American political leaders as well as other black individuals who stood up to economic exploitation and disfranchisement. Second, the "pedestaling" of the white female, in turn, resulted in her being stripped of her own self-determination, for protection by white males also implied dependency. Third, invoking the alleged hypersexuality of African American females, it tended to cloak the very real acts of rape of black females by white males. And lastly, it served to obscure the fact that, historically speaking, so-called racial miscegenation in American society was infinitely more the result of liaisons forced upon black women by white men, than white women by black men.

It is with this background that we can more fully analyze Clarence Thomas's assertion, at the beginning of the second round of hearings on October 11, 1991, that he had been subjected to a "high-tech lynching": "I will not provide the rope for my own lynching, or for further humiliation," said Thomas, in a prepared statement.[2] Later in the day he described the proceedings as a "high-tech lynching for uppity blacks who think for themselves."[3] But it was in his October 12 testimony, in a reply to Senator Orrin Hatch, that Thomas attempted to link the stereotypes of sex and race to the accusation of sexual harassment leveled at him:

> And if you want to track through this country in the 19th and 20th century the lynchings of black men, you will see that there is, invariably, or in many instances, a relationship with sex, and an accusation that that person cannot shake off. That is the point that I am trying to make, and that is the point that I was making last night, that this is a high-tech lynching. I cannot shake off these accusations, because they play to the worst stereotypes we have about black men in this country.[4]

Clarence Thomas's attempts to picture himself as a victim of "high-tech lynching" is opportunism of the most cynical stripe—akin to that of George Bush's nomination of him in the first place.[5] First, the connection between the lynching of black males and racial stereotypes had to do with the alleged rape of white females, not the sexual harassment of black ones. I know of no historically recorded instance of a black man's being lynched for sexually harassing or even raping a black female. Second, Thomas's self-description as "uppity" and as "thinking for himself" is as laughable as the support given him by arch-racist Senator Strom Thurmond of South Carolina, who, among other perfidies, has taken as his vocation the attempted blocking of virtually every piece of Civil Rights legislation to pass through Congress since the 1940s. Rather than being "uppity," Clarence Thomas is—if you will forgive my invoking of yet another stereotype—more akin to the contented, favored slave of the master, rather than a rebellious Nat Turner, to say the least. Third, the sordid spectacle posed by the Senate Judiciary Committee hearing from Friday, October 11, through the early hours of Monday, October 14, may have been many things, but it was *not* a lynching. That it eventually and sadly took the form it did—with all its lurid, public details of apparent sexual misconduct—occurred *not* because of racism, but because of the failure of the Senate Judiciary Committee to take charges of sexual harassment seriously. And it was that very failure that led to another round of hearing concerning Thomas's fitness to sit on the Supreme Court. In the improbable case that Anita Hill's charges are not true—and I say this based on the corroborated testimony of Angela Wright, who was disallowed a public hearing at the last moment—the very most that Clarence Thomas might claim in any case is "high-tech character assassination," which is a far cry indeed from a "high-tech lynching." On the other hand, if anyone at the committee hearings was smeared by stereotypical casting, it was Anita Hill.

ERNEST ALLEN, JR., Ph.D., is associate professor of Afro-American Studies at the University of Massachusetts, Amherst. He is co-editor of two forthcoming projects: Unite or Perish, *a compilation of black radical and nationalist writings from 1954 to 1975; and* The Black Freedom Struggle in the United States: An Encyclopedia.

NOTES

1. Alessandra Stanley, "Erotomania: A Rare Disorder Runs Riot—in Men's Minds," *The New York Times*, November 10, 1991, p. 2E.
2. *The New York Times*, October 12, 1991, p. 10.
3. *Boston Globe*, October 12, 1991, p. 1.
4. *The New York Times*, October 13, 1991, p. 31.
5. In her unsworn testimony Angela Wright "recounts being present when Thomas offered advice to another black in the office on how to cope with his financial difficulty—'mortgage or whatever,' she says. According to Wright, Thomas told him: 'Well, you know why you can't get any money? Because you're not black enough. Now, if you grew an Afro and put on a Dashiki, you would get all the government money you want'." Sidney Blumenthal, "The Higher Hustle," *The New Republic* (November 11, 1991), 46.

Time to Heal the Wounds of Pornography

Robert L. Allen

The recent furor over charges that Supreme Court nominee Clarence Thomas sexually harassed a female assistant, Anita Hill—now a University of Oklahoma law school professor—focused national attention on the issue of sexual harassment. It also compels us to consider pornography.

Prof. Hill stated that Thomas made unwanted sexual advances and pressed graphic descriptions of pornographic materials on her. Thomas denied that any such thing happened.

The dramatic accusation and denial provoked intense debate, but the fact is that thousands of women are sexually harassed every day, a great many of them women of color and poor women who are most vulnerable in the jobs which sexist and racist discrimination force them to take—domestics, clerical workers, farmworkers, sweatshop and factory workers. Not only are these women especially vulnerable to sexual harassment, but they also have less access to the levers of power needed to seek redress. The majority of the crimes against them are not reported because they fear revenge from their employers or they know their complaint will be dismissed. They are doubly oppressed: subjected to abuse and then constrained to remain silent about it.

As an African American man I am outraged by the sexism and racism that make so many of my sisters who must work to support their families targets for sexual attacks by bosses and supervisors and other men in power.

However, incidents of sexual harassment are not unrelated to the flood of pornography that has invaded even the corner market. Pornography is a multibillion dollar business. I suspect that for every man who sexually harasses a woman in the workplace there must be hundreds if not thousands of us who occasionally or habitually buy pornography. If questioned we may rationalize it on the grounds of its being a safe fantasy alternative to unsafe sexual practices (which is exactly what some porn mags now proudly claim to be) and point out that the violence in commercially distributed porn has been eliminated or at least toned down (some mags carry a tag proclaiming their "non-violent explicit action").

We cannot continue to evade the recognition that even "tasteful" pornography demeans and degrades women and men by exploiting our sexuality and making a commodity of the most intimate physical connection between two human beings. Studies show that it also elicits feelings of sexualized aggression in men who view it, no doubt contributing to the epidemic of sexual violence against women that stalks our communities. But studies and statistics and even discussions with friends can be kept at a distance—safely impersonal and intellectual. It becomes possible to separate knowledge from action: an intellectual understanding of pornography as poison having no apparent effect on the practice of using it.

But when porn comes home it is hard to evade the contradictions. A short time ago I discovered a pornographic magazine tucked under my teenage son's bed. Knowing that pornography is so pervasive I was not shocked, but finding it was a "softcore" magazine *I* had purchased bathed me in shame. At first I was tempted to hide my guilty feeling by getting mad at my son and dumping my discomfort on him. Fortunately, a moment's reflection made possible by the fact that he was not home when I discovered the magazine allowed me to think of a better approach. After all, his interest in the magazine stemmed from an adolescent's emerging and normal interest in sex. I decided to tell him I found the magazine and to have a talk with him about sexuality. I also gave him a copy of *The Joy of Sex*. I didn't have the courage to talk about why I had bought the magazine.

Recently I returned from a trip to New York City. While there I took my eighteen-year-old niece to dinner and we talked about her career. A beautiful and intelligent young woman, she is struggling to succeed in the highly competitive business of professional modeling. It is something she has diligently pursued since as a pre-teen she appeared in amateur fashion shows at the local malls. Of course, the family has been worried about her vulnerability to sexual exploitation by the clients, photographers, and other men with whom she must work. Her mother, who lives in another city, calls every few days to check on her.

My niece showed me her "book," a portfolio of photos showing her in various poses and clothes. Sometimes the clothes were a bit skimpy, but the poses were always tasteful. Many of the photos were stunning and vibrant, revealing her youthful beauty and poise. But I became uncomfortable as I thought about how these photos used her body to sell products. Even more discomforting was my realization that for some men the distance between these photos and the images in some of the more "tasteful" porn magazines was not all that great. Knowing of my niece's struggle to make a living, I was sickened by the thought that she might feel pressured to do other kinds of "modeling" to survive. Of course, my niece would never do this, but I was deeply disturbed by the recognition that she might be economically pushed in that direction and that I, as an occasional consumer of pornography, helped create the economic pull that would draw her or others into it.

I hope my niece will be okay. But the fact is that many young girls are pushed into pornography and prostitution simply to survive. And the racist exploitation of black women and other women of color in pornography and prostitution is notorious. As a black man I feel I must stop being complicit with a system that would demean and degrade my niece and other women whom I cherish.

It is not that difficult to truly see (rather than merely ogle) the women (and men) who appear in porn mags. Look at the eyes rather than the body. Then you will see the pain, the anger, the feigned enjoyment on the women's faces; the vacantness and forced leers on the faces of the men. Even if you look only at the bodies ask yourself, Are these images the way I want my son to see sexuality, to see women, to see men? Would I want my niece or my daughter or my partner to be one of the images on the page?

Pornography corrupts our sexuality, our most intimate relations with other human beings. That is reason enough to consider it a major personal problem. That it also harms women and children and men by fostering sexualized aggression and abuse makes it a major social problem.

We need to heal the wounds of pornography. Through community education and action, legislative initiatives, and support groups for victims of harassment and recovering porn "addicts," the problem must be addressed.

It is time for pornography to come out of its hiding place in the bedroom closet of our collective psyche, and finally—with no second thoughts or lingering doubts—be thrown into the trash.

ROBERT L. ALLEN, Ph.D., is an author and editor. His books are Black Awakening in Capitalist America, The Reluctant Reformers, *and* The Port Chicago Mutiny. *He is senior editor of* The Black Scholar.

I Dare to Hope

Maya Angelou

Now, as America's mighty marketing machines are being oiled and checked to begin selling and celebrating Christopher Columbus's feat of 1492, some people are examining with amazement and alarm another achievement that took place in Europe two decades later.

In the early 1500's Niccolo Machiavelli, exiled and out of favor in Italy, wrote a slim manual on power: how to gain it, how to wield it, and how to keep it. He named the handbook *The Prince* and dedicated it to Lorenzo de Medici. The ideas therein so captured how to use what was base, weak and ignoble in the human psyche that for hundreds of years hence when a person, event or action was deemed devilish or satanically manipulative it has been called Machiavellian. The advice Machiavelli offered, which has been used so successfully against the powerless and which interests me today, can be paraphrased as: Divide the masses that you may conquer them, separate them and you can rule them.

The recent vocal opposition to the nomination of Clarence Thomas to the Supreme Court and the reams of media coverage the nomination has generated have sent me again to *The Prince*. I wag my head in soreful disbelief over the present-day relevance and use of ideas summarized nearly 500 years ago for the sole purpose of instructing the mighty on the management of the powerless.

Today, the African-American community whirls in eddies of debate, demolition, disagreement, accusation and calumny over the matter of whether an African-American man with a lamentable reputation and impressive credentials should be seated on the highest court in the land.

Judge Thomas, chosen by President Bush, has demonstrated that he is as conservative as the President and the Administration, else he would not have been selected. The African-American savants know that, and we know as well that if efforts to scuttle his appointment are successful, another conservative possibly more harmful, and one who has neither our history nor culture in common with us, will be seated firmly on the bench till death or decision rules otherwise.

Judge Thomas has given his adversaries every reason to oppose and distrust him. Many of his audacious actions as chairman of the Equal Employment Opportunity Commission were anti–affirmative action, anti-busing and anti–other opportunities to redress inequality in our country.

In a Federal court case, as Assistant Secretary of Education for civil rights, he reportedly testified that he had deliberately disobeyed a court order requiring his department to conduct speedy reviews of discrimination complaints. That admission along with his behavior of indifference to African-American issues has given even his most ardent supporters pause.

Judge Thomas, a poor black from Pin Point, Georgia, has reached proximity to America's highest court because of the very laws his forefathers fought to have written and enforced, and which he has treated so cavalierly.

It follows then that many African-Americans ask, How can we advance if one we have sent forth in the vanguard ignores our concerns?

In these bloody days and frightful nights when an urban warrior can find no face more despicable than his own, no ammunition more deadly than self-hate and no target more deserving of his true aim than his brother, we must wonder how we came so late and lonely to this place.

In this terrifying and murderous season, when young women achieve adulthood before puberty, and become mothers before learning how to be daughters, we must stop the rhetoric and high-sounding phrases, stop the posing and preening and look to our own welfare.

We need to haunt the halls of history and listen anew to the ancestors' wisdom. We must ask questions and find answers that will help us to avoid falling into the merciless maw of history. How were our forefathers able to support their weakest when they themselves were at their weakest? How were they able to surround the errant leader and prevent him from being co-opted by forces that would destroy him and them? How were they, lonely, bought separately, sold apart, able to conceive of the deep, ponderous wisdom found in "walk together, children . . . don't you get weary."

The black youngsters of today must ask black leaders: If you can't make an effort to reach, reconstruct and save a black man who has graduated from Yale, how can you reach down here in this drug-filled, hate-filled cesspool where I live and save me?

I am supporting Clarence Thomas's nomination, and I am neither naive enough nor hopeful enough to imagine that in publicly supporting him I will give the younger generation a pretty picture of unity, but rather I can show them that I and they come from a people who had the courage to be when being was dangerous, who had the courage to dare when daring was dangerous—and most important, had the courage to hope.

Because Clarence Thomas has been poor, has been nearly suffocated by the acrid odor of racial discrimination, is intelligent, well trained, black and young enough to be won over again, I support him.

The prophet in "Lamentations" cried, "Although he put his mouth in the dust . . . there is still hope."

MAYA ANGELOU, a poet, is professor of American Studies at Wake Forest University. This article is reprinted from The New York Times*, August 25, 1991.*

A Radical Double Agent

Derrick Bell

After a careful analysis of the civil rights writings and statements of Clarence Thomas, I am tempted to support his nomination to the Supreme Court. I have concluded that Judge Thomas is not really a conservative, but, rather, a committed black revolutionary. I am convinced that he plans to use right-wing dogma to spark racial revolt, a revolt he evidently sees as a dangerous but urgently necessary response to this society's growing hostility to African Americans.

Initially, I had a number of grave concerns. I was baffled by Judge Thomas's opposition to affirmative action and other civil rights remedies that advanced his career.

I cringed at his advocacy of capital punishment when blacks are given that irreversible penalty in such disproportionate numbers.

I wondered how he could condemn poor black people—including his own sister—for relying on Government assistance to feed, clothe and house their children at a time when so many Americans are dependent on the Government to spend billions of dollars to insure savings that have been put at risk by ill-managed banks and savings and loans.

Even his anti-abortion advocacy seemed to fly in the face of reality. State limits on a woman's choice contradict his espousal of free enterprise without government interference. Such limits also ignore the fact that state-mandated restrictions fall heavily on the poor, among whom black women are disproportionately represented.

Then I realized that Judge Thomas's seemingly ridiculous statements must be part of a carefully conceived conspiracy. No black man with his roots and knowledge of the nation's dire employment situation could actually believe that today's poor can find a formula for success in a "self-help" ideology advocated by those born into wealth or privilege or both.

Many liberals hope that, if seated on the Supreme Court, he will take a more realistic and sympathetic position on issues concerning minorities and other disadvantaged groups. Large numbers of blacks also hope for a post-confirmation conversion. They support him based on his race and his impoverished childhood and despite his disavowal of all race-based selection processes. Such hopes are futile.

Indeed, his value as a revolutionary double agent depends on his strict adherence to the positions that persuaded President Bush to mock both merit and good sense by claiming he was the most qualified candidate.

An all-white Supreme Court hostile to racial issues is one thing. But a Court with its lone black Justice joining the majority in its anti–civil rights decisions will send a clear message: It is useless to continue seeking relief through law for America's still rampant racism.

Militant arguments that blacks now have no alternative except disruptive protests and boycotts will be invulnerable to more moderate responses. The Court's action will even give legitimacy to claims by some extremist leaders that black people must respond with violence to the violence inflicted on them by an uncaring society.

History reveals no precedent for a black man in a position of real power advocating racial policies that are so at odds with the convictions of a great majority of his people. Thus, Judge Thomas must expect fierce criticism, first from blacks and then—when they realize the racial chaos his decisions will create—whites as well. His stand will require personal courage.

The brilliance of his scheme lies in the following: It will work even if he denies—as he probably will—that his conservatism really masks a radicalism to which most blacks do not adhere but to which an ever-increasing number will subscribe within months after he takes his seat on the Supreme Court.

DERRICK BELL is a visiting professor at the New York University Law School. Reprinted from The New York Times.

Clarence Thomas and the Apartheid Connection

Herb Boyd and Don Rojas

While the Judge Clarence Thomas and Professor Anita Hill confrontation is popularly seen as a bout between contending forces, the two opponents have more in common than meets the eye. What is indisputably clear and ironic in the complex Clarence Thomas affair is that both the leading players espouse conservative values, are champions of "self-sufficiency," worked dutifully for the racist Ronald Reagan, and supported the rejected Supreme Court nominee Judge Robert Bork, himself a dangerous reactionary.

This confrontation was not a feud between two black persons with diametrically opposed approaches to the struggle for black progress and social justice in America. It was not a face-off between contending political philosophies. This was no liberal/conservative conflict, no radical/moderate debate, which it should have been for it to have lasting historical value.

Neither Justice Thomas nor Professor Hill has demonstrated any desire to reform a judicial system rife with racism, inequality, and corruption. Both are successful "careerists" who will defend the system to its last gasp because they both have vested interests in it. They are inextricably bound and beholden to the current legal apparatus—one teaching the laws of the capitalist system, the other now ensconced on the highest court where he can continue to defend and uphold these laws.

There is, of course, nothing surprising about all of this, but it is startling and painful for us when the drama unfolds in blackface. Why should black America be upset or embarrassed by this bourgeois spectacle? Is it a consequence of our being a racial minority that we still wish to be judged by the values, norms, and mores of white American society?

The real outrage and anger should come, not from the embarrassment of a black man and a black woman accusing each other in full public view, but from the ultimate irrelevancy of this event to the everyday realities that the majority of black people struggle to improve all across the nation. This was not a passion play about poverty and social inequality—the greatest immoralities in America today. It was a lurid tale of "sex, lies, and videotape."

Neither Judge Thomas, whose nomination in many respects is a reprise of Bush's Willie Horton caper, nor Professor Hill, who is being touted as the Rosa Parks of sexual harassment, is representative of mainstream black American working men and women. Thomas and Hill are members of the black elite, what W. E. B. Du Bois called the "talented tenth." These two climbed the ladder of success from humble origins—a minority within a minority and exemplars of the fulfillment of the American dream for a precious few—while the vast majority of black Americans continue to live the horrors of the American nightmare.

Very few black Americans were surprised by the outcome of the Senate Judiciary Committee's confirmation hearings. The certainty of approval was virtually assured once it was clear that the Senate panel would offer no rigorous scrutiny of the nominee's legal qualifications or any of the charges brought against him.

There is no need to discuss Justice Thomas's weak judicial background, the fact that there were several black jurists far more qualified than he was to fill the post vacated by the retiring Thurgood Marshall. Nor is it necessary to expound on the fiasco with Anita Hill. This issue like the previous one has been amply discussed elsewhere. However, nowhere has there been any assessment of Justice Thomas's connection to paid representatives of the South African Apartheid regime—an issue only a few alternative and black newspapers covered with any consistency.

During the summer of 1991 it was disclosed that Thomas had served on the editorial advisory board of the *Lincoln Review,* the journal of the Washington-based, neo-conservative Lincoln Institute, a black think tank.[1] The Lincoln Institute was founded in 1978 by J. A. Parker, who headed President Ronald Reagan's transition team at the Equal Opportunity Employment Commission. It was through this affiliation that Thomas became acquainted with Parker and his associate William Keyes—both of whom are registered lobbyists for the South African government. And, in fact, Thomas would later claim Parker as his political mentor, a man who many consider to be the founding father of the contemporary black conservative movement.[2]

In 1988, while chairman of the EEOC, Thomas told an audience at California State University: "But even in the face of this [the hold of the liberal left on black Americans], a few dissidents like Thomas Sowell and J. A. Parker have stood steadfast, refusing to give in to the cult mentality and childish obedience that hypnotizes black Americans into a mindless political trance. I admire them and only hope I can have a fraction of their courage and strength."[3]

Perhaps it was this same "strength and courage" that aided Parker and Keyes when they made a pact with apartheid. As registered agents for the South African government, Parker and Keyes began to develop a web of organizations—IPAC (International Public Affairs Consultants), the Lincoln Institute and its *Review,* and the Abe Lincoln Foundation—all of which support right-wing activity. From 1985 to 1988 IPAC received well over a million dollars, courtesy of the South African government through its Washington embassy.[4]

According to the *National Catholic Reporter,* Parker was also vitally connected to the WACL (World Anti-Communist League), an "international organization often described as a network of 'emigré' collaborators of Hitler, Latin American death squad leaders, and apologists for apartheid, the Moonies, and other fascist and anti-Semitic elements."[5] Thomas's relationship with registered agents should give us all pause, for in the long run it could play an important role in the opinions he writes.

In Thomas, as Dan Levitas, executive director of the Center for Democratic Renewal in Atlanta observed, the far right has an advocate on the Supreme Court, and it "should raise questions about the maturity of his judgments . . . already Thomas seems to have failed to distinguish between fascism and conservatism."

There are at least two verified reports of Thomas's being present at functions sponsored by the Lincoln Institute in which funds were being raised to support various reactionary governments.[6] These issues could have been further examined if the Senate Judiciary Committee had had the guts or inclination to pursue the extent of Thomas's association with Parker and Keyes.

However, there is good reason to believe that even if such a relationship could have been fully disclosed, it would still have had no effect on the outcome of the hearings. And yet, if information as publicly accessible as this was passed over, the question remains, how much more did the senators ignore? Why, for example, didn't the committee raise questions about Thomas's failure to excuse himself during a review of the *Ralston-Purina* v. *Alpo* case? Thomas's impartiality as an appeals judge was clearly compromised since he was a protégé of Senator John Danforth of Missouri, whose grandfather was a founder of Ralston-Purina.

Thomas's association with Parker and Keyes is the most immediate evidence of his link to neo-conservative thought. But he has clearly been on this path of reaction for several years, despite confessed flirtations with the ideas of Malcolm X and the civil rights movement. As for the current litmus test for rightist tendencies—affirmative action, black "victimization," and welfare—Thomas passes with flying colors. He is a sworn opponent of affirmative action, believes that black people are largely responsible for their social and economic plight, soft-pedals racism, and has criticized so-called "welfare queens."

If Professor Hill possesses conflicting feelings about some of these touchstones of neo-conservative thought, she has not made them available to the public. Although it is our opinion, given her past affiliations and actions, that she is a dyed-in-the-wool proponent of right-wing ideology.

Black neo-conservative thought is becoming increasingly fashionable nowadays, and there is no refuting the indirect impact of the Thomas-Hill encounter. There have been a number of black Republicans and neo-conservatives who have pointed with pride to them as role models in the new age of politics in which blacks are no longer expected to be automatic supporters of the Democratic Party. This is certainly the thinking of CORE's Roy Innes, TV commentator Tony Brown, and housing advocate Robert Woodson.

Though now forever estranged personally and politically, Thomas and Hill still share a common bed. But there is one critical distinction. While secure within their niche of the black bourgeoisie, there are two main differences between Justice Thomas and Professor Hill that move beyond gender and into human nature. Thomas personifies power without respectability, and Hill reflects respectability without power. You need no reminder of who will be the overall winner in capitalist and sexist America.

HERB BOYD is a reporter at the New York Amsterdam News, *and DON ROJAS is an editor at the same newspaper. Boyd and Rojas are currently co-editing a collection of essays on the Los Angeles Rebellion.*

NOTES

1. The most incisive and exhaustive discussion of Clarence Thomas's association with J. A. Parker and William Keyes has been done by researcher Russ Bellant. This information came from Bellant's article in the *National Catholic Reporter,* August 2, 1991.

2. Allan Brownfield, *Washington Inquirer,* August 23, 1991.

3. This excerpt is from a speech delivered by Thomas at California State University, San Bernadino, California, April 25, 1988. The quote is part of Thomas's attack on black liberals and leftists. "Those on the left," he said, "smugly assume blacks are monolithic and will by force of circumstance *always* [his emphasis] huddle to the left of the political spectrum. The political right watches this herd mentality in action, concedes that blacks are monolithic, picks up a few dissidents, and wistfully shrugs at the seemingly unbreakable hold of the liberal left on black Americans."

4. Juan Williams, *Washington Post,* November 21, 1985. Williams centers most of his attention here on how William Keyes became a lobbyist for the South African government, charging nearly $400,000 a year for his services.

5. Bellant, *op. cit.*

6. *Human Events,* June 6, 1987.

Collard Greens, Clarence Thomas, and the High-Tech Rape of Anita Hill

Melba Joyce Boyd

On the second day of the Clarence Thomas–Anita Hill hearing I telephoned Rain, an old friend and college roommate, to talk about the scuttlebutt. After a long first day, it was time "to kick it" with a sister. Her husband answered the phone and said I should come over and watch the event with them. The need to experience the hearing in a communal setting intensified the significance of the moment as the clash of the sexes and sexuality was staged on television live, and in living color.

For me, the hearing was as much a personal, political issue as it was a topic critical to my work as a professor of Afroamerican Studies. In the background of my thoughts, effacing this conflict, were my most recent classroom lectures and discussions about the sexual exploitation, abuse, and rape of the slave woman. I could hear the echo of Linda Brent's complaint in *Incidents in the Life of a Slave Girl* as Anita Hill alleged the indignities of the sexual harassment she had suffered at the whims of the aspiring Supreme Court Justice Clarence Thomas. The setting: An all white, all male senate committee, sitting in a row, cross-examining a black woman attorney, testifying in precise and perfect "standard" English. It was a scene straight from the theater of the absurd, aptly embellished on "Saturday Night Live" and "In Living Color."

Having just returned from her father's garden, Rain was loaded down with collard and turnip greens to be cleaned, cooked, and distributed to family and friends. Rain worked at the kitchen sink and stove with her back to the television, while I sat at the round table. With biting sarcasm, we "dogged" Thomas, the usual backward, insidious intelligence of the government, and the media's blind ignorance. "Who's lying?" was our rhetorical refrain, as the African American Republicans lined up for the camera as Yale's neat elite (we call them "e-lites" in Detroit).

Rain's husband, an ex–factory worker and now a successful contractor, and Rain's father, a ninety-year-old labor union veteran, felt a sense of male kinship with Thomas. They wanted Anita Hill to be lying basically because Thomas was a black man. Grabbing on to any suggestion to discredit her testimony, they believed Thomas's situation was a typical, racist scenario—a comfortable resolve in lieu of the alternative.

But, for me and Rain, there was no question about the lie. As she washed the grit and grime from the collards we cracked on the shame-faced Senator Kennedy, framed on the right side of the TV screen, impotently silent and to the left of the committee chair, Senator Biden. Intermittently, Rain, a social worker in a public school system, unloaded horror stories about sexual abuse in homes, in schools, and in the workplace. Most important was her critique of American society's psychological acceptance of sexual transgressions against women and children. Indeed, I held too many memories of distressed women who were too ashamed for themselves and their perpetrators to defend their dignity and self respect. The lie that festers below the sexual psychosis of America's complicit silence is more frightening than the trauma of the Thomas-Hill hearing. (Subsequently, a Miss America, the quintessential virgin queen, shatters another sexual illusion and reveals the anguish of being an incest survivor, and the startling statistics of "one in five" children reiterates the severity of a maladjusted, repressive social order.)

The subterfuge of America's sexual psyche is so deep-seated that women who have been victimized are victims even before the assault. The woman is not to be believed at any cost, especially the black woman, whose sexual legacy in this country has been the Jezebel—the loose woman who instigates her own rape. The periphery of comments made by many women and men, even when they believed Anita Hill was harassed, is reflexive of a cultural code that dictates: "As a black woman, she should have checked him and got him straight from the get go, but she should have *never* exposed him in front of white America." In addition to being accorded so little respect and consideration, black women are still expected to eradicate the onslaught of male madness and to endure indignities simply because to reveal the truth about the devils in the camp would be an embarrassment for the "race." Conversely if black Americans exhibited stronger political and moral positions on such issues, we would not continue to be consumed by the deluge of contradictions that, historically, have blamed the victim instead of the perpetrator. And in our case, what could be more evident than the fact that slavery is still used by bigots as a reference to demean and degrade us instead of American democracy.

Why is it that women are denied full humanity and must shoulder the weight of everybody else's weaknesses, especially when the character in question is perfectly prepared to sell us and even his own mother and sister down the river in order to achieve fame and prestige by cavorting with the anti–Civil Rights president and his New World Order?

The incapacity of human beings to evolve beyond the superficial, beyond the arbitrary categories of race (which, in our case, were contrived by the slaveholding class to perpetuate our enslavement and subsequent second class citizenship) and deal with the truth is directly related to the confusion and conflict revealed in responses to the Thomas-Hill hearings. The stratification of race, gender, and class can no longer be assessed by token representation. The New World Order is the Old World Order constructed to the benefit of global corporations. Representation in the hierarchy by people of color, women, and even homosexuals too often reflects a careful selection of well trained, articulate functionaries who facilitate the expectations and directives of that ruling order.

This is not a new phenomena, as an appraisal of most of our public and private institutions indicates the installation of "conservative" blacks, who refute the necessity for affirmative action with the same fabrications and disinformation as reactionary "whites." They function both as an illusion of equal opportunity and as spokespersons for the "race." As the old folks would say, "He may be my color, but he ain't my kind."

Clarence Thomas—the nouveau pork chopper, the black-gowned equalizer of reverse discrimination—represents the tip of the iceberg. In the face of high unemployment, homelessness, and crack-cocaine genocide, the president of the United States throws the B.U.P.P.I.E.S. a bone, while they wait in line to shake the hand of Strom Thurmond, the same Dixiecrat who fought for months to stop the Supreme Court appointment of Thurgood Marshall, a brilliant litigator and human rights activist. What has been filtered out in this picture is the legacy of freedom, which views "blackness" as a perspective derived from the circumstances of the disenfranchised.

Meanwhile, Anita Hill returns to her lectures at The University of Oklahoma, having met her "call to duty."

With all due respect to Hill's humiliation and the nation's shame and tongue-tied politicians, the new Negro has a Ph.D. or law degree from the cobwebs of the Ivy League and is conditioned to take a place of prominence while the People sleep in the streets, without an address, without relief, or a voter's registration card. Understand, the New World Order has altered the dynamics of Struggle and has united the disenfranchised under a true multiculturalism of poverty.

The lesson to be learned is that a black woman's justice is the people's justice, the legacy of self defense secured at sundown in the parking lot, after a serious plate of collard greens.

MELBA JOYCE BOYD, D.A., is associate professor of African-American Studies and director of African-American Studies at the University of Michigan, Flint campus. Her latest publication is a book of poems, Inventory of Black Roses.

Taking Sides Against Ourselves

Rosemary L. Bray

The Anita Hill–Clarence Thomas hearings are over; Judge Thomas is Justice Thomas now. Yet the memories linger on and on. Like witnesses to a bad accident, many of us who watched the three days of Senate hearings continue to replay the especially horrible moments. We compare our memories of cool accusation and heated denial; we weigh again in our minds the hours of testimony, vacuous and vindictive by turn. In the end, even those of us who thought we were beyond surprise had underestimated the trauma.

"I have not been so wrenched since Dr. King was shot," says Jewell Jackson McCabe, the founder of the National Coalition of 100 Black Women, an advocacy group with chapters in twenty-one states and the District of Columbia. "I cannot begin to tell you; this thing has been unbelievable."

The near-mythic proportions that the event has already assumed in the minds of Americans are due, in part, to the twin wounds of race and gender that the hearings exposed. If gender is a troubling problem in American life and race is still a national crisis, the synergy of the two embodied in the life and trials of Anita Hill left most of America dumbstruck. Even black people who did not support Clarence Thomas's politics felt that Hill's charges, made public at the 11th hour, smacked of treachery. Feminist leaders embraced with enthusiasm a woman whose conservative political consciousness might have given them chills only a month earlier.

Even before the hearings began, the nomination of Clarence Thomas had taken on, for me, the quality of a nightmare. The particular dread I felt was one of betrayal—not a betrayal by President Bush, from whom I expected nothing—but by Thomas himself, who not only was no Thurgood Marshall but also gradually revealed himself to be a man who rejoiced in burning the bridges that brought him over.

I felt the kind of heartbreak that comes only to those of us still willing to call ourselves race women and race men in the old and honorable sense, people who feel that African-Americans should live and work and succeed not only for ourselves but also for our people.

The heated debates about gender and race in America have occurred, for the most part, in separate spheres; the separation makes for neater infighting.

But black women can never skirt these questions; we are their living expression. The parallel pursuits of equality for African-Americans and for women have trapped black women between often conflicting agendas for more than a century. We are asked in a thousand ways, large and small, to take sides against ourselves, postponing a confrontation in one arena to address an equally urgent task in another. Black men and white women have often made claims to our loyalty and our solidarity in the service of their respective struggles for recognition and autonomy, understanding only dimly that what may seem like liberty to each is for us only a kind of parole. Despite the bind, more often than not we choose loyalty to the race rather than the uncertain allegiance of gender.

Ours is the complicity of guilty survivors. A black man's presence is often feared; a black woman's presence is at least tolerated. Because until recently so much of the work that black women were paid to do was work that white men and women would not do—cleaning, serving, tending, teaching, nursing, maintaining, caring—we seem forever linked to the needs of human life that are at once minor and urgent.

As difficult as the lives of black women often are, we know we are mobile in ways black men are not—and black men know that we know. They know that we are nearly as angered as they about their inability to protect us in the traditional and patriarchal way, even as many of us have moved beyond the need for such protection. And some black men know ways to use our anger, our sorrow, our guilt, against us.

In our efforts to make a place for ourselves and our families in America, we have created a paradigm of sacrifice. And in living out such lives, we have convinced even ourselves that no sacrifice is too great to insure what we view in a larger sense as the survival of the race.

That sacrifice has been an unspoken promise to our people; it has made us partners with black men in a way white women and men cannot know. Yet not all of us view this partnership with respect. There are those who would use black women's commitment to the race as a way to control black women. There are those who believe the price of solidarity is silence. It was that commitment that trapped Anita Hill. And it is a commitment we may come to rue.

As I watched Hill being questioned that Friday by white men, by turn either timid or incredulous, I grieved for her. The anguish in her eyes was recognizable to me. Not only did she dare to speak about events more than one woman would regard as unspeakable, she did so publicly. Not only did she make public accusations best investigated in private, she made them against a man who was black and conservative, as she was—a man who in other ways had earned her respect.

"Here is a woman who went to Sunday school and took it seriously," says Cornel West, director of the African-American Studies department at Princeton University and a social critic who felt mesmerized by what he called "the travesty and tragedy" of the hearings. "She clearly is a product of the social conservatism of a rural black Baptist community." For black women historically, such probity, hard-won and tenaciously held, was social salvation. For white onlookers, it suggested an eerie primness out of sync with contemporary culture.

In the quiet and resolute spirit she might very well have learned from Sunday school, Hill confronted and ultimately breached a series of taboos in the black community that have survived both slavery and the post-segregation life she and Clarence Thomas share. Anita Hill put her private business in the street, and she downgraded a black man to a room filled with white men who might alter his fate—surely a large enough betrayal for her to be read out of the race.

By Sunday evening, Anita Hill's testimony lay buried under an avalanche of insinuation and innuendo. Before the eyes of a nation, a tenured law professor beloved by her students was transformed into an evil, opportunistic harpy; a deeply religious Baptist was turned into a sick and delusional woman possessed by Satan and in need of exorcism; this youngest of thirteen children from a loving family became a frustrated spinster longing for the attentions of her fast-track superior, bent on exacting a cruel revenge for his rejection.

These skillful transformations of Anita Hill's character by some members of the Senate were effective because they were familiar, manageable images of African-American womanhood. What undergirds these images is the common terror of black women out of control. We are the grasping and materialistic Sapphire in an "Amos 'n' Andy" episode; the embodiment of a shadowy, insane sexuality; the raging, furious, rejected woman. In their extremity, these are images far more accessible and understandable than the polished and gracious dignity, the cool intelligence that Anita Hill displayed in the lion's den of the Senate chamber. However she found herself reconstituted, the result was the same. She was, on all levels, simply unbelievable.

Anita Hill fell on the double-edged sword of African-American womanhood. Her privacy, her reputation, her integrity—all were casualties of an ignorance that left her unseen by and unknown to most of those who meant either to champion or abuse her. As credible, as inspiring, as impressive as she was, most people who saw her had no context in which to judge her. The signs and symbols that might have helped to place Hill were long ago appropriated by officials of authentic (male) blackness, or by representatives of authentic (white) womanhood. Quite simply, a woman like Anita Hill couldn't possibly exist. And in that sense, she is in fine historical company.

More than a century earlier, black women routinely found themselves beyond belief, and thus beyond help, solace, and protection. In 1861, the most famous of the few slave narratives written by a black woman, *Incidents in the Life of a Slave Girl,* was published. (The book was regarded as fiction for more than 100 years, until in 1987 Jean Fagin Yellin of Pace University completed six years of painstaking research substantiating the existence of its author, Harriet Jacobs, and her harrowing story.) Writing under the pseudonym "Linda Brent," Jacobs outlined for the genteel white woman of the nineteenth-century the horrors, both sexual and otherwise, that awaited the female slave. Jacobs spent close to seven years hiding from her master ensconced in a garret, with food smuggled in by her recently freed grandmother.

In the story of Harriet Jacobs, the powerful man she fears is white. In the story of Anita Hill, the powerful man she fears is black. But the vulnerability of each woman is a palpable presence in the stories they tell. Jacobs's tale is enlivened by the dramatic structure of the nineteenth-century sentimental novel, Hill's accounts are magnified through the image of her presence on television. Indeed, Jacobs's first lines are a plea to her audience to be taken seriously. "Reader, be assured this narrative is no fiction. I am aware that some of my adventures may seem incredible; but they are, nevertheless, strictly true."

Later she recounts the beginning of her owner's pursuit of her, the year she turned fifteen: "My master began to whisper foul words in my ear. Young as I was, I could not remain ignorant of their import. I tried to treat them with indifference or contempt. . . . The other slaves . . . knew too well the guilty practices under that roof; and they were aware that to speak of them was an offense that never went unpunished. . . . I longed for some one to confide in. I would have given the world to have laid my head on my grandmother's faithful bosom, and told her all my troubles. . . . I dreaded the consequences of a violent outbreak; and both pride and fear kept me silent."

Harriet Jacobs had good reason to fear; even free African-American women of the nineteenth century possessed no rights that anyone was bound to respect. Regarded as immoral and loose, black women spent an inordinate amount of time in the years after slavery in attempts to establish themselves as virtuous women, as a rebuke to the rash of hypersexual images that flooded contemporary consciousness in those days, images that rationalized the routine sexual abuse of black women—both slave and free—by white men.

It was a stereotype that had consequences for black men as well: "Historically, the stereotype of the sexually potent black male was largely based on that of the promiscuous black female," explained Paula Giddings, in *When and Where I Enter,* her history of black women in America. "He would have to be potent, the thinking went, to satisfy such hot-natured women."

Such myths of sexual potency and promiscuity, written and disseminated by trained nineteenth-century historians, fueled the widespread fears of black men as rapists of white women—and provided the engine for a campaign of terrorism against newly freed black people that included a rash of lynchings. Thus, it was especially troubling that Clarence Thomas should refer to the second round of hearings as "a high-tech lynching."

Thomas evoked one of the most emotional images in African-

American consciousness, flinging himself across history like Little Eva clinging to an ice floe and, at the same time, blaming a black woman for his troubles. A century earlier, it was the courageous and single-minded investigative reporting of a black female journalist, Ida B. Wells, that finally galvanized a recalcitrant United States into taking lynching seriously.

Incidents in the Life of a Slave Girl would have made far more instructive reading for the Senate Judiciary Committee than *The Exorcist.* It was, after all, the Senate's appalling lack of familiarity with what it feels like to be powerless, vulnerable, and afraid that rendered Anita Hill and her behavior incomprehensible to most of them. In her preface, Jacobs writes that she has "concealed the names of places and given persons fictitious names. I had no motive for secrecy on my own account, but I deemed it kind and considerate toward others to pursue this course." It is likely that she is more fearful than she lets on.

But it is just as likely that Jacobs evokes a way of seeing the world that transcends nineteenth-century female gentility, that Jacobs is acting out of Christian charity to those who have persecuted her. And it is just as likely that she held on to her fragile dreams of connection, however slight, to home and friends, however frightening the context in which she enjoyed them.

Studying this connected way of seeing the world has been the work of Carol Gilligan's professional life. The author of *In a Different Voice: Psychological Theory and Women's Development,* she has written extensively on women's psychological development and the issues of justice and care that characterize the relationships of many women, both personal and professional. Thus she did not find it implausible that Anita Hill might have experienced the events she described, yet continued to work with Judge Thomas.

"It amazed me that no one understood the underlying logic of what she did," Gilligan says. "Her basic assumption was that you live in connection with others, in relationship with others. Now, her experience of that relationship was one of violation; it was offensive to her. But she was making the attempt to work it through in the relationship; trying to resolve conflict without breaking connection." The possibility that such an ethic might have motivated Anita Hill in her choices is rarely voiced in discussions about her.

It may be that this low-key approach does not fit the image of the black woman who stands ready to challenge and confront offensive behavior. The surly black wife with a frying pan in her hand is the flip side of the nurturing mammy, and it is abundantly clear to millions by now that Anita Hill is neither.

Thus her profound self-possession, particularly in the face of the behavior she ascribed to Thomas, seemed impossible to observers—in large part because her response was not the conditioned one for black women. Hill showed no signs of the Harriet Tubman Syndrome, the fierce insistence on freedom or death that made Tubman an abolitionist legend. Anita Hill grabbed no blunt objects with which to threaten her superior, she did not thunder into his office in righteous anger or invoke the power to bring suit. She was not funny, or feisty, or furious in response to the behavior she described. She was disgusted, embarrassed and ambivalent. Therefore, it must have been a dream.

"It was quite fitting that the bulk of the hearings took place on the weekend that Redd Foxx died," says Stanley Crouch, a cultural critic and author of *Notes of a Hanging Judge: Essays and Reviews 1979–1989*. "A bunch of the material sounded like stuff from a Redd Foxx–Richard Pryor–Eddie Murphy routine."

But few people were laughing. That week in October, my phone rang nonstop. Friends called to talk about their stories of sexual harassment, their memories of vengeful, jealous women who lie, their theories of self-loathing black men who act out their hostility toward black women while lusting after white women. My sister, Linda, called from Chicago the night before the vote, then used her conference call feature to add her good friend to the line, with whom she had been arguing for an hour already. "I already know you believe her," Linda announced to me. "I just want to hear you tell me why."

The buses and trains and elevators were filled with debates and theories of conspiracy. Hill set up Thomas to bring a black man down. Thomas was a man; what man didn't talk about his prowess? In a Harlem restaurant where I sat with a cup of tea and the papers that Saturday, the entire kitchen staff was in an uproar. The cook, an

African woman, wanted to know why Hill waited ten years to bring it up. The waitress, an African-American woman, said she couldn't tell what to think.

A young black man in his twenties announced he had a theory. "Clarence got jungle fever, and she got mad," he said with a laugh. Jungle fever is the code term, taken from the Spike Lee film of the same name, for a black man's desire to sleep with a white woman. Clarence Thomas's second wife is white, therefore Anita Hill was overcome with jealous rage and hungry for revenge.

"We all know that the animosity of black women toward black men who marry white women is on the level of the recent fire in Oakland," Stanley Crouch said. "That's a major fact. They might be as racist about that as white people used to be."

Then again, some black women might not care at all—a reasonable assumption, given the statistics indicating that interracial relationships between black women and white men have more than tripled in the last twenty years.

Some black women may feel rejected or betrayed by black men lured by a white standard of beauty few of them could emulate. Some may just hate white women. But there is no real evidence to suggest that any of these scenarios apply to Anita Hill and her galvanizing testimony. Most people with an opinion about why she stepped forward regard it as a matter of ideology, not, as some people still want to think, romance.

Yet the issues of race and sex illuminated by the hearings remain. So, too, do the myriad ways in which race and gender combine to confuse us. But for the first time in decades, the country has been turned, for a time, into a mobile social laboratory. A level of discussion between previously unaligned groups may have begun with new vigor and candor.

Segments of the feminist movement have been under attack for their selective wooing of black women. Yet many of these same women rallied to Hill with impressive speed. Some black women who had never before considered sexism as an issue serious enough to merit collective concern have begun to organize, including a group of black female academics known as African American Women in Defense of Ourselves. And even in brusque New York, people on opposite sides of this issue, still traumatized by the televised spectacle, seem eager to listen, to be civil, to talk things over.

"I am so pleased people are starting to ask questions, not only about race and gender, but about the America that has frustrated and disappointed them," says Jewell Jackson McCabe. "People who had become cynical, people who have not talked about issues in their lives are talking now. I think the experience was so bad, it was so raw. I don't know a woman who watched those hearings whose life hasn't been changed."

"It was an international drama," says Michael Eric Dyson, assistant professor of ethics, philosophy, and cultural criticism at Chicago Theological Seminary. "Anita Hill has put these issues on the American social agenda. She has allowed black men and women to talk freely for the first time about a pain that has been at the heart of our relationships since slavery. Black wives are beginning to tell their husbands about the kind of sexism they have faced not at the hands of white men, but black men."

What was most striking about the hearings, in the end, was the sense of destiny that surrounded them. There was something rewarding about seeing what began as a humiliating event become gradually transformed only in its aftermath. Two African-Americans took center stage in what became a national referendum on many of our most cherished values. In the midst of their shattering appearances, Anita Hill and Clarence Thomas each made us ask questions that most of us had lost the heart to ask.

They are exactly the kinds of questions that could lead us out of the morass of cynicism and anger in which we've all been stuck. That is an immensely satisfying measurement of the Hill-Thomas hearings. It would not be the first time that African-Americans have used tragedy and contradiction as catalysts to make America remember its rightful legacy.

ROSEMARY L. BRAY is an editor of The New York Times Book Review. She is working on a book of essays on black identity.

On the Clarence Thomas Hearings

Vicki Crawford

As I watched the Clarence Thomas hearings, what I found most striking was the continued devaluation of black women and the absence of our voices from news commentary, round-tables, and the many discussions around the hearings in both print and broadcast media. With few exceptions, rarely was there consideration given to the analysis of the issues from a black woman's standpoint. Did not the analysis of black women warrant air time or sufficient news coverage? After all, there were several columns and air time afforded to the expertise of white male psychiatrists who ventured to speculate about Anita Hill's psychological state. At the request of various members on the Senate Judiciary Committee, these experts attempted to build a case against Anita Hill's sanity, putting forth a bizarre range of theories, some of them so arcane that it's questionable that they ever existed outside some textbook of psychiatry: Anita Hill as delusional, as a victim of transference, as schizophrenic, as erotomanic, as a revengeful scorned woman, as depressed, an overachiever—all these diagnoses without having even met the woman, let alone having clinically examined her.

My point here is that the coverage of the events taking place the week of October 10th was governed by a set of assumptions about black women that are shared by news reporters and their editors, mostly white men, members of the Senate Judiciary Committee, and, unfortunately, many people in this country. To make the point, one column in particular comes to mind. Writing in the *Boston Globe* on October 13th, a reporter recounts Clarence Thomas's charge of being a victim of racial stereotyping. He explores the notion of sexual stereotyping about black men, but fails to probe the level and extent to which a counter-stereotypical image of black women exists. Nowhere in this article is there any mention of the absurdity of such a charge, to wit, the reporter interviews black Boston University economist Glenn Loury, who attempts to render commentary in favor of Thomas, this despite the fact that Loury, himself, has been accused of sexual violence against women. I want to call attention to the white male media's bias in terms of who gets interviewed, who is called upon to be an expert, and what angles of a story get covered, all of this shaping public opinion and reaction formation.

In the process of trying to unravel the complexity of issues surrounding the Anita Hill–Clarence Thomas case, I wanted to hear the expert analysis of other African-American women. What would Eleanor Holmes Norton have to say, former chair of the EEOC, in more than a sentence or two? What about Faye Wattleton, president of Planned Parenthood? What about the venerable Judge Constance Baker Motley? What about the black women whom I had met who worked in the cafeteria at the University of North Carolina–Chapel Hill? What are their thoughts? Concerns? What, indeed, about my black women friends who are psychologists and psychiatrists? Do they think Anita Hill delusional or erotomanic?

Why not a treatment of black women's distinct place in American history that is uniquely situated at the crossroads of race, class and gender? Why didn't someone write a piece about the mythic images of black women as mammies, jezebels, tragic mulatoes, hottentot venuses? The list of insulting degrading stereotypes goes on. Why didn't someone write about how Anita Hill stands on the shoulders of courageous black women like Ida B. Wells, Sojourner Truth, Fannie Lou Hamer, Ella Baker, Vivian Malone Jones, even if she doesn't know it? Women who were outspoken and took risks. Why not a feature story on Emma Mae Martin, Clarence Thomas's sister, who he publicly ridiculed as being angry when her welfare check arrived late. Single parenthood is the reality for many African American women struggling in this country. To my mind, as unfortunate and sad as they were, the events occurring the week of October 10th were a teachable moment. Why not take an opportunity to let the present serve as a guide towards interrogating the past?

Just a few weeks prior to the hearings in my course on "Black Women in U.S. History" we read Debra Gray White's book, *Aren't I a Woman: Female Slaves in the Plantation South*. She begins her discussion of black female slaves with a chapter titled "Jezebel and Mammy: The Mythology of Female Slavery." Here, White, writing about the experiences of black women more than a century ago, traces the origins of pernicious stereotypes surrounding black women's sexuality back to the antebellum period. Sexist ideologies served to buttress the systematic oppression of black people. Yet, amazingly enough, here was a real live, modern-day case study where in 1991 these same myths and stereotypes were used to inform public opinion and debate around the Thomas hearings.

Where do we go from here? I don't know, really, but, to sum up I'd like to suggest three considerations. First, that the cultural memory of black women's resistance and struggle in this country be preserved: that we must work consciously to keep alive the collective memory of women, like Ella Baker, who spent a lifetime organizing for civil rights and fighting oppression; women like Fannie Lou Hamer who was brutally thrown into a Mississippi jail cell just because she attempted to register to vote; and eighty-six-year-old Modjestka Simpkins, a freedom fighter in South Carolina; Ruby Doris Smith Robinson who died young, in her thirties, having given her best years to the freedom struggle. If anything, the events of this week underscore the need for African American history, in general, and black women's history, in particular. For students, it is to know this history to the extent that none could possibly see Thomas as a lynch victim. That simply totally erases Anita Hill and black women out of historical memory. Second, I want to insist on the indispensability of black women's voices to the future of political organizing and social progress in this country, the indispensability of our voices on the front lines of change. Finally, that as black women we need to continue to work in our communities, to organize, to talk, to direct our energies inward for a change, to attend to our physical, psychological, and spiritual selves, and to form networks of support like our nineteenth-century sisters and like Black Women in Defense of Ourselves, a group of black women and supporters who took out an ad in *The New York Times* to speak to the treatment of Anita Hill. Basically we need to keep the things stirring, as ex-slave Sojourner Truth remarked over a century ago.

VICKI CRAWFORD, Ph.D., is assistant professor of Women's Studies at the University of Massachusetts, Amherst. She is currently writing a book on black women activists in the southern civil rights movement of the 1950s and 1960s.

The High-Tech Lynching and the High-Tech Overseer: Thoughts from the Anita Hill/Clarence Thomas Affair

Henry Vance Davis

The Anita Hill/Clarence Thomas affair was charged with pertinent topics. The sexual harassment issues were of great importance to every office in America. The Senators' bungling was an embarrassment not only for the Senators but also for the government. The weakness of the Democrats' performance must have sent Democrats all over the nation scurrying for cover. But what continues to intrigue and concern this writer are thoughts that were generated by nominee Thomas's usage of the high-tech lynching imagery.

When Clarence Thomas invoked his right of protection from a twentieth-century, high-tech lynching, he obscured the effort to determine if he was a twentieth-century, high-tech overseer. I am afraid that where African American people are concerned, the latter is of much greater concern than the former.

Thomas had every right to rail against the lack of due process in the hearings. He was, in fact, asked to prove his innocence at the same time that his accuser was asked to prove his guilt. This kind of "even-steven" judicial process is not consistent with the American way. However, his use of the high-tech lynching imagery to defend himself was troubling. While I found the comparison of the attack on his good name with the taking of life that occurred during a lynching a bit overdrawn, I can overlook that Judge Thomas was under stress. A little hyperbole can be understood. What was more troubling was that Thomas did not seem to be railing in a search for the truth; his was a search for self-protection. This would explain his truncated description of the virile, sex-craved, black buck stereotype which undergirded his imagery. He very carefully selected a description of the stereotype that would buffer his case, omitting elements that might cause him embarrassment. The whole truth was not disclosed. While some might consider this smart, I suggest it was unethical and ask, Is this proper behavior for a Supreme Court Justice?

The implications of what he left out are even more troubling. The stereotype not only entails the description of the large body parts of the black buck and the buck's lust for sex, which Judge Thomas detailed. It also claims the buck's predilection for white women, which Thomas ignored. The white woman's role in these affairs is well documented. History reveals that the vast majority of African Americans lynched during the height of lynching in this country (1890–1910) were accused of some type of sex crime against a white woman. Those African American men did not get lynched for raping, misusing, or harassing African American women, nor did any whites. Not one lynching would have occurred if only African American women had been violated. (Indeed, I find it difficult to believe that the good old boy network in the Senate is significantly more concerned today than in the past with protecting the virtue of African American women.) Why did Judge Thomas choose to leave this very well known dimension out of his description? Could it have been because Ms. Hill is not white? Could it have been because Thomas's wife is white? While this writer does not sanction sexual harassment against any women, be they black or white, neither does this writer condemn a black man for falling in love with a woman who happens to be white. Justice Thomas's omission is troubling because it smacks of "selective blackness." It appears that he dons, and sheds, the elements of blackness as it suits him. While this seems both unethical and disloyal to this writer, there is a still larger concern.

This "selective blackness" is troubling because it is a symptom of a greater malaise that is sweeping higher education, politics, and business. A malaise that is common, at the dawn of the twenty-first century, in the person of one who might be termed the twentieth-century high-tech overseer. Like the person who worked the slave for the master during slavery, in the twentieth century the high-tech overseer has become a person with black skin who will stand between oppressive policies and the majority of African Americans. This person acts as a gatekeeper, letting the appropriate Negroes into the "big house" and sending selected resources out to the masses. He/she often facilities this by slipping in and out of various shades of black—selective blackness. She/he can be anything from "yo' bro', what's happenin'?" to Warrington Mostuphigh III, Esq., if the price is right.

These high-tech overseers publicly profess their blackness under banners such as community self-help, the virtues of independence, or the need for African Americans to feel that their degrees are earned on an equal footing with whites. They have learned to market themselves via opposition to affirmative action, minority set asides, admittance standards, the welfare cheat, and political correctness. (Sounds like David Duke.) Privately, while they profess their difference from "them blacks," they market themselves as willing to do the right thing: If he is not "qualified," he will not get admitted. If she does not have the "experience," she will not get the job. If they are not "team players," I will do the firing. If the money has to be cut, I will make the "hard decisions."

These are among the most dangerous African Americans in America, because quite often they are used to stall and retake the gains that the struggles of millions have earned. And unfortunately, the African-American, high-tech overseer is gaining both wider use and more sophistication among closet racists and neoconservatives. Let us look at college campuses, for example. How often is a salaried position the first thing granted to demonstrating students by college or university administrators? A position that can often be titled "Head Nigga In Charge" (HNIC). I would venture, as a conservative guess, that in over 90 percent of the demonstrations by African American students that gained concessions, an African American has gotten a job. While the majority of these workers are well qualified and well meaning, quite often they are selected for the wrong reasons. Too often they are not hired because of their proven commitment to the position of the demonstrators. Too often they are not accountable to African Americans. Paradoxically, they *are* accountable to the administration that the demonstrators had to demonstrate against. Additionally, they often are committed to constraining the demands of the demonstrators within "reasonable" parameters. The administration receives a bonus, because often the students will not hold the HNIC to the same standards of performance and commitment to equity that they would hold a white in the same position.

The administration comes up smelling like a rose. They have hired an African American. Any problem can be referred to that person who, incidentally, is going to receive the benefit of the doubt (to a fault) from concerned students. If the hired African American has learned to slip into and out of blackness as it suits him/her, the administration has a superstar, a twentieth century, high-tech overseer. In exchange for their struggle, African Americans have a person inclined to restrict the growth of many of the programs earned by their blood and sacrifice. Little wonder the Civil Rights era has not produced more lasting gains.

George Bush knew exactly what he was doing when he picked Clarence Thomas to become the next justice of the Supreme Court. Clarence Thomas was an affirmative action admittee to Yale who subsequently repudiated affirmative action. He is a man who has distanced himself from the average African American at every opportunity and yet would invoke selected portions of the most feared and controversial black stereotype to protect himself. Thurgood Marshall knew exactly what he was doing when he recently answered a reporter's question with a question. The reporter asked if Justice Marshall would rather have a black or a white replace him on the Court. In reply, the judge asked the reporter whether he would rather be bitten by a black snake or a white snake.

African Americans cannot continue to allow their leaders to change colors at will. African Americans must learn to require the same standard of excellence and commitment to equity from African Americans in power positions that they do of whites. They must also extract the same price for failure. Until they do, those who seek to derail development of the pluralistic multicultural community will continue to throw a twentieth-century, high-tech overseer into the breech.

This writer shares the concerns of those who originally questioned Judge Thomas's confirmation. Be he conservative or liberal is of little concern. There is a much more pertinent question: Is he a twentieth-century, high-tech overseer?

HENRY VANCE DAVIS, Ph.D., is assistant professor of history, Western Michigan University in Kalamazoo. He is preparing a manuscript, The Black Press: From Mission to Commercialism, 1827–1929*, and has received a research grant for his project, "Black Periodicals of the World."*

The Clarence Thomas Hearings and the Entertaining of America

David J. Dent

Clarence Thomas is now the Supreme Court Justice with the most tarnished image. His name is synonymous with sexual harassment. As Willie Horton became a symbol of recidivism and violent crimes of sex in the 1988 presidential campaign, Judge Thomas became a symbol of another putrid form of sexual misconduct in the confirmation process. But, just as Willie Horton wasn't the nation's only recidivist, Thomas, if guilty, wasn't the first high profile male boss to make disgusting advances toward a female employee. As one friend of mine said, "Thomas just got caught with his pants down." But it isn't out of the American ordinary for a black man to become the sacrificial lamb of a major issue. This is the USA.

The Thomas saga was another chapter in America's history of the manipulation of blacks by a political system dominated by whites. This time, a criminal like Horton wasn't the pawn in the match to win points in the public opinion game. Two well educated African Americans were the spectacles for television viewers and the fighting tools of two opposing political agendas. Once again, the issues of racism and sexism were not treated with the kind of depth and sincerity that might help lead to the annihilation of those problems. Instead, those issues were treated pretentiously. And, like Horton, Thomas and Hill, the evils of racism and sexism were manipulated to benefit the futures of white politicians.

Just look at American politics in the wake of the Thomas-Hill throwdown. Now, many GOP pollsters are bragging publicly that the Thomas episode may help some Republican candidates garner 25 percent of the black vote in 1992. And what have African American voters gained in exchange for such support? We have Clarence Thomas on the Supreme Court and a new, but weak, civil rights law, as electoral politics in this country dangerously ticks into the past with David Duke. President Bush and countless other Republicans tried to distance the mainstream of the party from the Duke campaign. But those are tardy and hypocritical gestures. Through Willie Horton, George Bush promoted the climate that helped David Duke breeze into the Louisiana Governor's race, and may even boost Duke's presidential campaign.

Thomas and Hill were placed on what seemed like a political dart board. While the two bled, Senators sat in judgment. The Judiciary Committee members often prolonged the dirty confirmation hearing with speeches denouncing the process, even though it was a process that gave the senators several hours of free advertising and the chance to superficially clean up their own images with shallow, but seemingly eloquent, rhetoric.

Although Clarence Thomas was victimized in the process, I find it hard to sympathize with him. Thomas allowed himself to be exploited by white conservatives, which is consistent with his career. Thomas often has been a bullet begging white conservatives to fire him into black America, apparently thinking he was an immortal part of the target—until the hearing. Isn't it ironic that the man who once attacked Thurgood Marshall claimed to be a victim of racism? Out of desperation, Thomas conveniently uttered words of racial consciousness at the hearing: "In this country, when it comes to sexual conduct, we still have underlying racial attitudes about black men and their views on sex," Thomas said in the hearing. "And once you pin that on me I can't get it off . . . And this plays into the most bigoted, racist stereotypes any black man will face."

True, the image of the dangerous black stud lives on in the minds of many whites, e.g., Willie Horton. Does Thomas now realize that he shares a commonality with Horton? Will his votes in the High Court reflect that realization? The Horton commercials indeed were a form of bigoted and racist stereotypes—something one might expect from the David Duke campaign. But the commercials were engineered by the presidential campaign of the man who nominated Thomas to the High Court.

The Bush machinery has a history of exploiting the threat of black male sexuality. However, a different type of exploitation emerged during the hearings. Politicians who once used negative black male stereotypes to incite fear in whites and garner votes in the ballot box suddenly became mendacious sympathizers with the victims of such stereotypes—black men. Politics transformed Willie Horton manipulators into Ida B. Wells wannabees. They skillfully used Thomas to appeal to African Americans, whose support helped influence wavering Democrats to vote for Thomas. Thomas offered white conservatives like Republican Senator Orrin Hatch (who opposed the Civil Rights Act of 1990) the platform to stage an apocryphal interest in how the stud image plagues the lives of black men.

After Thomas assaulted his liberal opponents with the race issue, Hatch picked up the cue and attempted to champion the cause through his questioning of Thomas. "Well, this bothers me. Bothers me," said Hatch, questioning Thomas. "I saw—I didn't understand the television program—but there were two black men . . . and one of them said, 'She's trying to demonize us.' I didn't understand that at the time. Do you understand?"

Perhaps Hatch would have understood and would have saved some minutes of the hearing if, before the Thomas testimony, he had taken a look at the Willie Horton demon in the commercials.

The major hypocritical element of the Thomas-Hill debacle occurred when Hatch and white conservatives called Thomas a victim of racism and denounced the ugliness of racial prejudice. Where were they when the Willie Horton commercials were created and aired? Where was Thomas? Unfortunately, many of Thomas's African American supporters probably didn't ask themselves that question. The Thomas testimony just pulled them into the conservative corner similar to the way the Horton commercials pulled many whites onto the Bush wagon in the 1988 campaign.

Professor Hill's fellow conservatives failed her in the process. But remember, Hill, the spark of the alleged "high-tech lynching," wasn't a white Southern belle like the sparks of the real lynchings that real American heroes like Ida B. Wells fought against. I wonder if Hatch and others would have seen things the same way if Anita Hill wasn't only a conservative like them, but also white like them—liberal or conservative. Was it easier for many white conservatives to support Thomas—despite his white wife—since the alleged victim of sexual harassment was black? We can only guess the answer to that question. Based on my experiences as an African American male, I would guess yes.

I remember covering a rape case when I was a television reporter in Nashville, Tennessee. Two black star football players at a rural high school outside of Nashville were accused of raping two teenage girls, whose names were not released. Many students and school officials, eager to see the football team go all the way, were behind the boys. In a taped interview with a school official, I received a standard line: "I can't comment until all the facts are in." Once the camera was off, the official privately told me: "It's not going to be a big thing. You know the girls are black."

Of course Anita Hill's charges became "a big thing." Although she's a conservative who supported Judge Bork's nomination, Hill became the ammunition of feminists, white Democratic senators and other liberal forces seeking the demise of the black conservative Bush nominee. The he-said-she-said fight can be compared to a typical boxing match between two African Americans. Hill and Thomas entertained America by slugging it out. By the final round, both were exhausted. But, for the benefit of their mostly white supporters, they were still trying to knock out each other's characters, which were barely standing in the end. It was the kind of battle that probably produced a smile on David Duke's face.

DAVID J. DENT is an assistant professor of Journalism at New York University and a freelance writer based in New York City.

Clarence Thomas: Loyal Foot Soldier for Reaganism*

Hermon George, Jr.

The nomination of Judge Clarence Thomas to the Supreme Court of the United States is a sign of the times, of the nation's elite's turn to the right. But, it is also symbolic of another historic trend, first played out over eighty years ago.

In that earlier time in 1903, in *The Souls of Black Folk*, W. E. B. Du Bois commented on Booker T. Washington's program for black advancement by noting, in part, that

> . . . on the whole the distinct impression left by Mr. Washington's propaganda is . . . [the] future [of black people] depends primarily on [their] own efforts. [This] . . . is a dangerous half-truth. The supplementary [truth] must never be lost sight of . . . [that] while it is a great truth to say that [blacks] must strive and strive mightily to help [themselves] . . . , it is equally true that unless [their] striving be not simply seconded, but rather aroused and encouraged, by the initiative of the richer . . . environing group, [they] cannot hope for great success. (p. 47)

Clarence Thomas is a modern-day parody of Booker T. Washington. But, to paraphrase Karl Marx, "History repeats itself, first as tragedy, then as farce." Thomas is a farce being perpetrated on African Americans, and on all Americans.

His nomination represents President Bush's manipulation of American racial politics as a conscious goal of the ruling class. Bush seeks to redefine the content of race relations in the 1990s so that

*This article is based on a speech delivered at a National Lawyers Guild forum on the Thomas nomination at Denver University Law School, September 25, 1991.

"black" will mean "loyal, inferior, conservative American" in the minds of *the white majority*, especially white males. Winning black votes (for the GOP, generally, and for the 1992 presidential elections, specifically) is a decidedly obvious, though distinctly secondary, concern. After all, in the presidential elections of 1980, 1984, and 1988, the Republican candidates garnered only about 5 to 10 percent of the black vote. Bush's larger goal is to neutralize legitimate white concern about rising racial inequality (the signs of which are increasingly visible everywhere) by deflecting white angst onto black bootstrappers ("Look. *They've* made it. The system works.") and, thereby, silencing the civil rights leadership, its white allies, and black progressives. Historically, the Thomas nomination is another sign of the defeat of the Second Reconstruction (1953–1985) and the consequent rise of black capitulationism ("accommodations"), i.e., neo-Bookerism, in an age of reaction.

But, who is Clarence Thomas and what is his judicial and political philosophy? To the first query, Anthony Lewis ("Which Judge Thomas?," *The New York Times*, September 16, 1991) has responded:

> He has never been in the private practice of law. He has never been a teacher, a scholar. He has never argued in a case in an important court. He was the highly ideological chairman of a Federal agency (EEOC), spending much of his time making 150 political speeches, and then a Federal judge for one year.

Additionally, other facts may be stated about his background. He was born in 1947 in Pin Point, Georgia, and educated at a private Catholic school in Savannah. He was admitted to Yale Law School *under an affirmative action program* in 1971, graduating in 1974. He was appointed an Assistant Attorney General for the State of Missouri in 1974, serving until 1977. He left this position to become an attorney in the law department of Monsanto Corporation, 1977–1979. Then, Senator John C. Danforth became his mentor, making Thomas his legislative assistant, 1979–1981. The Reagan administration next sought his services, appointing him as Assistant Secretary for Civil Rights in the Department of Education (1981–1982), and then, Chairman of the Equal Employment Opportunity Commission, where he served eight years. President Bush appointed Thomas to the U.S. Court of Appeals for the District of Columbia in February 1990, and nominated him to the U.S. Supreme Court in July 1991. In sum, for a decade, 1981–1991, Thomas has been, in the words of Stanford Law School Prof. Charles Lawrence, "a loyal foot soldier for Bush and his predecessor, Ronald Reagan, and . . . [he has] always sought to please his political benefactors." (*The New York Times*, September 18, 1991).

Moreover, when we seek answers to the second query about his judicial and political philosophy, we may begin with his own evaluation. Speaking to the right-wing Heritage Foundation in June 1987, he offered that his areas of legal expertise are "energy, taxation, and general corporate regulatory matters." Yet, he has won praise from the right because he endorses the ambiguous concept of natural law, using it to support his own anti–abortion rights view as when he approvingly cited Lewis Lehrman's use of the concept to the same end in Lehrman's April 1987 *American Spectator* piece. Thomas wins praise from the right because he professes the doctrine of narrow individualism under capitalist democracy, declaring that the "principle of freedom and dignity" applies *only* to *individuals*, *not* to *groups*. The practical consequences of this view are seen in his behavior as EEOC chairman. He de-emphasized class action suits as a percentage of all EEOC lawsuits filed, from 66 percent in 1980 (218 of 326, before Thomas was director), to 35 percent in 1983 (75 of 211), to 28 percent in 1986 (148 of 525), after dismantling the systemic litigation unit within the EEOC in 1985 and allowing it to lose over half of its twenty-five attorneys. Thomas also, while EEOC chair, shifted the burden of proof from employers to employees in cases involving waivers of employees' rights and he discouraged group remedies as in March 1987, when he decided that Xerox Corporation not be prosecuted, *against the EEOC staff's recommendation*, for illegally targeting older, higher-paid workers for forced early retirement in the case of *Lugardi* v. *Xerox*.

Thomas wins support from the right because he espouses an anti–affirmative action politics, since he believes that, "For Lincoln and for the Declaration of Independence, equality [of individuals] led to the principle of government by consent, limited government, majority rule, and separation of powers." (Clarence Thomas, "Toward a 'Plain Reading' of the Constitution—The Declaration of Independence in Constitutional Interpretation," *Howard Law Journal* 30:4 (1987) p. 984). Again, the consequences of this view are seen in his behavior as EEOC chair. In 1984–1985, he refused to require mandated "goals and timetables" in EEOC settlements, even after three favorable Supreme Court rulings in May-June, 1986. At EEOC, from 1987–1989, Thomas refused to fully investigate age discrimination charges, letting cases lapse and then lying to the Senate Committee on Aging about the agency's backlog of ADEA (Age Discrimination in Employment Act) cases. He first reported a backlog of seventy cases (September 1987), then admitted to 900 cases, then 1,603 (March 1988), then 7,500 (June 1988), then 8,900 (November 1988) and finally admitted to more than 13,000 (May 1989). Under Thomas's chairmanship, a 1988 GAO report found that between 41 percent to 82 percent of EEOC field office charges were not fully investigated. The GAO report also found that total EEOC case backlog and processing time had grown under Thomas: from a 31,500 case backlog in 1983, to 46,000 cases in 1989; processing time lengthened from four to seven months in 1983, to almost ten months in 1989.

In sum, Clarence Thomas represents the *perversion* of black self-reliance. One need only compare, for example, Du Bois's 1934 call for a black cooperative commonwealth maximizing black communities' economic and political strengths under segregated living conditions while *simultaneously* urging black folks' continued struggle for full democratic rights, to Thomas's apologia for continued white supremacist practices as when he claimed, as EEOC chair, that "most [EEOC] cases involve discrimination by a *particular* manager or supervisor, rather than a 'policy' of discrimination . . ." (emphasis added). Thomas espouses these views against an historical backdrop of worsening socioeconomic inequality, as the government dole for the rich expands, as seen in public trough-fed militaristic corporations, tax loopholes, and interest on the national debt, while working class income shrinks and its tax burden increases. These trends are appreciably worse for African Americans, like James Douglas, a sixty-five-year-old retired postal worker, who declared:

> I can remember when the water fountains were marked "white" and "colored." But I can also remember why they are not that way now. He [Thomas] benefited from all the civil

> rights battles, but he says we don't need that anymore. Well, I don't know anybody who thinks we need him, and I sure don't need Clarence Thomas on the Supreme Court. (*New York Times*, September 16, 1991, p. A3.)

And adding her voice to those in the black community who oppose Thomas's nomination, Dorothy Hubbard, a fifty-eight-year-old real estate agent, commented:

> It's nice that he talked about how somebody called his granddaddy "boy," but so what? Why didn't he talk about his own experiences of discrimination? He keeps taking the attention off himself, which makes me wonder if we are getting the whole story. I can't put it together. (*The New York Times, supra cit.*)

What we—those who oppose Thomas's nomination to the Supreme Court—must "put together" is a cogent presentation of the basis for opposition to this nomination. We must oppose Thomas's nomination because of his assault on civil liberties, such as the equal protection and due process clauses of the Fourteenth Amendment as revealed in his EEOC tenure. We must oppose him for his right-wing pandering to white supremacy and sexual oppression. He is a useful, opportunistic token in the right's backlash against affirmative action and abortion rights. As Tom Teppen has remarked:

> White racial conservatives love few people more than a black man who will cover their tails. Additionally, Bush's promotion of Thomas with one hand lets the president and his cadres claim racial bona fides even as they fight substantive racial justice [e.g., by opposing the Civil Rights Act of 1991] with the other hand. (*San Francisco Daily Journal*, July 9, 1991.)

We must oppose Thomas's nomination for his ahistoricalness, a crucial element in the right's re-definition and re-articulation process of American racial politics. Thomas seems to believe, as does the right, that people must forget history, or be taught to lie about it. Thus, in his 1987 *Howard Law Journal* article, he apologizes for the framers' white supremacist defense of slavery, noting that neither "slave" nor "slavery" appears in the Constitution, and claims that the 3/5 clause (Article II, section 2) actually *diminished* slave states' power. Thomas, however, conveniently neglects to mention that twenty-nine of sixty-five, or 44.6%, of the representatives in the first Congress were slavocrat Southerners. This numerical dominance of the South in national affairs led to a long train of shameful conciliations to slavocrat interests such as the Wilmot Proviso of 1820, the Fugitive Slave Law of 1850, and the Missouri Compromise of 1854.

We must oppose Thomas's nomination for his opportunistic black conservatism, in reality a stalking horse for the right. As Carl Rowan argues, echoing Du Bois eighty-eight years ago:

> It horrifies me that the country might have to endure forty years of opinions of a black man . . . Who hasn't the guts to acknowledge that "self-help" isn't enough in a milieu of institutionalized racism . . . (*Baltimore Sun*, July 4, 1991.)

And, finally, we must oppose him for his adherence to the regime of austerity capitalism and its reactionary social agenda, filled with the psycho-social sexual panic of the white male capitalist ruling class. This panic is the common thread which defines the right's anti–affirmative action position, anti–abortion rights position, anti–bilingual education, pro–English only stance, anti–minimum wage hostility, and anti–cultural democracy, pro–"political correctness" hysteria.

In conclusion, even if Thomas wins confirmation, we must fight, despite the daunting odds. If murderers come to kill you, you do not say, "I cannot oppose the next stab wound because my life is already forfeit." No—you fight for your life! And, working class people, poor people, and political progressives must fight Thomas. They must fight for their lives. They must fight for the future.

The U.S. Supreme Court does not need "diversity." It needs "the voices of adversity." Ultimately, a black face alone is not enough.

HERMON GEORGE, JR., Ph.D., is professor of Black Studies at the University of Northern Colorado. His essay, "Black Power in Office: The Limits of Electoral Reform," was recently reprinted in Black Studies: Theory, Method, and Cultural Perspectives *(1990). He is currently at work on a research project concerning race relations in the Americas.*

Breaking the Silence: A Black Feminist Response to the Thomas/Hill Hearings (for Audre Lorde)

Beverly Guy-Sheftal

There are a number of disturbing issues raised by the recent appointment of Clarence Thomas to the Supreme Court even if Anita Hill's allegations of sexual harassment had not surfaced: his unfitness to serve on the High Court due to inadequate judicial experience and overall mediocrity; his views on affirmative action and abortion; his record at EEOC; his disavowal of deeply held, frequently stated right-wing views; his portrayal of his hard-working, supportive sister as a disgusting welfare mother; and his obvious lying—he claims not to have read a report opposing abortion which he signed, or having ever discussed *Roe* v. *Wade*. In a historic statement in support of Anita Hill which appeared in the November 17, 1991, issue of *The New York Times*, entitled "African American Women in Defense of Ourselves," 1642 black women[1] reminded the nation of Thomas's persistent failure, despite his own racial history and professional opportunities, to respond to the urgency of civil rights for disadvantaged groups in this country: ". . . this consolidation of the conservative majority on the Supreme Court seriously endangers the rights of all women, poor and working class people, and the elderly . . . we know that the seating of Clarence Thomas is an affront to African American women and men and all those concerned with social justice."

The overwhelming reaction among blacks to Anita Hill's sexual harassment charges against Judge Thomas during the nomination proceedings, despite what the polls may have revealed, seems to have been that even if the allegations were true, she should have remained silent. I have encountered very few blacks, men or women, who believe that Thomas was telling the truth when he categorically and unequivocally denied having engaged in sexually inappropriate conduct, including pressuring Hill for dates and making offensive sexual comments, while he was her boss. I became even more convinced of the "reality" of my observations when I asked my eighty-year-old father who has lived in Memphis, Tennessee, all his life and understands the painful reality of racism and the particular plight of Southern black men, about his reactions to what he saw on television. He responded, very quickly and calmly and without any racial references, this way: "Well, of course Thomas is lying, and Hill is a very good girl. Anyone should be able to see that. Men have been taking advantage of nice girls for as far back as I can remember." When I asked him whether he thought Hill should have come forth after being pressured to do so by the Judiciary Committee, he stated, very forcefully, "Of course." Even conservative Orlando Patterson, a black Harvard professor and one of Thomas's most ardent supporters, argues, much to my dismay, that "Judge Thomas was justified in denying making the remarks, even if he had in fact made them. . . ."[2]

Perhaps the best explanation of this tendency on the part of large numbers of African Americans, men and women, to vehemently oppose Anita Hill's public exposure of Thomas's sexual harassment of her (I wonder if the response would have been different if the hearings hadn't been televised) is that she violated a deeply held black cultural taboo which is that we shouldn't air our racial dirty linen in front of white folks. This prohibition has engendered the most anger when it is black women "breaking the silence" about our experiences, especially sexual, with black men. I am reminded at this point of the need to contextualize the Thomas/Hill hearings and to analyze them within a framework which enables us to see this drama as part and parcel of a larger scenario which has been brewing for more than a decade.[3]

Twelve years ago (August 27, 1979, issue of *Newsweek*), "a new black struggle" was chronicled. This came on the heels of Ntozake Shange's award-winning Broadway play "For Colored Girls Who Have Considered Suicide/When the Rainbow is Enuff" (1976) and Michele Wallace's controversial book *Black Macho and the Myth of the Superwoman* (1979), and both writers were demonized among large segments of the black community:

> It's the newest wrinkle in the black experience in America—a growing distrust, if not antagonism, between black men and

> women that is tearing marriages apart and fracturing personal relationships. . . . But while the strains between blacks are much the same as those between the sexes in general, their impact on (blacks) seems unusually severe.

The issue of sexual politics within the African American community soon became a hotly debated topic in such publications as *The Black Scholar* (March/April 1979), *Freedomways*, and *Black Books Bulletin*, and provided the catalyst for the founding of a short-lived bimonthly magazine, *Black Male/Female Relationships* by Nathan and Julia Hare. A decade later, the controversy continued and grew more virulent, the most obvious manifestations of which were loud and angry litanies, especially among black professional men, about the portrayal of black male characters by contemporary black women writers. Alice Walker's novel *The Color Purple* (1982) and Steven Spielberg's film adaptation sparked the most vitriolic responses. Shahrazad Ali's self-published *The Blackman's Guide to Understanding the Blackwoman* (1990) is the latest and most disturbing publication in this decade-old family battle and reminds us, once again, of a perceptible but unspeakable misogynist strain in African American thinking.

Black women too often become suspect and discredited in our communities when we raise issues of sexism, such as sexual harassment, rape, incest, battering, date rape, or when we speak openly and honestly about what we have experienced as women under patriarchy, a structure of domination which exists in the larger society and also within the black community. We become associated with the "F" word—feminism—and are assumed to be man-hating or worse, lesbian. Historically, we have been accused of being traitors to the race when we align ourselves with women's liberation struggles, as we've consistently done since the nineteenth century despite the racism of white women and the scorn of many black men and some black women. And so, as one black feminist activist reminds us in her analysis of the ironies embedded in the Thomas/Hill hearings:

> Black women must always put duty to the race first. No mention was made of how Clarence Thomas had failed in his duty to the race, especially to Black women. This deeply held ethic that Black women have a duty to the race while Black

> men are allowed to have a duty only to themselves, can only be challenged by a black feminist analysis that emphasizes the importance of black women's lives. (Hammonds, p. 6)

As we prepare ourselves for the most difficult time of our sojourn in America since slavery, it is imperative that black men and women rid ourselves of all ideas and behaviors that will result in our individual and collective underdevelopment and debasement. There are deadly dragons to slay, and men and women must be prepared equally for struggle, especially in this menacing Republican era made worse by a Supreme Court seemingly dedicated to undoing the work of Justices like Thurgood Marshall with respect to the rights of minorities and women. Black men do not need subservient women who remain silent about the abuse and suffering they experience, no matter who is the victimizer. We must reject antiquated and counterproductive notions of manhood which dictate that men maintain power over women and prevent them from speaking, even in their own behalf. The black community will continue to survive, despite the recent hearings, though we will fare better when we commit ourselves to dealing honestly with our problems—whether it is the racism and sexism in the dominant culture or the internalized racism and sexism within our own communities. We must heed the admonishment of Audre Lorde to her sisters: "So it is better to speak remembering we were never meant to survive."[4]

BEVERLY GUY-SHEFTAL, Ph.D., is director of Spelman College Women's Research and Resource Center, and an associate professor of English. She has published in such journals as Signs, Southern Exposure, *and* Journal of Negro Education. *She is the founding co-editor of* Sage: A Scholarly Journal on Black Women.

NOTES

1. Though black female voices were conspicuously absent as commentators during the Thomas/Hill hearings, a number of important statements by enlightened black women are beginning to emerge in print. See Jill Nelson, "Back Talk: Hill Versus Thomas," *Essence,* December 1991, p. 134; Evelynn M. Hammonds, "Viewpoint: Who Speaks for Black Women?" *Sojourner: the Women's Forum*, November 1991, pp. 7–8. Upcoming publications include a Forum on the Thomas/

Hill hearings in a special issue of *SAGE: A Scholarly Journal on Black Women* on relationships which will include essays by Gloria Wade-Gayles, Nellie McKay, and others; and a collection of essays edited by Toni Morrison which will include Paula Giddings, Cornel West, and others.

2. See *The New York Times* Op-Ed, "Race, Gender and Liberal Fallacies," October 20, 1991.

3. This part of my analysis was sparked initially by my revulsion at the publication of Shahrazad Ali's *The Blackman's Guide to Understanding the Blackwoman* (1990), one of the most blatantly misogynist and racist texts which has appeared in print during this period. See my essay, "Exacerbating the Problem," in *Confusion by Any Other Name: Essays Exploring the Negative Impact . . .* , edited by Haki R. Madhubuti, Chicago: Third World Press, 1990.

4. See her "A Litany for Survival," *The Black Unicorn.*

The Clarence Thomas Hearings

Nathan Hare and Julia Hare

The Senate Judiciary Committee hearings on live television generated a flip-flop in the relationship of Judge Thomas to black people. However, the pro-Thomas fervor was not so much a crown for Thomas as a thorn in the flesh of white liberals so arrogant that even a black intellectual could detect their dastardly doings.

On the one hand, white-oriented assimilationist ("coconut") feminists and their hangdog male cohorts were quick to point and snicker at the judge's white wife, the same one Professor Hill had called to congratulate Thomas for having married. By contrast, angry black nationalist women (or at least those not living on feminist-dominated college campuses) were inclined to say that, inasmuch as they were going to have to make a choice, they'd rather deal with Thomas's white wife than the National Organization of Women.

Black women (apparently the majority of them) would wish us to caution black intellectuals and other elements of the colored cognoscente and all the "people of color" (high-tech colored people) against the possibility of being misled by white feminist rhetoric to make too much of a distinction between the white woman and the white man.

If white women and black people share a common foe, then the white woman sleeps with the enemy. Otherwise, the white woman is merely the white man in drag. The relationships of Hill and Thomas to the black community may not be anything to write to high heaven about in either case. Both derived from rural Southern upbringings, and both appeared to come under the influence of whites as teachers and—at least in the case of Anita Hill—classmates, beginning in high school.

The necessity for choosing between two up-and-coming black individuals was clearly wrenching to black people on individual and collective levels. They either saw it as a choice between two impressive, even if misguided, black "role models," or a profound choice between the lesser of two evils.

The black community was divided by the hearings but not along gender lines so much as along ideological interpretations. As in the case of voting in electoral politics (despite the mythical type of a "gender gap"), the gap, especially in the election of Reagan and Bush, was racial, with white males and females voting for Bush and Reagan, with a slightly higher male vote for the conservatives: while black males and females voted for the opposition (the inert democratic candidates, Ms. Ferraro and Mr. Dukakis, for whom the more qualified Jesse Jackson had been sacrificed). Likewise, there was no serious split between black male and female voting.

In the Clarence Thomas/Anita Hill controversy, it is true that black women who themselves had experienced harassment on the job were inclined to feel considerable sympathy for Professor Hill, but this was insufficient in the majority of cases to offset their siding with Thomas on other grounds. Many black women (including those who sympathized with Professor Hill) had mixed emotions and couldn't see why—as they themselves had done so many times—Anita couldn't have put her hands on her hip, let her backbone slip, and told Clarence where to get off.

Many assumed that the charges were true but concluded they didn't matter enough to block the nomination. Some figured Professor Hill was a woman scorned, though neither she nor the judge saw it expedient or wise to reveal that they had actually carried on some kind of relationship beyond his stopping by her apartment to help her hang her pictures, or her multiple telephone calls, including one call just to say "congratulations on your marriage." On another occasion, "I'm in town and in room . . . call me tonight." They wondered why the professor invited the man out to Tulsa and volunteered to escort him back to the airport in a private car in which they would be alone together.

The ideological split seemed to ignore traditional political divisions. Once you left black feminists proper (themselves also multi-ideological since about 1980 though more heavily integrationist), people appeared to divide on the basis of their impression of Clarence Thomas on "civil rights" or whether he embraced the conventional wisdom on affirmative action as a tool for black uplift. (At the risk of erroneously appearing "conservative," we remind the reader that research shows that affirmative action has appeared to help the "black bourgeoisie" and white women more than black people at large).

Thus, according to the polls, black people as a group gave Thomas a majority decision.

Before siding with Thomas, many black persons had to decide that, as one person on the Supreme Court, Thomas would have no more impact than Thurgood Marshall's role of dissenting with white colleagues. Many concluded that Bush, a conservative, wasn't going to appoint a liberal to the Court and that Thomas was probably the last black male Supreme Court judge that black boys and girls would get a chance to see in this lifetime.

Other blacks who went for Thomas didn't think the Supreme Court matters as much for blacks as civics teachers try to make out. Many blacks have grown considerably disenchanted by the Supreme Court's flagship black decision of 1954. Either they marvel at the slow and elusive pace of "desegregation with all deliberate speed," or hold heavy disaffection for the latent consequences of school integration (or disintegration) itself.

Once you got past the black bourgeoisie, the hearings presented black people little more than an overblown "People's Court." For some it was just one more big unhappy sitcom or one more that wasn't really funny. It was clear that, though the press tried to pitch it as a simple matter of "which do you believe," it was not that simple.

The bottom line is as follows: The Person (or should we say "perdaughter" or "persibling?") from Mars descending to Earth would see a black man (Clarence Thomas) approach a body of seven white men and one white woman (the Supreme Court) seeking admission to their coveted company. Then a crowd of white women, led by three white women and one black woman (Planned Parenthood's Fay Wattleton), rush to another body of white men (the Senate subcommittee) asking them to block the black man's admission because he opposes abortion (objectively the termination of a fetus's development, either the life or the possibility of life, premature infanticide, regardless of the fact that we ourselves uniquely were advocating the legalization of abortion ten years before it was legalized. But we are aware of its ambiguous involvement in black genocidal reproductive control strategies by white society today).

However, this new epidemic in which white feminists marshal a black woman or two to stop or bring down a black male advancement was already well in motion. It surfaced when the National Organization for Women's Legal Defense Fund and the Women's Division of the American Civil Liberties Union sent black female spokespersons to stymie the all-black male school movement that had caught fire in Detroit with the blessing of the black female superintendent of schools. It surfaced when white feminist lawyer Gloria Allred stepped up to represent the inept-acting young black woman bringing down the first black Catholic cardinal in the history of the United States. It surfaced when a San Francisco black, off-campus but school-connected Boy Scout Program was blasted away because the national Boy Scout office (unlike the black San Francisco program) does not admit girls and gays.

When the abortion ploy failed to derail the nomination of Thomas, white feminists scurried over to a group of black men and women (the NAACP's national board), and, against the initial better judgment of one black male executive officer (Benjamin Hooks) and entire local chapters, endeavored to persuade the NAACP board to accompany them to the white Senate chamber and act to negate the black man's admission to the Court on grounds that he questioned the efficacy of what most people admit to be a fallible or assailable program of "affirmative action" for African Americans up to now. The labor unions could also, in turn, agree to go along without appearing to be racists, once the National Association for the Advancement of Colored People had opened the way. (The Person from Mars could see all of this but wasn't privy to the intricacies and particulars of the arguments, inasmuch as people from Mars don't speak English.)

However, people on Mars, like black people down here, do believe in plain old-fashioned fair play; especially when a black man has already won something fair and square. But, when the affirmative action ploy didn't work, the mob of white women hurried to the white men and women of the ACLU with a "privacy" argument. When that too failed, the white women feverishly combed the country, flinging around newspaper ads; finally came up with a lone black woman, Anita Faye Hill, out in the hills and dales of Oklahoma. They lured her back to the white men of the Senate Committee in the hope they could block the black man's admission on lukewarm ten-year-old charges of "sexual harassment." The pro-abortion feminists (now buttressed of course by hordes of knee-jerk liberals) then demanded a forum live on television that was watched singlemindedly for days by the entire country.

The ten-year-old charges were mainly hearsay, patently unproved and unprovable, depending on whether you wanted Thomas on the Supreme Court or wanted somebody to keep him off. Objectively, if a man's telling of a bad joke is a constitutional violation of a woman's civil rights, this leaves liberals unbecomingly on the side of those who now risk treading on freedom of speech, just as many feminists have curiously turned up fighting pornography (a role traditionally left to conservative passions), while today's conservatives not infrequently may be found picketing and protesting and bombing clinics while flabbergasted liberals lurk sheepishly in the background openly and unashamedly pleading for law and order.

Yes, Anita, the world is being turned upside down—proving that all change is not progress, even when advocated by self-proclaimed "progressives" unconsciously adapting to the socioeconomic needs of white domination in the postmodern society. However, in the end, the puzzled Person from Mars was able to see that, just this once at least, black people as a group had stood impressively tall and (even if only briefly) justice had triumphed in black America.

NATHAN HARE *has two doctorates, in Sociology and Psychology. He is the author of* The Black Anglo-Saxons *and numerous essays.* JULIA HARE, Ed.D., *is a media consultant and expert in black education. Together, the Hares operate The Black Think Tank in San Francisco, an institution devoted to identifying and solving problems of black Americans and publishing monographs on its findings.*

Clarence Thomas and the National Black Identity

Charles P. Henry

The individual Clarence Thomas has replaced on the United States Supreme Court was the last and one of the best personifications of our national black identity. Thurgood Marshall was a liberal, a civil rights advocate, and a defender of victims—both black and white, male and female. These are all labels attached to values that fashionably are under attack in neo-conservative circles and unfortunately in the wider political arena. To be politically correct is somehow to be unAmerican (under current criteria Indians would be unAmerican!).

Yet the liberal champion of civil rights image was only a part of Marshall's national appeal. A product of segregated schools, there was no question of his ability to compete in the wider society or serve on the Supreme Court. Through discipline and hard work he had overcome tremendous odds. But his upward mobility did not separate him from his black identity. His individual skills were not used for personal enrichment but for the benefit of blacks and all believers in democracy and civil rights. Thus, Thurgood Marshall represented a real and substantial constituency that was, and is, lacking on the nation's highest court.

Clarence Thomas represents none of the qualities that made Thurgood Marshall a personification of the national black identity. Thomas has been ranked last among twenty-three recent Supreme Court nominees in terms of qualifications by the American Bar Association. Thomas has worked for the Federal bureaucracy and benefited from affirmative action—the very institution and program he attacks. He has had neither a distinguished legal practice, teaching career, nor judicial experience. In short, he represents no significant constituency in the black community.

By nominating a candidate for the Supreme Court as clearly unqualified and hostile to traditional black interests as Thomas, President Bush has effectively split the black community. He has offered up the most flagrant example of affirmative action abuse while appealing to the most superficial sort of skin-color nationalism. Liberals have been reluctant to attack his credentials because of his race, civil rights organizations have proferred only lukewarm support or opposition because of his race, and conservatives have warmly embraced him because of his political views.

This remarkable dissolution of the national black identity would have gone largely unnoticed had it not been for Anita Hill's willingness to confront Thomas with charges of sexual harassment. Whether or not the charges are true, the hearings have led to unprecedented soul-searching in the black community. Issues of class and gender that have been simmering below the surface since the sixties have now burst into the open. The parade of black Yale law school graduates before an all-white male panel of Senators should tell us a number of things about our contemporary situation.

First, despite conservative claims that politics have failed the black community and that self-help economics are the way forward, the virtual absence of women and minorities in the Senate indicates that neither group is represented in politics at the national level. What reception would Thomas have received if fifty of the senators were women and ten were black?

Second, the parade of conservative black professionals before the television cameras revealed the success of the civil rights movement and affirmative action. Does anyone honestly believe the doors of Yale would have opened without either of these stimuli? However, more profoundly than William J. Wilson, it raises the question of whether those who have benefited most from civil rights have forgotten those who were unable to "break the cycle" of poverty and poor education.

Third, the attack on Thomas by many women's groups and the defense offered by many blacks—women and men—reveals a split that has been growing over two decades. This split has class implications as well. Simply put, the question is, to what extent is the agenda of the major women's groups the same agenda as the majority working class women and (as seen in the hearings) some middle class black women? The same question might be asked of the major civil rights organizations in regard to the agenda of the black working class and underclass.

Fourth, the attack on Hill by Thomas supporters demonstrates that sexual harassment is still not taken seriously by large numbers of people. As Orlando Patterson has suggested, although there are larger numbers of women in the workplace we have yet to devise a non-sexual discourse for intimate work relationships. Moreover, cultural differences in current discourse or any future discourse need to be carefully examined.

Fifth, while conservatives like Clarence Thomas and Shelby Steele have stated that the latter agenda is one of victimization, they are unlikely models for the new national black identity. The victimization syndrome that Steele says blacks use as a shield to avoid competition with whites is too real and too often reinforced by incidents like the Rodney King beating to be dropped. In addition, none of the black conservatives embrace the positive themes and strengths that define us as a people. Indeed, the obvious career opportunism of a Clarence Thomas or John Doggett or, to a lesser degree, Anita Hill, is precisely opposed to the values embodied in Thurgood Marshall.

Finally, is the loss of a national black identity a bad thing? I think it is, unless we believe that this country as a whole currently embodies those values and goals we seek to be identified with. If it does not, then we must seek to present alternative values and goals as forcefully as possible. This struggle is not new. At the turn of this century, Booker T. Washington firmly identified himself with the optimism, pragmatism, and materialism of the great corporate leaders of the day. Over a twenty-year period his leadership produced no marked improvement in the quality of life for most African Americans. Opposed to Washington was W. E. B. Du Bois who, while not opposing industrial education, challenged the values of the larger society that denied blacks full equality. It was Du Bois, not Washington, who served as an inspiration for the leaders of the civil rights movement. And it will be Thurgood Marshall, not Clarence Thomas, who will inspire us to move forward into the next century.

CHARLES P. HENRY, Ph.D., is professor of African American Studies at the University of California at Berkeley. He is the author of Jesse Jackson: The Search for Common Ground *(The Black Scholar Press) and* Culture and African American Politics *(Indiana University Press).*

Breaking Silences*

Calvin Hernton

The sex war and the race war in the United States have always been ruled by the politics of a common ideology—the Ideology of Race First and Sex Second.

The machinations of this ideology have been indelibly manifested in three historical moments of truth. First, the long struggle for freedom bore fruit between 1865 and 1870. For both women and men, the 13th Amendment abolished slavery. But the 14th and 15th Amendments, which granted citizenship, equal protection, and the ballot to black men, deliberately excluded women, rendering them without any civil rights whatsoever. A half century later, in 1920, women won the vote with the passage of the 19th Amendment, marking the second moment of truth in which, again, black women were effectively excluded, since "women" meant white women only. The third time around, the Civil Rights *cum* Black Power Movement of the 1960s and early 1970s was thoroughly dominated by men whose values and practices relegated women to the "prone position." Women were objectified as being either "queens" or "bitches," which meant anything from a house-serving, baby-producing, "glorified slave," to a subservient, stamp-licking "piece of ass." Indeed, from slavery until now, at the close of every cycle of racial upheaval in America, the nefarious machinations of the ideology of race first and sex second have resulted in black women getting "screwed" every time.

The ideology of race first and sex second fosters both white supremacy and male supremacy, and it underpins the racial oppression of black women and men. At the same time it underpins the sexual oppression of both black and white women. Specifically, in terms of race this Hydra-headed ideology empowers white over black and, in

*This piece is an excerpt from a much larger work entitled *Locomotion Split: The Dance and The Music*, slated for publication in the fall of 1992.

terms of sex, it empowers male over female. Race is sexualized and sex is racialized, but race is ranked higher than sex, which means that racial equality between white and black men is more important than the "lesser question" of sex equality. Thus, race and sex are abstracted and "polarized," then they are manipulated and played off against one another. But the politics of sex and the politics of race are one and the same politics. The most recent enactment of the vulgarity of this politics was the televised gang rape of Anita Hill before the gaze of the world.

Because it is impossible to separate their sex from their race, and since they are at once sexually and racially oppressed, the primary target of the ideology of race first and sex second is black women. Their sex and race are split in two, which requires them to choose and be loyal to *either* their race *or* their sex. In this fashion the ideology of race first and sex second verifies and denies that sexual oppression exists, and it prohibits and penalizes anyone who says that sexism and racism are intertwined and that they should be fought as one. Vitiating and deforming their sex and race, the ideology of race first and sex second seeks to smear the integrity of being a woman.

The mandate that authorizes the sexual abuse of women is implicitly coded and explicitly sanctioned in the ideology of race first and sex second. Sexually, this ideology empowers men over women; it teaches that the penis is first and the vagina is last; that the "dick" is supposed to be all-powerful and the "pussy" is supposed to be powerless. In its most barbaric form, male power is the penis seeking to subdue, conquer and ravish women as objectified "pieces of ass." Male power over women is "dick over pussy," where ideas such as "Long Dong Silver" and a battery of men's "dirty" jokes and references are designed to degrade women sexually and pornographize the act of coitus.

Sexual harassment then is merely the tip of the iceberg. For the power that men wield over women consists of more than sexual insults and insinuations by individual men. All male power is located in and backed up by the institutional orders and cultural *norms* of society; male domination over women is realized in and through these institutions, particularly in the economic and political structures of the Corporation and State.

Men first, women second, moreover, is individually and collectively vested in the concept of Manhood, which is significantly based on and actualizes itself in the sexual degradation of the female sex. Altogether, male power is *patri-power*, where the ideas, feelings, beliefs and practices of violence against femaleness are embodied in and authorized by hierarchal structures of patriarchy throughout society and culture. In a patriarchy, men are the officers of power, and women are viewed as spoils of the powerful. Accordingly, women are supposed to be attracted to power and to the men who claim this power as theirs alone. Especially in political jobs women are regarded as sexual game. This is particularly true in bureaucratic places like the nation's capital where women—secretaries, typists, stamp-lickers, filers, and so forth—exist as a colony of sex for men in command of the most powerful patri-structures in the world. But, in all work places where men predominate—from the halls of academe to the fire department, from the corporate board room to the sweat shop, and from the auto plant to the halls of Congress—women employees are constant victims of sexual intimidation, vulgarity and profanity. This is the key, the power to exploit and degrade women in all places of work. For the work place is the traditional bulwark of penis power. No matter what the job or the status, sexual exploitation of women is taken for granted as a built-in benefit, a "perk" and a privilege for men.

Women and men are never treated as equals, only people with penises can be equals; never mind how much money a woman might earn, no vagina can ever be equal to a penis. When the signs read: "Men at Work," it means, "Penises at Work." Whoever heard of "Vaginas at Work?" Such a sign would be taken that prostitutes were in the area. These are the living sexways of the ideology of race (men) first and sex (women) last. Thus, we witnessed on television the sexual and racial *smearing* of Anita Hill by members of an all-white-male Senate Judiciary Committee, along with a black man and his supporters, including a majority of the public, as reported by the polls.

Race first and sex second is a misogynist ideology that mandates male appropriation of women's bodies as objects of pornography and abuse. Sexual harassment, politically considered, is a power variant and is a manifestation of the macho politics concocted, practiced and exemplified by the Reagan-Bush regime. The Reagan-Bush men make up a typical locker room gang; football is their metaphor and paradigm. Every man is a jock with a killer instinct. Bush and his jocks have "kicked ass" from Grenada to Libya to Panama and back to Iraq. The locker room attitude and behavior in the political world are matched by the locker room attitude and behavior in the world of men and women—for, like football, sex and women are regarded as "sport" for men. In the locker room, profanity, vulgarity and pornography. In the locker room, men "joke" with themselves about "sex" that is always degrading to women. Derisive palaver about "faggots," "freaks," "nymphomaniacs," "sucking dick" and "eating cunt" are standard pastime activities among men. Just to say "fucking bitch," to feel these obscenities on the tongue and in the mouth, and to hear oneself say them, socializes in men a hateful, violent, and righteous feeling of *power* over women.

This is the ethos that characterizes all places where women and men work. This is the world in which Anita Hill works and lives. Lawyers, doctors, professors, preachers, judges, politicians, business men, as well as construction workers and garbage men, black and white, yellow and brown, share the attitude and the behavior that men are primary and righteous, and women are secondary and profane.

Three boys come upon a cabin in the woods. They go in and overpower a black woman writer and rape her for nearly four hours. Fearing to report it to the authorities, the writer shared it with some of her close peers who gossiped among themselves that perhaps the writer had "made up" the story, or had "embellished" it—after all, the writer was known to have a "vivid imagination." On October 12, 1991, women sympathetic to Anita Hill held a demonstration in front of the U.S. Supreme Court. A man yelled to them that they were interfering with him watching football. "Fuck you, bitches!" he yelled to them.

Let's face it. Very few if any black folk, let alone white folk, doubt that Clarence Thomas did what Anita says he did. What turned people away from Hill was their perception of her as "uppity" by class position, education, job, presumed equality in a world of men. The public got mad at Hill for jeopardizing a black man getting his piece of the American pie. Anita Hill was supposed to devote her energies to fighting white racism, and do nothing about black or white sexism. But by breaking the silence, inadvertently or not, Anita Hill put her sex and humanity and the sex and humanity of all women on par with men and race. Hill's translation of silence into words and action was perceived as insubordination and a challenge to male power.

The ideology of race first and sex second means that no act that a man commits against a woman can warrant the woman telling on the man. When a woman does tell, as Anita Hill told, the whole race reacts as if the woman told on the entire race. The ideology of race first and sex second decrees that women belong to a race, which is to say that they belong to men, and not vice versa, the first identification then, is with men and the only loyalty is to the race. Not only would Anita Hill be punished. Women feared that all women who took her side would be punished, they feared that men would backlash them. So they turned away from Anita and sex, and supported Clarence and race.

Punishment consists of re-victimization where the victim, the one who tells, is made to be the criminal. When a Cleveland woman kills her batterer of fifteen years, she is labelled a traitor to the race for aiding white men in destroying black males. Women are *blackmaled* into silence for fear of being attacked as "sluts," "whores" and "nymphos." Classic examples are slave women who often broke the silence on their white masters at the risk of their lives. Branded as not merely a traitor to her race, but as being a mentally unstable, love-starved sex-teaser and fantasizing liar, the punishment dealt to Anita Hill was a message to other women not to follow in Hill's footsteps. Every woman testifying for Thomas told of having been harassed by every employer they ever had, *except Thomas*! Thomas was supported by not just the spectre of the entire black and white male population, but there was Senator Danforth in person. During slavery a free Negro was behooved to have some influential white man as his protector-guardian. Because everybody knew he was Ole Massa John's nigger, you did not mess with such a Negro. There is little need to argue that Hill herself is a cut off of the same block as Thomas. The only difference is that Thomas is a black man and Hill is a black woman, which is all the difference in the world. The primacy of race before sex demands that black women split themselves in two, and that they deny their sex and behave as if race is everything and their sex is worth absolutely nothing. Nearly every black man in America, and a majority of women too, would have us believe that black women are oppressed solely because of their race and not because of their sex. Historically, the ideology of race first and sex second has been utilized to divide and conquer. Black women are stigmatized by two "negatives"—femaleness and blackness, and are required to split themselves and become "schizophrenic." Race *vs.* sex as an *either/or* proposition has always rendered black women on the bottom of the power structure in America.

On the other hand, women identifying with Hill are organizing. One such organization is African American Women in Defense of Ourselves. They recognize that sexual harassment is part and parcel of the mores and practices of male violence and women's oppression the world over. For feminist or womanist/feminist women, Hill's breaking of silence has greatly raised and illuminated their awareness and strengthened their commitment. In *Sister Outsider*, Audre Lorde has written, "Your silence will not protect you. I am not only a casualty, I am also a warrior. And of course I am afraid, because the transformation of silence into language and action is an act of self-revelation. . . . For it is not difference which immobilizes us, but silence. And there are so many silences to be broken."

CALVIN HERNTON is author of Sex and Racism in America. *His most recent book is* The Sexual Mountain and Black Women Writers. *Hernton is professor of Black Studies at Oberlin College.*

The Thomas Hearings and the Nexus of Race, Gender and Nationalism

Gerald Horne

"Justice Thomas is the first black-skinned man ever to hold such a major post in American history. 'It's a victory of the black men over the yellow men,' said the source, aware of the sensitive nature of his comment. 'Light-skinned blacks down through history have dominated the scene. During slavery, the blacks were the field hands. Then came the age of mulattos. Now the mantle of self-imposed color limitation has been lifted. We don't have to rely only on black people who are light skinned.' " (*Jet*, 4 November 1991.)

The bitter struggle to confirm Clarence Thomas to the U.S. Supreme Court has revealed dangerous fault lines, and not just within African American discourse. The quotation cited above was mirrored in the November 1991 edition of *Essence* that queried if lighter-skinned sisters were preferred by brothers. Such a query is the unfortunate but logical corollary of a narrowly nationalistic form of thinking that has not been interrogated sufficiently within an African American community that since the dawn of the Red Scare has been dominated intellectually by various forms of nationalism, be it progressive, reactionary or bourgeois. The U.S. ruling elite, not unaware of this tendency, has decided in jujitsu fashion to turn this tendency back against us on the assumption that we will drink the poison if it comes in a black bottle.

The fact is that theories positing the negative implications of the relative absence of melanin are all the rage within certain Afrocentric circles. Such theories received the ultimate validation when trumpeted in a recent "Public Enemy" album. But it was inevitable that such a theory, designed ostensibly to analyze white supremacy, would be taken to the next step: after all, Clarence Thomas appears to have more melanin than Thurgood Marshall, Roy Innis has more than Julian Bond, so maybe we should be supportive of the former and hostile to the latter. (I'm still trying to figure out what this theory tells us about Louis Farrakhan.)

The larger question obviously involves more than just this popular theory. It involves the marginalizing of figures like W. E. B. Du Bois, Paul Robeson and Claudia Jones over the past thirty-five years; it involves the marginalizing of the way they examined and interpreted the world. This devastating process was a precondition to civil rights concessions. However, now that this process has been concluded—when the Black Panthers rose in the 1960s in an attempt to continue the Robeson tradition in their own way, they were shot down—the time has come to replace our remaining leadership with the likes of Thomas, Robert Woodson (recipient of a MacArthur "genius" grant, would you believe), Shelby Steele (nominee for numerous awards and prizes), and others.

African American intellectuals, rappers, and politicos have been consumed with the question of race in recent times. Yet as the twentieth century is coming to a close it is apparent that despite—or perhaps because of—this analysis they have managed to miss the most important "race" story of contemporary history: how Washington and its European allies destabilized "white" Moscow and thereby prepared the way for "non-white" Tokyo to go to the head of the line of the capitalist nations in the twenty-first century. Many in our community missed the implications of the old Jack Benny joke; he is accosted by a potential robber who barks, "Your money or your life!" Benny replies, "I'm thinking, I'm thinking . . ." The U.S. elite values lucre above life itself and somehow many of us have forgotten this simple lesson.

To be sure, the rise of David Duke tells us that we cannot be indifferent to the question of race at any time. But look at South Africa: there Duke's comrades have been in power for decades. But, unlike the situation here, the African National Congress refused to break its alliance with the organized left, including the South African Communist Party. The rise of Clarence Thomas and the black conservatives is the inevitable result of Faustian bargains—acquiesced to by many of us—concluded in the 1950s when Washington decided that Jim Crow was a handicap in fighting the Cold War and in attempting to portray Moscow as the embodiment of all that was evil.

And akin to what is happening today in Eastern Europe, the erosion of left influence within the African American community set the stage not only for the hegemonic influence of various forms of nationalism, it also led directly to the devaluation of the gender question. African empires in place thousands of years ago have been valorized as the *ne plus ultra* of our existence, with little regard to the subjugation of women during that era. Rap music and videos have been praised unduly for their "energy" and "nationalism," while their treatment of women has been assessed as an irrelevant detail or minor flaw. Black males are referred to as the "endangered species" with the inference left that somehow women are doing swimmingly, thank you. Hence, we have reached the point that in many respects "Afrocentrism" is barely distinguishable from "andro-centrism."

Yet, it would be equally one-sided to just leave the analysis at that; this would be just another brand of the "blame the victim" psychosis so fashionable nowadays. Take our friends in the civil liberties community, for example. We are told that we have to tolerate racist speech, for if we seek to circumscribe it, we would have to bar anti-racist speech as well. Images of the "thought police" and "tyranny of the politically correct" are trotted out at such moments. Nevertheless, the kind of sexual harassment that creates a "hostile working environment" is no more than speech and I have yet to hear those same civil libertarians claim that we must allow such filth.

Michael Thomas, columnist for the *New York Observer*, was called anti-Semitic by Alan Dershowitz when he claimed that stating that street crime was committed disproportionately by black youth is deemed a sociological observation but suggesting that insider trading seems to be committed disproportionately by Jewish stockbrokers is deemed bigoted. The fact is that in U.S. intellectual circles, if one wants to devalue a principle, a piece of legislation (*cf.* the Civil Rights Act of 1991) or whatever, all one has to do is invoke the devalued people—African Americans. Anita Hill has become the Rosa Parks of sexual harassment but the fact that she is of African descent probably accounts for why her allegations were not given more weight—even within her own community.

The only perverse pleasure I receive from this scenario (and it is quite limited) is that racism—which has been so essential to the construction of this nation—will now play a role in its demise; for it

tion in that quasi-legal setting. She might well have been the rape victim at the precinct—in the days before feminist agitation checked the worst outward manifestations of abusive sexism. Patriarchy naturally inclines toward defensive disbelief about what women say about sex/sexuality, particularly if it casts doubt on the *status quo*. Almost *a priori*, the instinct is to discredit women and the narratives of our experience. Having to talk as a woman—and a *black* woman—about gross sexual matters, not only in public but before national television cameras, forced Anita Hill into an almost "prim and proper" self-presentation. Even more importantly, it compelled her to subdue her emotions and behavior and deaden her affect. Unfortunately, deadening her affect also helped kill her power. Unlike those early women crusaders, she could not then rise to the kind of outraged righteousness which gave force to their personalities and platforms. Whether the way she acted her part emanated from her own nature or was adopted strategy, it edged her into a type of nice girl persona.

I want to make it clear that the interpretation I have presented here is not a criticism of Professor Hill (even though I am aware that some people may still feel that she comes off badly in this analysis). I believe that she is a brave woman who did us all a great service. And she is certainly not responsible for the macho morals and ethical barbarism which block appreciation of her fine behavior. What I intended was to offer a gendered reading of her and Thomas's conduct during the sexual harassment hearings because this angle interested me. In the final analysis, I think I have been forced to conclude that being a nice, good girl got Anita Hill what all "nice girls" usually get: nothing—but further abuse.

GLORIA T. HULL, Ph.D., is professor of Women's Studies and Literature at the University of California, Santa Cruz. She is one of the 1,603 "African American Women in Defense of Ourselves" who united to sponsor the November 17, 1991 statement in The New York Times *protesting the Thomas appointment and Hill-Thomas hearings.*

is clear that in the new global paradigm of economic competition this nation will be unable to compete unless "human capital" is deployed more efficiently, which means affirmative action. But it is precisely the gutting of that policy that caused George Bush to nominate Clarence Thomas to the U.S. Supreme Court. The presence of Thomas's dark visage is supposed to reassure that such a demarche is not racist.

The Thomas-Hill hearings have been so stirring because they have disturbed the remote subconscious. Like an abused child, the African American community has repressed so many distasteful memories—particularly what happened during the Red Scare—but now, like the adults we are supposed to be, it is time to confront those nightmares and draw the appropriate conclusions. Above all, Clarence Thomas should force us to think a bit more profoundly about questions of nationalism, racism, and gender, and their explosive intersection.

GERALD HORNE, Ph.D., is former executive director of The National Conference of Black Lawyers; he most recently published Studies In Black: Progressive Views of the African American Experience, *and has two forthcoming works:* Black Liberation/Red Scare: Ben Davis and the Communist Party, *and* Fire This Time: The Watts Uprising and the Meaning of the 1960s.

Girls Will Be Girls, and Boys Will . . . Flex Their Muscles

Gloria T. Hull

I wish to comment on only one aspect of the Anita Hill–Clarence Thomas debacle: how the two of them acted out traditional gender role conventions and what impact I think this made on how they were perceived and treated.

This perspective occurred to me as I reflected on how upset I had become during the segment of the hearings when the scurrilous John Doggett affidavit about Hill at the Washington, D.C., party was newly introduced. Even though this development was yet one more unexpected piece of tripe to handle, Professor Hill was willing to open herself up to immediate questioning about it. A "friendly" Judiciary Committee member pointed out her option of taking time to read and consider the document, but she continued to say, "I can respond to that now." Here was one of those moments when I yelled advice at the television screen: "Take your time. Yeah, take your time. You don't have to deal with that now. Steady, sister. Easy, slow. Take your time."

I wanted her to pace the proceedings and give herself a break. I viewed such a response as being more dignified and powerful, as exhibiting the kind of deliberative, quasi-legal cool which communicates "I have my time to think about this, I'm going to take what is due me, and I'll get to it when *I'm* ready." If nothing else, this would have shown an unwillingness/refusal to be so totally accommodating, no matter what. As it was, Hill's response further demonstrated the openness, forthrightness, and niceness which made such a positive impression on people who were inclined to take her seriously and give her a fair hearing. It also enhanced her grace-under-pressure, poise-under-fire image—which I and many others admired.

Judge Thomas, on the other hand, gave up nothing from beginning to end of his confirmation process—nothing, that is, except the tired bootstrap narrative which bored and embarrassed me. And in his

appearance before the Committee after Hill's testimony, he took aggressive offensive, letting his anger out in intemperate attitudes a language. Every hard word and clench of the jaws was meant convey, "I'm pissed at all of you for f—ing with me." This was hig male dudgeon at its best.

Women have been socially conditioned to try to please (evei when displeasing). Men are encouraged to "act out" and think oi themselves. These poles of behavioral patterning could easily be seen in the contrasting deportment of these two characters. Clarence Thomas came out swinging for Clarence Thomas—his integrity, his reputation, his career, his future. Anita Hill said she came forward not for herself, but in the interest of "truth." Thus, she took recourse to a higher authority to sanction behavior which transgressed patriarchal norms, as "uppity" women have done for centuries—women such as the early evangelists and social reform crusaders who dared to speak in public.

Unfortunately, this society runs on values which accord greater respect, weight, and efficacy to the masculine stance. I am even aware of the possibly contradictory nature of my own desire that Professor Hill had acted less "feminine" when confronted with the affidavit. Apparently, Thomas being individualistic and tough on his own behalf backed off some attacks, deflected others, and heightened his stature in the eyes of many. It more strongly convinced me that he was a complexly constructed, perhaps complexly damaged man whose possible use of supreme judicial power was frightening to consider. Hill's accommodation seemed to additionally license ever more insulting questions and general inconsideration.

Thus far, I have discussed these gender issues in terms of what Clarence Thomas did, what Anita Hill did—that is, as socially constructed but ultimately personal behavior. However, I should also point out that the scenario was only a small part of a drama much larger than their two individual selves. Further considering these larger forces brings special understanding to Hill's role. In the first place (as I have implied but wish to state outright), she was automatically disadvantaged by the play being set in and directed by the rules of a male power domain. Thus, all of her admirable qualities carried little weight.

Secondly, the subject being sex inherently compromised her posi-

"Them Against Us": Anita Hill v. Clarence Thomas

Jacquelyne Johnson Jackson

PULLING FOR THOMAS

Totally absorbed by the Hill-Thomas cataclysmic hearings and often biased print and electronic media-reported news and commentary, I unabashedly pulled "all the way" for now Associate Justice Clarence Thomas, just as once during my bachelor's and master's years back in the early 1950s at The University of Wisconsin I zealously cheered for any black football player on our team *and* on any opponent's team. When a doctoral student in the late 1950s at The Ohio State University, blacks were somewhat more commonplace on the best and most prestigious collegiate football teams outside of the still racist South, so I just earnestly cheered for blacks and non-blacks alike on our team. The Hill-Thomas cataclysm aroused my old football (*read* black) feelings.

My lasting impression of Hill, formed when I saw her very first televised press conference, was she's "them against us." My female antenna bristled at her flippant dismissal of a reporter's inquiry about Phyllis Berry Myers's comment about her in the previous Sunday's *New York Times*. Hill glibly intimated she knew not that black female, so Myers knew nothing about her. Yet, as it was later revealed, they were acquaintances and EEOC co-workers in Washington: Hill knew her and knew she knew her. Far from suave at that conference, Hill was passively aggressive, even subtly vindictive, so I wondered, "What gives?" Why does she want to block Thomas's appointment? Had he really "done her wrong"?

I supported Thomas's confirmation, not because he was the most qualified (not a criterion), but because he was George Bush's *only* black star. If not Thomas, I reasoned, then an equally or more conservative Hispanic, white female, or white male. Thomas was surely as qualified as most Supreme Court nominees and better than many. Reared in Alabama, I knew Hugo Black's Ku Klux Klan membership did not prevent him from being a good and decent Associate Justice. A conservative black Georgian can be another Hugo Black.

Besides, given the Court from which Thurgood Marshall retired, Thomas is more likely than a Marshall clone to move it toward racially equitable compromises on such controversial issues as affirmative action. Whether Thomas might vote to overturn *Roe* v. *Wade* is not germane to me; if overturned, the U.S. Congress can and should legislate legal abortions. So I viewed Thomas's shrill feminist opposition based on his unknown abortionist views, as well as abortive attempts by some Democratic Judiciary Committee members to uncover such views, as a masquerade to derail him because he was not *the* black or, more likely, non-black they wanted on the Court.

HILL LIED

Now, on to the "them against us" hearings before fourteen obviously august white male senators, including the pious and devout Edward Kennedy and Howard Metzenbaum, saved only (to end the jest) by Joseph Biden's generally decent mien, Orrin Hatch's plucky emotional and partisan defense of Thomas, Alan Simpson's caustic wit, and, above all, Arlen Specter's judicious and legally competent destruction of Hill's gravamen against Thomas. Specter's astuteness and wisdom have long impressed me, including his vote several years ago against impeaching the then (now impeached) Floridian black Federal Judge Alcee Hastings.

Moreover, but for the legalism that recanting false testimony before ending testimony is not perjury, Hill and her star white female witness Susan Hoerchner (a Worker's Compensation Judge in Norwalk, California) would have committed perjury. Hoerchner uncharacteristically became amnesiac when Specter justly sought the approximate date (even just the year or where she was living) when Hill informed her of Thomas's allegedly sexual harassment. Hill's much touted passing of a lie detector test is also questionable in the absence of any expert certification that she used no drug-altering or other means of manipulating physiological reactions to the test or was not prone to lie.

Hill lied: she fantasized herself as a scorned woman, was a liberal-feminist conspiratorial tool to derail Thomas's confirmation by any

means necessary, or both. Hill, the Yale graduate, coyly played the "young dumb female" bit by supposedly being unaware of her federal career employee rights. But she had to know that her continuing federal employment back in 1981 was decidedly not dependent upon following Thomas from the U.S. Office of Education to the U.S. Equal Employment Opportunity Commission.

About forty-eight of my black female and male friends and acquaintances (mostly social scientists) telephoned me from far and near during the Hill-Thomas cataclysm to see what I thought. We all agreed that Hill lied. Applicable public polls also convincingly show that most blacks—female or male—sided with Thomas, not with Hill. Yet most of us think something "went down" between them. We do not dismiss sexual innuendos by Thomas, but we question both Hill's situational descriptions of when they occurred and her own behavior toward him in those settings and her linguistic description of them. Would a black male of Thomas's background refer to a pubic hair on a Coke top or "Long Dong Silver?" Or would he use speech more common to his black roots and generational stratum? That is an "iffy" question since both Thomas and Hill may have sexually spoken as "Yalies" speak.

But even if Thomas or Hill used such sexual language, Hill was unconvincing. Hill's gravamen of verbal sexual harassment was not then legally recognized as such. There was no disclosure of Hill's possible "come-on" to Thomas, where she might have been the villain, not victim. Her humdrum behavior and looks and typically incredible witnesses lent credibility to black attorney John Doggett's highly believable assertion that, considering Thomas's political ambitions, Hill was "not worth Thomas's risk." I accept that assertion.

I also deeply respect constitutionally protected statutes of limitations, rights of defendants to face their accusers, and interracial marriages (including Thurgood Marshall's). Hill apparently does not. Even if she had a legitimate charge, the statute of limitations had long expired; her desire to hide herself as Thomas's accuser is suspicious, devious, and definitely not the "American way"; and Thomas had the right to remarry and, although I personally hate to see black men of his stature do so, marry white.

"CHANGING OF THE BLACK GUARD"

So, on to "them against us" by concentrating briefly on just three of the intriguing and interrelated questions *The Black Scholar* posed to forum respondents, all of which clearly point toward "the changing of the black guard" by racial representation, racial integration, and black female-male relationships.

Racial representation. First the Thomas and then the Hill-Thomas hearings unequivocally and irrevocably demonstrated publicly that Native American Blacks are not ideologically or politically monolithic, nor do we all march to the same drummer, whether that drummer be the Congressional Black Caucus, National Association for the Advancement of Colored People, or the National Baptist Convention, U.S.A., several of whose pastors incredibly and irresponsibly chastised Thomas in their testimony before the Judiciary Committee because he was not a black church member. So what! As a sociologist, I doubt that black pastors were ever the leaders of each and every Native American Black residential community (and I know that most black pastors and churches were *not* active and refused to be active in the black civil-rights movements of the 1950s and 1960s).

Also as a sociologist I know of the rising gap between the opinions of "ordinary blacks" and aged black civil-rights establishment heads, such as Benjamin Hooks, John Jacob, and Joseph Lowery, and the self-appointed or self-anointed black leaders, such as Jesse Jackson. This rising gap has been partly driven in recent years by the substantially large—and welcome—rise of extremely well-educated and articulate black women and men who know national issues and are critical thinkers or at least "think for themselves" or their vested interests.

These types of "new blacks" (whom *The Black Scholar* describes as "the new generation of post–civil rights blacks, notably those cultivated during the last twenty years") and many "old blacks," such as myself, know and respect black diversity. More importantly, we know that technological and other advances in communication and public opinion polls no longer mean that one or two or three or four or even the double-handful members of the Congressional Black Caucus can pretend (and get away with it) that they speak for and represent all

Native American Blacks. *That, quite frankly, is history and herstory.* Racial representation must now be based upon real racial representation, so those who purport to be such representatives must really represent the majority opinion, not just their opinions.

Racial integration. The Black Scholar call to this forum queried, had the politics of racial integration been reduced to a politics of racial inclusion? I share and know well such fears, because that is precisely what has happened in far too many instances on prestigious college and university campuses and elsewhere, including many of President Bush's black appointees. But this is not a new pattern nor one peculiar to higher education and the Bush administration. The historical record clearly shows that most black racially integrated appointees, hirings, et cetera, have always been "safe niggers" or "Uncle Toms and Aunt Thomasinas" (which is how I see Hill). Make no mistake about it: Most blacks who support blacks, such as Doggett, are unacceptable to whites and, if employed in white-controlled establishments, are quickly labeled as arrogant, uncooperative, and unacceptable employees. Just think of the myriad ways in which many whites, including many gay and lesbian whites, have tried to discredit "Magic" Johnson's forthright announcement of his HIV infection. Ye gads!

The unadulterated truth of the matter is that, despite the notable achievements of racial desegregation during the past several decades, Native American Blacks are not and cannot be empowered as such in the United States. Thus, it is fitting and proper that we recognize the fact that Native American Blacks are highly diversified by various physiological, psychological, sociocultural, and political factors. Our recognition of this diversity is long overdue, and, until we accept it we will falter by the road in just believing that because you are black you are committed to blackness. That is a false assumption. Most blacks, and particularly those in "high places," are not and cannot be committed to "blackness." If they were, they would not be in "high places."

Black female-male relationships. Among Hill's major faults, perhaps her two most crucial ones were her apparent belief that slavery's legacy of the highly peculiar triangle of black male, black female, and white male relationships meant that white males were more partial to black females than to black males; and, as a corollary, that white males always support black females over black males, notwithstanding their own actual or alleged sexual or other transgressions.

The "them against us" hearings undoubtedly showed that most blacks—female and male alike—objected to Hill's witting or unwitting acquiescence to white male superiority, improper use of black females against black males, and the extension of that peculiar triangle into a rectangle of conniving white females who, no matter how cleverly they try to disguise it, absolutely oppose any black women or men whom they cannot control and who vehemently compete against blacks for political offices. After all, whenever to their advantage, don't they keep saying that "We are just like the blacks" and we can represent them?

CONCLUSION

So Hill was, for whatever reasons, "them against us." She sided with some whites against some blacks and with some white women against one black man, perhaps because she was a woman scorned or because her anticipated personal and monetary benefits outweighed whatever benefits she might have accrued, even as a law school professor, from supporting the constitutionally protected rights of statutes of limitations and the rights of defendants to face their accusers. In my judgment, Anita Hill and *Anita Hill* v. *Clarence Thomas* do not represent Native Black America's "finest hour." We can and must do better in the future. We must recognize the diversity of Native Black Americans and act accordingly. We must not upset ourselves by the traitor Hill just because she is black and female, nor because Thomas is conservative and married white.

"The old black guard" is changing and rapidly becoming extinct. They cannot and ought not represent "new blacks." The National Urban League has long pouted about low wages, but its Washington Urban League recently opposed a proposal by an official body of the District of Columbia to raise minimum wages for clerical and related workers from $4.25 to $7.25 per hour ("too much," said the Washington Urban League). There are many diverse black guards today, so we must all now pull for Thomas to be, if not better than, at least a Hugo Black. We must forgive and forget Hill, but not the continued fight for racial *and* sexual liberation, including for black women freedom from and ample monetary compensation for racial and/or sexual harassment.

JACQUELYNE JOHNSON JACKSON, Ph.D., is associate professor of Medical Sociology, Department of Psychiatry, Duke University Medical Center.

Tom, Buck, and Sambo or How Clarence Thomas Got to the Supreme Court

Llenda Jackson-Leslie

George Bush's expertise at racial stereotyping is well known. His *piece de resistance* however, was the transformation of a colorless, color-blind Clarence Thomas into an outraged black man. The use of racism to garner political support from white voters is not new, but Bush manipulated the prejudices and fears of African Americans as well.

The first and most enduring image is Clarence Thomas as the noble, loyal and faithful Uncle Tom, derived from the original Harriet Stowe novel. Thomas's opening statement to the Senate Judiciary panel was a depiction of the sober, dignified, hard-working black man, proud to be a slave. Stowe's Uncle Tom, cruelly sold by his master, nearly dead from starvation and brutality, insists, "he will hear not one word against old massa." Clarence as "Tom" stoically told of the social and economic deprivations suffered by his sharecropper grandfather.

Few things appeal to white men more than a long-suffering black man. Reporters, pundits, and correspondents fell over themselves describing Thomas's compelling testimony.

Although willing to wax poetic on the injustices of his youth, Thomas fell silent about the injustices brought before him as the Secretary for Civil Rights. Thomas was even more reticent about his earlier claims that natural law superseded the constitution, or his opinions on *Roe* v. *Wade,* which he claimed never to have discussed.

Tom had evolved into Sambo, that colorful, comic minstrel character who can remember nothing without his master's help. The white senators and white media were persuaded because Thomas's disingenuity coincided with their own opinions about black intelligence. Thomas became the invisible black man, devoid of any inner life or consciousness, a mere reflection of his master's desires.

The third stereotype, less accurate but effective nonetheless, was that of Anita Hill presented variously as a scorned, vengeful or tragically psychotic woman. Although Hill's behavior and demeanor did not conform, she was portrayed as a black woman bringing a "good" black man down. Like Lena Horne's sultry temptress in "Cabin in the Sky"; Dorothy Dandridge's amoral gold digger in "Carmen Jones"; or Fredi Washington's tragic mulatto in "Imitation of Life," Hill just didn't know her "place." Hill bore the brunt of intraracial hatred: the resentment of black men toward upwardly mobile black women; the contempt of black men who view all black women as bitches, skeezers and hoes; the envy of black women who are less talented and less attractive. The campaign to undermine Anita Hill's credibility succeeded because of historical divisions within our community. Men against women; educated against uneducated; middle class professionals against working class; light skin against dark skin.

The underlying racist presumption that all black women are too immoral, too loose to be raped or sexually abused helped inform white opinion. This presumption is as old as slavery and as contemporary as Tawana Brawley. Thomas's colorless position and his status as Bush's manservant ensured Hill's allegations were treated as black women's complaints of sexual abuse are almost always treated, with silent contempt. Once the allegations became public, Bush and his imagist began the re-creation of Anita Hill and the recasting of Clarence Thomas as a proud and angry black man.

But like the Toms and Sambos of stage and screen, Thomas's anger was carefully channeled. His hostility was principally directed toward a black woman.

Thomas's reference to a "high-tech legal lynching" of an "uppity black man" bore no historical relation to the real, legal lynchings of Paul Robeson, Marcus Garvey, Adam Clayton Powell or Judge Alcee Hastings. Thomas was not comparing himself to the more than 4,000 black elected officials who have been systematically harassed by the federal government over the past two decades. They are not Thomas's historical antecedents, nor would he willingly claim them. This well-chosen phrase was calculated to arouse the protective instincts of the African American community, to remind us that Thomas is still a black man, just as his earlier posturings were to assure the Senate that he was not.

A beneficiary of Yale's affirmative action program, Thomas opposed affirmative action as a public official. A sharecropper's grandson, Thomas proclaimed natural law, a concept once used to defend slavery and segregation, superior to the U.S. Constitution. Thomas was no more a victim of "legal lynching" than the Operation Rescue fanatics are heirs of the Civil Rights Movement.

This reconstituted, angry black man received his strongest support from Strom "segregation forever" Thurmond. A former South Carolina judge who routinely denied any semblance of justice to thousands of African Americans was Thomas's chief defender.

How do we resolve this paradox? First, the alleged harassment was against a black woman, in Thurmond's eyes, as in the distorted vision of other racists, no crime at all. Second, the equation of power must be considered, both as Hill's boss and Bush's manservant, Thomas had more power than Hill. In the mentality of a Strom Thurmond, Thomas had the same right to abuse Hill as the white master to abuse and debase his female slaves.

The final image is that of Thomas as "Buck," a virile, insatiably sexual black man who satisfies his casual lusts with black women but whose heartfelt desire is for white women. Buck is seen on film as Mandingo, and the male protagonist in almost any 1970s blaxploitation film. Buck also had a reputation for being bad and uncontrollable, but in plantation films dating back to "Birth of a Nation," the desire for white women proved Buck's undoing.

Thomas's ascension to the Supreme Court provides a paradigm of racial and sexual stereotypes, introduced and embellished by George Bush. Buck is the only non self-ascribed stereotype pinned to Thomas. Ironically, it was the Buck stereotype and Thomas's histrionic reaction which made him finally appear in the eyes of African Americans as someone of color.

Thomas, the only African American of three possible nominees, was to be named only upon the resignation or death of Thurgood Marshall. Quotas of exclusion rather than inclusion motivated Bush's selection of Clarence Thomas.

Bush's stage managing of the Clarence Thomas affair leaves the African American community with the troubling dilemma of image as it shapes power. We still have not discarded the cultural shackles which allow us to be defined by centuries-old stereotypes. We have yet to heal the wounds of intraracial hatred, or define the parameters for

inclusion in our community. At what point do we shun those who disavow our common heritage and struggle? These are terms African Americans must set for ourselves, just as we must define our own image and future.

LLENDA JACKSON-LESLIE is a Detroit freelance writer who researches African-American media images. She has authored content analyses on the media image of Mayor Coleman A. Young and Mayor David Dinkins and has written extensively on the harassment of black elected officials.

Anita Hill: Martyr Heroism and Gender Abstractions

Joy James

Articles written about and rallies around Anita Hill as a feminist icon or role model are part of the spillover of the Anita Hill/Clarence Thomas hearings. Allegations of sexual harassment by Hill, a woman from Thomas's caste, were able to delay the confirmation of Supreme Court Associate Justice Thomas when his own political record—anti-black, anti-female, anti-poor/working class, anti-youth, anti-elderly—could not.[1] The spotlight on the hearings and the "gender consciousness" raised in the entertainment industry's coverage have made Anita Hill's name a symbol for reverence, respect, or ridicule in recent feminist and masculinist writing.

While the reverence and ridicule appear disconnected from reality and based more on gender abstractions, i.e., a notion of sexual politics conveniently and romantically severed from class and racial politics, the respect is a response to the fact that Anita Hill withstood the racist-sexist harassment of ultraconservative Senate Judiciary Committee members during nationally televised "hearings" on sexual harassment. Although their diatribes carried the virulent "authoritative" contempt that only members of the white supremacist patriarchy manages to spew, Anita Hill maintained her personal dignity. This certainly deserves respect and praise. Still both respect and praise are weighted with irony: for Anita Hill worked to implement the policies of white supremacy and patriarchy; she harnessed her career to Reagan-Bush ultraconservatism and its employee, her former employer, Clarence Thomas. To re-create Anita Hill as a martyr heroine for mobilizing women or feminists is only possible if (a) one disconnects Hill from the singeing racial and class politics she embraced (and likely still embraces) and/or (b) one maintains that racism and classism are abstractions to, that is irrelevant in, sexual politics. It is only possible to make her a symbol if one creates a martyr heroine as a gender abstraction.

Surviving and refusing to be silent about sexual victimization are courageous acts. Yet, survival or speaking out does not make one a public heroine; public responsibilities and commitments remain to be taken into account. In the making of heroines in gender politics, feminist or otherwise, race and class ideologies still count. For example, if a woman staffer in David Duke's campaigns were to courageously come forward with accounts of sexual harassment by Duke, who backed Clarence Thomas, although I would support her right to confront the abuser, I could not make her a heroine leaving the neo-Nazi Duke the only villain when they both espouse the same political ideology. Obviously the abuse of right-wing women building careers under the tutelage of right-wing men, implementing racist, classist and (hetero)sexist policies, needs to stop. But this hardly merits honoring such women with candlelight vigils (Northampton, MA) or lyrics to be sung to the tune of "Joe Hill" (*Village Voice*, November 19, 1991). Supporting Anita Hill's right to a fair hearing on sexual harassment reveals compassion and outrage concerning sexual abuse. Placing Anita Hill (who implemented Reagan policies, taught at Oral Roberts University Law School, and maintains that Robert Bork was unjustly denied a seat on the Supreme Court) on a pedestal reveals how analyses surrounding sexual-racial abuse and democratic politics have become inane.

To place Hill on a pedestal one has to imitate Clarence Thomas, Orrin Hatch, John Danforth, Arlen Specter, Strom Thurmond, George Bush and company in the wolfish cries of "lynching!" This time though, the cry of "lynching/rape!" would highlight Anita Hill. Following the opportunistic moves on political language, history and reality throughout the Hill/Thomas hearings, one could first make trivial and then manipulate the lengthy red record of racial-sexual violence and violent racist sexual imagery which African Americans struggle to survive (or mimic contortionists' claims in a "Tony Brown's Journal" episode with Phyllis Berry Myers and John Doggett, that Thomas was "lynched" while Anita Hill was "raped"). Rape and lynching are tied together in the history of African American women tortured and raped prior to and during lynchings; and lynched, along with African American men who assisted them, for resisting or avenging rape by white men. (Since manipulating history is a useful tool for denying reality, it is unsurprising how the political history and reality of African American men, engaged in sexual abuse of African American women, is equally manipulated and denied.)

The Hill/Thomas hearings provided, along with distortions and denials, equal opportunity for pedestals laden with right-wing role models—black and white, male and female. Anita Hill, who had overcome her personal victimization with testimony revealing dignity and restraint painfully lacking in Thomas and most of his (female and male) cheerleaders, was the most appealing. Consequently, in the November 12, 1991 issue of the New York–based weekly the *Village Voice*, African American columnist Lisa Jones, after describing the "Bush/Thomas lynch strategy" and the racist-sexist vilifications of African American women, writes "Anita Hill—shunning victimhood—is a role model."[2] Anita Hill—shunning or embracing victimhood—could not possibly be a role model if being one means having a responsible relationship to the African American community and democratic politics. For Jones, the class and racial politics of Hill are as irrelevant as Thomas's sexual politics are for the editors of the African American Brooklyn-based weekly, *City Sun*, who treat superficially the charges of sexual harassment while writing about the detrimental political relationship of both Thomas and Hill to African American communities: "The truth is that Clarence Thomas and Anita Hill are cut from the same cloth. . . . Black people's interests were not the motivating factor for either Thomas's or Hill's career move."[3] Both articles, based in gender abstractions, fail to present a discussion of sexual politics connected to racial and class politics and vice versa.

Reductionism is endemic to discussions in which the politics of sexual harassment are isolated from racial and class politics. When the African American experience was reduced to the African American male experience opportunistically performed by Thomas (which also became the *man's* experience since the woman victimized was of his caste), the *woman's* experience became reduced to the ("whitened") middle-class female experience uncritically worn by Hill. The irrational and irritating commentary on the hearings underscored how prevalent reductionism is: white women commentators on NPR would state that Clarence Thomas needed a "black" on the Senate Judiciary Committee whereas Anita Hill needed a "woman." Neither the fact that Anita Hill along with over half of the African American population is both "black" and female nor that there is no monolithic "black" or "women's" voice/vote (even among white women Senators—Nancy Kassebaum voted for and Barbara McCluskey against Thomas's confirmation) spared us the inanity of coverage spaced out in gender abstractions. Much of the analysis leaves one with models that obscure the political ties of gender to race and class and veil the racial and class politics of women and men mobilizing under the banner of sexual politics.

For example, on October 12, 1991, Margaret A. Burnham wrote in *The Boston Globe*: "In confirming Thomas in the face of Hill's odious, highly detailed and credible story, the Senate's clear message will be that women who complain of sexual harassment are not to be believed. . . . If an upstanding, articulate law teacher who knows the rules cannot get a group of men to hear her, can a secretary have much hope?" Burnham writes as if Hill had no race (although credibility is tied to race) and refers to class in an incomplete way: the secretary is likely to be believed if she is white and accuses the black janitor. Women harassed by men of their race and class have little credibility before the law; women with race and class privilege are more credible than the accused if s/he is someone with a "lower" status in the social hierarchy—which is a significant part of the history of lynching. Referring to Hill, as if she has no race or class (interests), "as a woman" gives her the guise of "respectability"—middle-class, white, and heterosexual womanhood. In isolating sexual harassment from a race and class analysis, it also reduces sexual harassment discussions to abstractions.

Rejecting both martyr heroines and gender abstractions with an analysis of sexual politics embedded in national racial and class politics, "African American Women in Defense of Ourselves," an ad hoc group organized by African American academic-activists Barbara Ransby, Elsa Barkley Brown, and Deborah King, have written and organized around the Anita Hill/Clarence Thomas episode. Ransby, Brown and King were instrumental in an educational and fund-raising campaign that produced a nearly full-page ad in the November 17th Sunday *New York Times*. Under the title "African American Women in Defense of Ourselves" their analysis demystifies abstractions by speaking out against the partnership between destructive U.S. policies and cynical racial-sexual posturings. By Bush, senators Hatch, Specter,

Danforth and their employees. Excerpted below and signed by over 1,600 women of African descent, it breaks the routine rally around media heroes/heroines and the diversion of gender abstractions:

AFRICAN AMERICAN WOMEN IN DEFENSE OF OURSELVES

As women of African descent, we are deeply troubled by the recent presidential nomination, confirmation, and seating of Clarence Thomas as an Associate Justice of the U.S. Supreme Court. We know that the presence of Clarence Thomas on the Supreme Court will be continually used to divert attention away from historic struggles for social justice through suggestions that the presence of a Black man on the Supreme Court constitutes an assurance that the rights of African Americans will be protected. Clarence Thomas' public record is ample evidence that this will not be true. Further, the consolidation of a conservative majority on the Supreme Court seriously endangers the rights of all women, poor and working class people, and the elderly. The seating of Clarence Thomas is not only an affront to African American women and men and all those concerned with social justice.

We are particularly outraged by the racist and sexist treatment of Professor Anita Hill, an African American woman who was maligned and castigated for daring to speak publicly of her experience of sexual abuse. The malicious defamation of Professor Hill insulted all women of African descent and sent a dangerous message to any woman who might contemplate a sexual harassment complaint. . . .

As women of African descent, we express our vehement opposition to the policies represented by the placement of Clarence Thomas on the Supreme Court. The Bush administration, having obstructed the passage of civil rights legislation, impeded the extension of unemployment compensation, cut student aid and dismantled social welfare programs, has continually demonstrated that it is not operating in our best interests. Nor is this appointee. We pledge

ourselves to continue to speak out in defense of one another, in defense of the African American community and against those who are hostile to social justice no matter what color they are. No one will speak for us but ourselves. . . .
—African American Women in Defense of Ourselves.

JOY JAMES, Ph.D., is assistant professor of Women's Studies at University of Massachusetts, Amherst. She recently edited with Ruth Farmer an anthology on African-American women in academia to be published by Routledge in 1993.

NOTES

1. The New York City–based Center for Constitutional Rights (CCR) maintained in a released statement that Clarence Thomas was unsuitable for the U.S. Supreme Court because of his lack of experience and anti-democratic bias. CCR reported that under Thomas's directorship as chair of the Equal Employment Commission (EEOC): class action suits declined dramatically compared to individual cases; in 1988 that 40 to 87 percent of cases were closed because they were improperly investigated by field offices/state fair employment practices agencies; case backlogs rose from 31,500 (1983) to 46,000 (1989); processing time increased from four to seven months (1983) to nearly ten months (1989); equal pay cases declined from thirty-five in 1982 to seven in 1989. Concerning affirmative action, Thomas changed the agency's practice of setting goals and timetables "for employers to make jobs available to white women and women and men of color," reinstating the policy only after the Supreme Court's summer 1986 decision upholding goals and timetables.

2. Lisa Jones writes that sexual harassment as "a more appealing middle-class women's issue than welfare rights" is the reason why fewer women rallied around Thomas's sister Emma Mae Martin, who Thomas, in true Lee Atwater fashion, publicly accused of welfare dependency: "She gets mad when the mailman is late with her welfare check." Jones observes in her article "The Invisible Ones: The Emma Mae Martin Story, the One Thomas Didn't Tell" that: "Thomas's distortion of his sister's life says a lot about him, but it says even more about America. No child-care or health-care system, dead-end jobs, dysfunctional schools, yes. But what of the political/media value put on the lives of women like Martin? Especially black women like Martin. The Martins of this country are pigeon-holed as sub-American, subfemale, subhuman." Lisa Jones, "The Invisible Ones: The Emma Mae Martin Story, the One Thomas Didn't Tell," November 12, 1991 *Village Voice.*

3. *City Sun* editorial, Oct 16–22, 1991, vol 9, no. 42, p.1.

We Have Heard: We Have Seen: Do We Believe? The Clarence Thomas–Anita Hill Hearing

Trellie L. Jeffers

Until we learned of his nomination to the United States Supreme Court from the media, we had never heard the name, Clarence Thomas, associated with causes that would inch the American people closer to a political or social goal. Certainly, the name had not surfaced in black America as belonging to one who had valiantly fought to rid our community of the various diseases that infest it from time to time. Yet, suddenly, the name had become a household word—the American conservatives had found the man whom they felt would help to keep sexism and racism as two viable institutions in the American society, a man they said represented black Americans, but a man whom they had chosen without consulting vocal representatives of the black community.

A temporary setback came when Nina Totenberg, an employee of National Public Radio, dug up "untiringly" a six-year-old sexual harassment charge made to the United States Justice Department by Professor Anita Hill, a law professor at the University of Oklahoma. Thus, overnight, Clarence Thomas was notorious, and the black Americans who had lambasted the Clarence Thomas nomination as an insult began to feel empathy as they watched a two-day scenario on television in "a high-tech lynching" entitled "The Clarence Thomas Hearings." During this time Thomas was asked amidst the Orrin Hatch and Strom Thurmond speeches whether in fact he did sexually harass Anita Hill. The most outrageous assumption associated with the incident was that anyone would believe that the Senators conducting the hearing wanted to discover what really transpired between Anita Hill and Clarence Thomas.

The question of Clarence Thomas's guilt or innocence of sexually harassing Professor Anita Hill as harangued continuously throughout the two days of the so-called hearings never became an issue, this writer believes, in black America. We were not naive enough to predict that such a sensitive and basic charge could be settled by biased people who had much to lose on both sides of the issues and who had no basic loyalty to either Professor Hill or Clarence Thomas and whose allegiance was to the personal causes that each served. For the simple fact that each of those involved in the hearings knew that a sexual harassment charge is an issue for the courts to decide and not to be aired on the Senate floor. Moreover, at best, the Thomas hearing could only be termed a fiasco whereby the Republicans, having "found their man," put on two days of charades through which they wrought embarrassment on black Americans in the name of "Confirmation." In so doing, those who staged the scenario may have felt that they created sympathy for Thomas, who faced stiff opposition in the black community due to his political ideology and simultaneously shamed many white groups who also opposed the Thomas nomination.

It is perhaps no accident that those of us who did oppose the Thomas nomination began to feel compassion for the man who had emerged from Pinpoint, Georgia (especially those of us who knew the racial climate of that section of the country), attended the Yale University Law School, and at age forty-three, was to be appointed to the highest court in America. There must have been awe and a sense of pride in black Americans that such a man had emerged from the "Souls of Black Folks" regardless of his political orientation. In addition, more blacks perhaps began to identify with him because they saw the hearings as the same type of insults that Thomas had to endure as a young black man in a small southern region.

But what about Anita Hill? She suddenly became a replica of the fate of a black, black woman. Though brilliant, articulate, and a graduate from the same law school, she could not possibly have expected to enjoy the success that Thomas enjoyed because she suffered a double jeopardy: she was black and female, and she had been brought in direct contact with some of the most powerful white men in this country. Perhaps Nina Totenberg did not realize the terrible dilemma in which she placed this woman when she spent her untiring moments searching for the six-year-old charge which the Justice Department had long forgotten. Thus Professor Hill did not have to prove her charge against Clarence Thomas; she had to battle to retain her self-esteem against the powerful Republicans.

What would Thomas's fate have been had his political views been different? Most of us can only imagine what an aspiration for a seat on the bench of the highest court in the nation involves, and we do not perhaps understand what it means to work for an aspiration and then have it snatched from within reach. This would have been the fate of Thomas had he been on opposite ends of his voting record. There are many important issues that will appear before the Supreme Court in this decade: tougher environmental standards, the death penalty, abortion, charges of racism and sexism, whether there should be a ban on certain literature and musical lyrics, whether surrogacy is a form of slavery, and many cases that will dismantle the gains of the Civil Rights Movement. Many cases will affect poor people and black people. When the Clarence Thomas hearings are placed in the context of what many people in America stand to lose with another conservative on the United States Supreme Court, we are momentarily saddened. But that is another issue.

I am sure that many women in black America are asking themselves, "Why would Professor Hill put herself through such an ordeal?" Could she have refused to appear before the Senate? Would her refusal have been interpreted as her having lied about the sexual harassment charge? It may be that she could not have possibly known beforehand that what the Senate intended was to drag hers and Thomas's honor through mire. Obviously both Professor Hill and Judge Thomas had had a relationship much different from the one that was described on television, so why and how did they justify a reason to Professor Hill for the ordeal that both she and Judge Thomas suffered? Surely she could not have expected that something positive would emerge from her discussing in detail her charges before men who had little interest in what she had suffered.

It may seem that this writer is blaming the victim, for many females are now claiming that Professor Hill's sexual harassment charge has given women courage to speak out against their similar horrors. In fact, the October 25 issue of *People* magazine included stories of women who have charged their supervisors (to the detriment of many of them) with sexual harassment. It may be, and I do hope for Dr. Hill's sake, that women did gain something from the

Thomas-Hill hearings. For black America, nothing positive came from the Clarence Thomas–Anita Hill hearings. Personally, I felt that black women were raped on national television, and black men were doused with gasoline and burned in front of one million viewers. There had to have been a better way to have settled nothing at all.

TRELLIE L. JEFFERS is professor of English at Talladega College in Alabama. Her article "The Black, Black Woman and the Black Middle Class" was published in The Black Scholar *in the spring of 1974 and again in the* Best of The Black Scholar *in 1982.*

Can I Get a Witness?*

June Jordan

I wanted to write a letter to Anita Hill. I wanted to say thanks. I wanted to convey the sorrow and the bitterness I feel on her behalf. I wanted to explode the history that twisted itself around the innocence of her fate. I wanted to assail the brutal ironies, the cruel consistencies that left her—at the moment of her utmost vulnerability and public power—isolated, betrayed, abused, and not nearly as powerful as those who sought and who seek to besmirch, ridicule, and condemn the truth of her important and perishable human being. I wanted to reassure her of her rights, her sanity, and the African beauty of her earnest commitment to do right and to be a good woman: a good black woman in this America.

But tonight I am still too furious, I am still too hurt, I am still too astounded and nauseated by the enemies of Anita Hill. Tonight my heart pounds with shame.

Is there no way to interdict and terminate the traditional, abusive loneliness of black women in this savage country?

From those slavery times when African men could not dare to defend their sisters, their mothers, their sweethearts, their wives, and their daughters—except at the risk of their lives—from those times until today: Has nothing changed?

How is it possible that only John Carr—a young black corporate lawyer who maintained a friendship with Anita Hill ten years ago ("It didn't go but so far," he testified, with an engaging, handsome trace of a smile)—how is it possible that he, alone among black men, stood tall and strong and righteous as a witness for her defense?

What about spokesmen for the NAACP or the National Urban League?

What about spokesmen for the U.S. Congressional Black Caucus?

All of the organizational and elected black men who spoke aloud

*Reprinted from *The Progressive*, December 1991.

against a wrong black man, Clarence Thomas, for the sake of principles resting upon decency and concerns for fair play, equal protection, and affirmative action—where did they go when, suddenly, a good black woman arose among us, trying to tell the truth?

Where did they go? And why?

Is it conceivable that a young white woman could be tricked into appearing before fourteen black men of the U.S. Senate?

Is it conceivable that a young white woman could be tricked into appearing before a lineup of incredibly powerful and hypocritical and sneering and hellbent black men freely insinuating and freely hypothesizing whatever lurid scenario came into their heads?

Is it conceivable that such a young woman—such a flower of white womanhood—would, by herself, have to withstand the calumny and unabashed, unlawful bullying that was heaped upon Anita Hill?

Is it conceivable that this flower would not be swiftly surrounded by white knights rallying—with ropes, or guns, or whatever—to defend her honor and the honor, the legal and civilized rights, of white people, per se?

Anita Hill was tricked. She was set up. She had been minding her business at the University of Oklahoma Law School when the Senators asked her to describe her relationship with Clarence Thomas. Anita Hill's dutiful answers disclosed that Thomas had violated the trust of his office as head of the Equal Employment Opportunity Commission. Sitting in that office of ultimate recourse for women suffering from sexual harassment, Thomas himself harassed Anita Hill, repeatedly, with unwanted sexual advances and remarks.

Although Anita Hill had not volunteered this information and only supplied it in response to direct, specific inquiries from the FBI,

And although Anita Hill was promised the protection of confidentiality as regards her sworn statement of allegations,

And despite the fact that four witnesses—two men and two women, two black and two white distinguished Americans, including a Federal judge and a professor of law—testified, under oath, that Anita Hill had told each of them about these sordid carryings on by Thomas at the time of their occurrence or in the years that followed,

And despite the fact that Anita Hill sustained a remarkably fastidious display of exact recall and never alleged, for example, that Thomas actually touched her,

And despite the unpardonable decision by the U.S. Senate Judiciary Committee to prohibit expert testimony on sexual harassment,

Anita Hill, a young black woman born and raised within a black farm family of thirteen children, a graduate of an Oklahoma public high school who later earned honors and graduated from Yale Law School, a political conservative and, now, a professor of law,

Anita Hill, a young black woman who suffered sexual harassment once in ten years and, therefore, never reported sexual harassment to any of her friends except for that once in ten years,

Anita Hill, whose public calm and dispassionate sincerity refreshed America's eyes and ears with her persuasive example of what somebody looks like and sounds like when she's simply trying to tell the truth,

Anita Hill was subpoenaed by the U.S. Senate Judiciary Committee of fourteen white men and made to testify and to tolerate interrogation on national television.

1. Why didn't she "do something" when Thomas allegedly harassed her?

The Senators didn't seem to notice or to care that Thomas occupied the office of last recourse for victims of sexual harassment. And had the Committee allowed any expert on the subject to testify, we would have learned that it is absolutely typical for victims to keep silent.

2. Wasn't it the case that she had/has fantasies and is delusional?

Remarkably, not a single psychiatrist or licensed psychologist was allowed to testify. These slanderous suppositions about the psychic functionings of Anita Hill were never more than malevolent speculations invited by one or another of the fourteen white Senators as they sat above an assortment of character witnesses hand-picked by White House staffers eager to protect the President's nominee.

One loathsomely memorable item: John Doggett, a self-infatuated black attorney and a friend of Clarence Thomas, declared that Thomas would not have jeopardized his career for Anita Hill because Doggett, a black man, explained to the Senate Committee of fourteen white men, "She is not worth it."

3. Why was she "lying"?

It should be noted that Anita Hill readily agreed to a lie-detector test and that, according to the test, she was telling the truth. It should also be noted that Clarence Thomas refused even to consider taking such a test and that, furthermore, he had already established himself as a liar when, earlier in the Senate hearings, he insisted that he had never discussed *Roe* v. *Wade*, and didn't know much about this paramount legal dispute.

Meanwhile, Clarence Thomas—who has nodded and grinned his way to glory and power by denying systemic American realities of racism, on the one hand, and by publicly castigating and lying about his own sister, a poor black woman, on the other—this Thomas, this Uncle Tom calamity of mediocre abilities, at best, this bootstrap miracle of egomaniacal myth and self-pity, this choice of the very same President who has vetoed two civil rights bills and boasted about that, how did he respond to the testimony of Anita Hill?

Clarence Thomas thundered and he shook. Clarence Thomas glowered and he growled. "God is my judge!" he cried, at one especially disgusting low point in the Senate proceedings. "God is my judge, Senator. And not you!" This candidate for the Supreme Court evidently believes himself exempt from the judgments of mere men.

This Clarence Thomas—about whom an African American young man in my freshman composition class exclaimed, "He's an Uncle Tom. He's a hypocritical Uncle Tom. And I don't care what happens to his punk ass"—this Thomas vilified the hearings as a "high-tech lynching."

When he got into hot water for the first time (on public record, at any rate), he attempted to identify himself as a regular black man. What a peculiar reaction to the charge of sexual harassment!

And where was the laughter that should have embarrassed him out of that chamber?

And where were the tears?

When and where was there ever a black man lynched because he was bothering a black woman?

When and where was there ever a white man jailed or tarred and feathered because he was bothering a black woman?

When a black woman is raped or beaten or mutilated by a black man or a white man, what happens?

To be a black woman in this savage country: Is that to be nothing and no one beautiful and precious and exquisitely compelling?

To be a black woman in this savage country: Is that to be nothing and no one revered and defended and given our help and our gratitude?

The only powerful man to utter and to level the appropriate word of revulsion as a charge against his peers—the word was "SHAME"—that man was U.S. Senator Ted Kennedy, a white man whose ongoing, successful career illuminates the unequal privileges of male gender, white race, and millionaire-class identity.

But Ted Kennedy was not on trial. He has never been on trial.

Clarence Thomas was supposed to be on trial but he was not: He is more powerful than Anita Hill. And his bedfellows, from Senator Strom Thurmond to President George Bush, persist—way more powerful than Clarence Thomas and Anita Hill combined.

And so, at the last, it was she, Anita Hill, who stood alone, trying to tell the truth in an arena of snakes and hyenas and dinosaurs and power-mad dogs. And with this televised victimization of Anita Hill, the American war of violence against women moved from the streets, moved from hip hop, moved from multimillion-dollar movies into the highest chambers of the U.S. Government.

And what is anybody going to do about it?

I, for one, I am going to write a letter to Anita Hill. I am going to tell her that, thank God, she is a black woman who is somebody and something beautiful and precious and exquisitely compelling.

And I am going to say that if this Government will not protect and defend her, and all black women, and all women, period, in this savage country—if this Government will not defend us from poverty and violence and contempt—then we will change the Government. We have the numbers to deliver on this warning.

And, as for those brothers who disappeared when a black woman rose up to tell the truth, listen: It's getting to be payback time. I have been speaking on behalf of a good black woman. Can you hear me?

Can I get a witness?

JUNE JORDAN, poet, is professor of African-American Studies and Women's Studies at the University of California, Berkeley.

Under the Camouflage of Color and Gender: The Dread and Drama of Thomas-Hill

Maulana Karenga

INTRODUCTION

If things were as they seem, there would be little need for critical investigation beyond the obvious and self-evident. If the sun actually rose, the discipline of astronomy would be less compelling and if the stick in the water were actually broken, there would be less need for the study of light refraction. So it is with the Clarence Thomas–Anita Hill controversy, obscured in its real meaning by its easily assembled vocabularies of blame, articles of indictment and partisans with little interest in the larger picture, only the immediate and unconditional defeat of the enemy. But invective is not analysis and choosing sides is the easiest effort one can make in a context of claimed injury and urgency, peppered with passionate anecdote and accusation and time-released rage.

Still, the Thomas-Hill affair is instructive in several ways which merit critical investigation as a lesson of history and struggle too meaningful to miss and too valuable to be reductively translated in the simplistic way each of the parties would have us do. The incident represents a study in race and gender relations, especially how instead of advocates of gender and racial justice finding common ground in the context of domination, race and gender became modes of contestation among the dominated with each group perceiving its interests as more urgent and oppositional. It is also instructive in terms of how the African American masses, justifiably sensitive to centuries of racial injustice and injury, focused on race rather than gender in this case, although they are historically not insensitive to gender issues. And it is also instructive how so many of us who are intellectuals, academics, professionals and self-defined critical thinkers of various political persuasions allowed for the most part others to set the parameters for our discourse and provide the conceptual hinge on which our thought and discussion turned.

In reality, the issue was never about Anita Hill and Clarence Thomas as persons. For they were essentially Black surrogates for others' agendas, self-destructive kamikazis for emperors and empresses who masked their identity, intention and discourse under the camouflage of color and gender. Liberals and feminists lined up on one side and conservatives on the other, claimed mutual injury and insult, and trotted out their respective Black troops to savage each other while the generals and politicians on each side, unwounded themselves, talked about the casualties to win points and to divert attention from the real issues. African intellectuals and professionals tended to choose sides according to their political links—liberal or conservative. But some of us chose according to what we considered it meant to African people as a whole, not to Anita Hill and Clarence Thomas, both Reaganites, conservative and with no record of progressive politics, literature or acts.

If one, then, looked beyond the frivolous and dishonest claims that Hill was a new Rosa Parks and that Thomas's main problem was his color rather than his competence and politics, one is left with the critical questions of, how does this benefit or harm Blacks and how do they participate in the process—as surrogates or self-conscious agents of their own life and struggle? The unavoidable conclusion is that the most damaged participants were Hill, Thomas and Black people and no one can seriously pretend Hill and Thomas were anything except surrogates in a war neither one of them seemed to know was going on or their contrived role in it. So in the analysis which follows, there is no choice of Hill over Thomas or vice versa. There is the choice of the interests of Black people and the interests of the larger ongoing struggle for a just and good society and the critical and courageous thinking and acting that are required to achieve this.

There are at least three major sets of issues in the Thomas-Hill controversy and it is the failure to clearly delineate and discuss these that choosing sides became a substitute for a more informed stance. These issues may be classified as: a) gender; b) racial; and c) systemic issues.

ISSUES OF GENDER

The issues of gender were raised by the feminists, Hill and their supporters and projected as an urgent criticism of the state of gender relations in society. However, it was a last minute ploy that was put in service when the arguments against Thomas's incompetence and politics seemed unlikely to block his move to be seated in the Supreme Court. This fact tended to cultivate an air of suspicious motives and eroded some of the moral force which advocacy of gender justice should and does command.

Nevertheless, it is important to state that the charge of sexual harassment is a serious one whether harassment is by physical assertion, quid pro quo proposition or creation and maintenance of a hostile environment. Moreover, Professor Hill has both the right to make a claim of injury if she feels she has suffered one and the right to a fair and effective hearing on that claim. Having said this, in the context of struggle to win justice, one must still raise the difficult and uncomfortable question of the appropriateness of the timing and the choice of forum. For the nature and late hour of the claim and the context in which it was raised tended to raise questions of suspicious motives and character assassination versus legitimate grievance. This remains a central concern even after conceding the fact that victims tend to be reluctant to raise such claims and the difficulty of establishing the credibility of such claims, especially by a Black woman. For if the case is already a difficult one, shouldn't one present it in the most promising circumstances? And should one attempt a victory that will be Pyrrhic at best to the person making the claim and at worst damaging to both her and the larger struggle with collateral and devastating damage to African people? Moreover, if the issue of sexual harrassment is as urgent, pervasive and ongoing as white feminists argue, then why have they not brought such a case against a white man of stature in similar political circumstance? It is this question in its various forms which invoked racial reservations and concerns about gender justice at the expense of African American people or the larger struggle for social justice.

Another important consideration on this issue is whether one wishes to put so much emphasis on sexual harassment that it tends to raise it to the level of importance (or beyond) of rape, wife battering, child molestation or other more serious crimes against women—not to mention the issue of reproductive freedom. Again, the last hour preparation and projection of the feminists and liberals left them in an uncomfortable position of expressing rage against multiform solicitation of sex and vulgar talk as if it were equal to the devastating physical violence visited in numerous ways on women daily or again somehow more important than the issue of reproductive freedom sure to be taken up soon by the Court.

Likewise, these advocates of gender justice who pushed the sexual harassment issue as the central concern, in spite of other issues before the hearing panel, should have been concerned with the possibility of the claim and discourse surrounding it suggesting a return of women to a special protective status. If women claim justifiably that they are equal, then it is important for them not to seem to be too delicate for the vulgar and infantile context many men create in their locker room, restroom and office fantasies of sex and power. What one must do is insist it not be directed toward her. But getting them to cease the discourse will take more than a week of hearings and insincere confessions of unprosecutable guilt. It is a lesson of moral intractibility the church, mosque, synagogue and temple have long discovered but cannot concede without encouraging greater infractions and suggesting theories of permanent masculine disorientation. The lesson here is that the struggle for gender justice like the struggle for social justice and human equality is a complex one, and in our theoretical and practical criticism of the established order, we can easily find ourselves, if not ever attentive, supporting arguments we are committed to disprove. Thus, Blacks who make too great a claim of whites' power over their lives often end up unintentionally denying their own moral autonomy and capacity for self-conscious, independent and successful action. And women claiming equality with men can and do in fact undermine the claim when they ask for privileged situations that divert from the questions of power and speak more to questions of general moral failure in society than inequality in male-female relations.

ISSUES OF RACE

The racial issues were raised by Judge Thomas as an eleventh hour *prise de conscience* or conversion to the faith after being mercilessly whipped by the ironic and hard hand of history and the parade of witnesses by the opposition. However, a majority of African Americans supported Thomas's claim of racial harassment and mistreatment and thus reflected a constant concern that issues not be raised and pursued at their expense in a racially biased society. And surely there was evidence of such a scenario. From street corner to college campus and back to barber shops and beauty parlors in the Black community, African Americans in the majority essentially saw this as a white issue played out by sacrificial Black surrogates. The questions asked again and again were: Who raised and pursued the issue, in whose interests is the struggle ultimately being waged, who are the real parties in the struggle, and most important, why raise the sexual harassment issue now and against a Black man, given all the previous opportunities of white women to raise it in similar contexts against white men and since everyone concedes both the pervasiveness and seriousness of the offense?

The conclusion was that it was again whites waging war against each other using Blacks as surrogate soldiers who went to war as throughout history for elusive gains only to return home to worse and more bewildering circumstances. The operative category here is surrogacy, for neither Hill nor Thomas took initiative in this struggle. Although she played her role with alternating passion and poise and no little amount of vengeance, once engaged, Hill admitted she did not originally consider the issue an important one. But the liberals and feminists courted and convinced her to step forward and accomplish for them with a gender issue what their arguments about competence and politics failed to achieve.

Likewise, Thomas was clearly put forth by Bush as another building block in the construction of a conservative Black leadership group which will serve as an alternative and counter to liberal Black leadership and serve in selective social silence the class and racial interests of their right-wing Republican mentors. It is important to note here that it is an established practice of ruling classes and groups to construct and place leadership buffers between the ruling regime and the masses of an oppressed people. So Democrats should take no pleasure in pointing to Republicans. For once upon a political time, when the Presidential office and apparatus were theirs, they too trussed up and trotted out Black surrogates and handed out patronage and plaques as the process requires. The issue here is when do Africans advance beyond simple and seductive patronage politics and create a truly independent politics, with both a particular and universal appeal to the poor, marginalized and less powerful? There was in recent memory once a Jacksonian option; it would be encouraging to hear it has not been enveloped and eroded by the durability and respectability demands of the established order.

But the key issue was race, not the patronage and propaganda which produced Thomas and declared him competent and committed to his people and perhaps even to the poor, in spite of the embarrassing abundance of evidence to the contrary. It was the stereotypes the struggle between Thomas and Hill as surrogates raised and reinforced. These had and continue to have a devastating impact on both discourse and relations between Black men and women and on society's and the world community's perception of us as a people. To speak graphically, it provoked a picking and scraping of scabs of war wounds suffered in prior battles of the sexes, occasioned by the discourse around Alice Walker's *The Color Purple* and Shahrazad Ali's *Black Man's Guide*. It recalled a discourse which posed these two texts as true and trustworthy in their depiction of Black male-female relations. Each in its turn became a kind of sacred text for the battered and bitter woman and man. And each offered little more than the balm of recrimination, self-deception and diversionary identification of alleged enemies we cannot avoid as friends and lovers, husbands and wives. And they offered us a strategy for victory over unredeemable Black villains that could only lead to our own personal and collective defeat. For a house divided against itself is a gift to the enemy. And the oppressor need not worry about his future or the challenge of the oppressed when the oppressed decide that they, themselves, are their real and perhaps only enemy.

The stereotypes which were raised and reinforced began with Hill being trotted out to attack Thomas. It is a well-established stereotype that the Black woman can be used repeatedly to undermine her man, that historically she has been willing to betray her man and through this, her people, for her relations with white men and, of late, white women. It is, of course, no more than a stereotype, but on international cable TV it takes on a life of its own. After all, who knows, remembers or cares about the history of Harriet Tubman, Sojourner Truth, Yaa Asantewa, Mary McLeod Bethune, Fannie Lou Hamer, Ruby Doris Robinson and the millions like them and the unnamed and unknown strong Black women who taught us by precept and practice to speak truth, do justice and walk in the way of righteousness, and to sacrifice for the struggle, be proud of our heritage and honor it by defending and developing it? It is Fannie Lou Hamer who taught us the morality of remembrance, but how clear is our memory and what has America made of our morality with its focus on money and machines, its disdainful disregard for the past and the fantasy of the detached individual stripped of peoplehood and culture and enveloped in an equal opportunity effort to invent him/herself?

The second stereotype raised and reaffirmed was that of the Black man ever perversely concerned with the size, length and next place in which he will put his penis, even on his way to the solemn and hallowed halls of the Supreme Court. And it is one of the most tragic periods in our history in which the stereotype was established in the blood and death of prehistoric lynching ceremonies by white men. It is here that they lynched Black men for alleged sexual crimes of thought, emotion and deed, cut off their genitals and burned them in rituals of savage rage while their women and children looked on.

The final stereotype raised and reinforced by the Thomas-Hill spectacle was the one of Black people's being crabs-in-a-barrel bent on self-destruction. It was a reaffirmation of the stereotypical contention that you need not attack Blacks yourself; you need only to throw them crumbs and they will picnic on each other in a most self-destructive way. The Thomas-Hill battle was in truth a *spectacle of mutual degradation*, a dreadful drama which captured even the shallow and shuttered minds of the soap opera community. And it is a testimony to the poignancy and power of Black sexual and relational imagery in a racist society, that unlike any other major interruption of the soap sagas—including the Papal visit, Persian Gulf Massacre and Challenger disaster—there were no major protests over this interruption. For in truth, here was a soap opera itself—with all its dread and drama, suspense and sordid tales of sexual fantasies, inflated genital size claims and declarations of profound sexual need—and all with the added advantage of being *in living color*.

One could not help but remember the Holocaust of Enslavement and the "buck fights" and "nigger fights" which whites staged for their own perverse entertainment. It is this spectacle of mutual degradation that made Black people reject Hill's eleventh hour appearance and all it stereotypically represented. It was for them a dread and drama they have seen so often and which they never get used to regardless of how often it is repeated. Here they were, two professional Blacks savaging each other on international television, not from their own initiative or even in the long run to their own interests and certainly not for the post-facto reasons of country, conscience and commitment to equality they developed in the process of engagement. A pathetic pair of seduced surrogates who eventually seemed to sense the futility and awesome cost of mutual savaging but could not choose when to exit, even as they did not choose when to enter the arena. Bound by common philosophy, past work together and a continuing commitment to the conservative politics of the Republican party, they were paraded before us as hero and heroine even though from the beginning it was evident that in such a context and contest there could be no victors, only victims, namely Anita Hill, Clarence Thomas and Black people. It is a reflection of the expediency of so much of what passes as politics, that even progressive feminists, nationalists and liberals did not notice or care about Hill's conservative commitments but lectured at length on Thomas' similar credentials. And it is clearly a reflection of the George Bush and conservative contempt for African American interests, that in addition to playing the Willie Horton card, resisting the Civil Rights Bill of '91 and giving David Duke pointers in racist politics, Bush would pretend a competence for Thomas he obviously does not have and choose him over even other conservative Blacks more qualified. It is Frederick Douglass who reminds us, however, that an oppressor will impose on the oppressed to the exact extent that they allow him. For as he explains, "power concedes nothing without demand," and the most definitive demand is effective struggle. Thus, it is the political stance of the Bush administration and his conservative constituency that must be challenged, and this leads to concern for the systemic issues raised by the Thomas-Hill controversy.

SYSTEMIC ISSUES

The systemic issues are essentially issues of ongoing struggle for social justice in the larger society. The first becomes one of how do we move beyond the increasing tendency to fight political battles in character assassination terms when even progressive forces seem to use this method of political contestation? A new and progressive politics must struggle to avoid charges which are suggestive of character assassination and stay instead focused on the real issues. Thomas's chastisement on the threshing floor of history has its strong and vulnerable points. On one hand, it might seem good to see him battered and pushed to the brink so that the only way he can escape annihilation is to declare his Blackness and use the shield of its history to defend himself. But it was a hollow pleasure because things declared under duress are not credible or constructive and conversions such as these are expedient, not eternal, and certainly without depth and reality. Moreover, the very personal nature of the attacks might seem warranted for an enemy, but clearly are not recommended or welcomed for friends. Thus, opponents who attacked and supported attacks on Thomas personally were enraged by personal attacks launched against Hill. Likewise, when each retreated under the camouflage and cover of color and gender, supporters of Thomas and Hill were expectedly outraged that their opponents were so devious. But one can no more deny that Thomas was treated in part the way he was because of his race than one can deny that Hill was treated in part the way she was because of her gender and race. The need, then, is not to deny the race and gender character of the opponent's attack, but to avoid aggravating the savagery of the process, catering to the discourse of character assassination and, rather, explore the critical social issues. One cannot yet gauge the impact of such a negative development in political discourse on potential candidates fearful of such a muddied and muddled process. But it cannot augur well for a society whose central political discourse is no more than mudslinging and whose central political practice is the vicious and televised personal destruction of opponents.

A second concern in the struggle for systemic change is the impact this process and spectacle has had on the debate or serious discussion on the issue of sexual harassment and other gender issues.

It was a premature claim by supporters of Hill that the controversy would create a new and more open discourse around this and other issues, for in fact this has not occurred. In the heat of the moment and in the context of rage, cowards and the devious will always cop out and confess—the first to escape pain and the second to escape more depthful inquiry and challenge to their power. Thus, politicians, in the light of women's rage, conceded a hearing, but did not fight with the faith of true believers. They even confessed the sexist nature of institution and practice. But in the final analysis, they did not change. Moreover, nor did thousands of women come forth and charge harassment, especially not against white men in power. Also, the very rawness of the process, like many previous major discussions of male-female relations, precluded real discourse and degenerated into essentially recrimination and mutual savaging. It is Martin King who taught that a real moral struggle seeks to win partners, not to leave victims. It is a lesson which at the same time is a challenge and a necessity, especially in the non-antagonistic struggles between women and men. Antagonism of class and race dominance might require harsher language and action, but living and sleeping together, building and hoping together should suggest and promote a softer language and more gentle exchange.

The process and claims of the Thomas-Hill spectacle were, in fact, deceptive and in part disarming. For they created a myth of effective action, claimed an easy victory, and thus masked difficulties of a complex and protracted struggle for gender justice. It is Amilcar Cabral who warned that we must recognize the awesome demands in time, effort and life of serious struggle. The struggle, he reminds us, is a long and difficult one, therefore we must "mask no difficulties, tell no lies and claim no easy victory." Furthermore, as Gil Scott-Heron has said, "the revolution will not be televised." In a word, the power of television lies not in its ability to create or sustain a revolution, but in its ability to divert and distract, confuse and misdirect those who would participate in it. Thus, in the final analysis, we must return to the people and as Kwame Nkrumah says, "start with what they know and build on what they have." This means rebuilding a movement similar to the sixties, but with an expanded knowledge rooted in lessons learned from the sixties.

This brings us to a final issue of importance in the struggle to change the system and create a truly just and good society. The division along racial and gender lines on the Thomas-Hill question reaffirms the reality that alliances among the dominated and marginalized are not automatic, and that great effort must be made to forge them on a solid foundation and sustain them in principled and cooperative practice. Certainly the leaders of the women's movement for justice and equality in this case cannot ignore the racial implications of it. Nor can they without explanation suddenly create a case with Prof. Anita Hill and ignore an enduring one at Harvard brought to our attention by Prof. Derrick Bell and which abounds across the nation, i.e., the systematic denial of Black women deserved space in academia. Again, how did this issue of Hill and Thomas become so important and merit more attention than Black women's equality of opportunity and placement in employment and the numerous other issues of major importance? And the Black Movement must continue to give weight to gender issues but not in opposition to, or at the expense of, the larger African American struggle. For there is no separate freedom or dignity for African men and women.

It is Sekou Toure who informed us that African freedom and dignity are indivisible. For as long as any African is wounded in his or her dignity or denied his or her freedom, all of us are somehow damaged and restricted by this. Thomas and Hill did not, of course, recognize this and suffered grievously because of it. This, however, is no call for the end, or the unwarranted restriction of, internal criticism. On the contrary, it is a call for a more responsible internal criticism, a criticism which reflects analysis rather than invective and is of our own initiative and in our own interests not that of others. For it is only in strength and self-determined thought and practice that we can build common ground with other progressive forces on the basis of the best we each have to offer.

MAULANA KARENGA, Ph.D., is professor and chair of the Department of Black Studies, California State University, Long Beach. He is also chair of US Organization, the director of the Institute of Pan-African Studies, Los Angeles, and the creator of Kwanzaa and the Nguzo Saba. He is author of numerous scholarly articles and eight books, including Introduction to Black Studies *and* Selections from the Husia: Sacred Wisdom of Ancient Egypt.

Cringing at Myths of Black Sexuality

Charles R. Lawrence, III

On Friday evening, Clarence Thomas called the Judiciary Committee hearings inquiring into Anita Hill's charges of sexual harassment a "high-tech lynching of an uppity black man." On Saturday, he called himself the victim of bigoted "racial attitudes about black men and their views of sex." Is this another confirmation conversion? Has this man who has scolded fellow blacks for complaining about racism suddenly discovered that he is still black? Is this the same man who invoked the racist stereotype of the black welfare queen to wrongly accuse his own sister?

I would like to believe that Judge Thomas has finally learned that he will never be free of racist stereotypes until the least of us is free. I would like to believe that his invocation of the most vivid symbols of racial oppression is more than a desperate attempt to divert attention from the serious and credible charges that have been leveled against him. I would like to believe that he is concerned not just for himself but for all of us. Los Angeles Congresswoman Maxine Waters echoed the sentiments of many of us when she spoke skeptically of this man who has so faithfully served a President who has made race-baiting his stock in trade.

Whatever his motivations might be, Thomas has called the nation's attention to one of its oldest and ugliest stories. This is a story of stereotypes about race and sex that are deeply embedded in the American psyche. It is a story of violence against black men and women motivated and justified by those stereotypes—a history of black men lynched and castrated, of black women raped—with no fear of consequences.

African-Americans cannot help but cringe as we hear the lurid details of Anita Hill's account of her harassment. We cringe because we know that the myths of black sexuality are alive and well in America. We cringe because we know that when this story is told about one black man, all black men are implicated. White America will hear this story not just as a lesson about the ubiquity of sexual harassment in the workplace. They will hear it as a story about oversexed black men.

Yet another story is being told as white America watches this Washington soap opera. This is the story of the way in which Americans have turned a blind eye to the rape of black women by propagating the myth that black women had no right to refuse the sexual advances of any man. When the man on the street says, "I don't believe Hill's story," it is in part because he believes the old, oft-told story of "unchaste" black women. When Sen. Orrin Hatch charges that her experience is the fantasy of a spurned woman, he is evoking this myth. When he implies that she tried to seduce Thomas by inviting him into her apartment, and when he reads the most lurid language in her account over and over again, all the while protesting his disgust, he is conjuring up these same racist images of the wanton black woman. An integral part of this story has been the historical use of violence against black women as a way to deliver a message of white domination to black men: "You are not a man in this patriarchal world if you do not control your women, if you cannot protect your women from white men, if you do not have control over and access to your women's sexuality as we do."

There is a third story here that is perhaps the most difficult for those of us in the African-American community to talk about. It is the story of black male violence against and degradation of black women. This is a story of our own internalization of racist myths, a story of black men taking the anger that wells up within us when we are humiliated and degraded by whites and turning it on the women within our own families and communities. It is a story that leads many in our community to believe Anita Hill even as we wish that we could say, "This cannot be true." There has been an unwritten code of silence that says we must not speak about this story outside of our communities because white men will use it against us. This is why so many blacks who believe Hill's story continue to wish that it had never been told.

The drama that is being played out in the Senate is much more than an inquiry into the credibility of two individuals. It is more than an important lesson about sexual harassment in the workplace. For black Americans, it raises the most difficult of dilemmas. How do we simultaneously fight the mutually reinforcing oppressions of racism and sexism in society and in our own community? How do we respond when these issues must be spoken to in the glare of television lights and under the pressure of newspaper deadlines? How do we talk about what is most difficult to talk about when the conversation about us, about who we are and what we think, is dominated by those whose primary concern is not our community's well-being?

As I've listened to folks from my community these last few terrible days, I hear anguish, hurt and anger in their voices. It is an expression of pain and dismay that seems much more genuine than the almost theatrical fury we have heard from Clarence Thomas in his new role as victim.

Judge Thomas is hoping that in taking on this victim's role he will appeal to the black community's sense of solidarity. He is trusting that in our desire to protect ourselves from racist stereotyping we will stand with him and blame Professor Hill for being the messenger who has been the bearer of the bad news. Many of us have felt, and some of us have said, "Why is she airing this dirty laundry?" But solidarity cannot mean silence. It will not serve us to fight racism by tolerating sexism within our own community.

Anita Hill is also one of our own. If her story is true, as I believe it is, she is the victim, and Clarence Thomas must not be allowed to use our collective racial victimization to blind us to that awful truth.

CHARLES R. LAWRENCE, III, a professor of law at Stanford, is currently a visiting professor at the USC Law Center. Reprinted from the Los Angeles Times, *October 15, 1991.*

Race as Commodity: Hill and Thomas as Consumer Products

Earl Lewis

The scene opens in a room of prominent, well-educated African Americans. The eye of reason zeros in on one of them. His face is churning, he is animated, proudly and defiantly proclaiming himself above the fray. The scene is riveting and disturbing at the same time. Why proclaim one's innocence so profusely, you ask? Before you can fashion a suitable answer, the lens tilts and in the corner of the field of vision you capture the image of the other, a demure, sophisticated, gifted woman, verbally sparring with a row of combatants. You sense that they are the protectors of the defiant one. You strain to focus but clarity is difficult. Their all-white dress is the only thing that is certain. It is clear, however, that this woman troubles the defiant one, although he never speaks her name. His protectors look for chinks in her armor of defense. The conversation turns on minute points. Yet even the minutiae is riveting. And then, like most dreams, you are suddenly awakened, frustrated, bewildered, and troubled by hints of what was.

The new age showdown between Clarence Thomas and Anita Hill had all the features of a dream sequence: events out of order, improbable characters, intrigue and fright, and irresolution. Like many dreams, you awake to discover that in the end you understood all and nothing at the same time. At least that is my interpretation after reading and listening to scores of post-hearing analyses. As a popular culture phenomenon brought to us live through the mediated and commodified vehicle of television, we discover that a fulfilling explanation awaits the next pop psychology theory. Until then we choke on the phlegm of social regret.

But what do the collage of symbols, signs, and cues culled from this manufactured social dream tell us about life in late twentieth-century America? Many things come to mind. Power remains consolidated in the hands of a few for the benefit of a few. George Bush had a domestic policy all along, one developed by Goldwater in 1964, defined by Richard Nixon in 1968, and refined by Ronald Reagan in 1980—race-baiting. That the extremism of David Duke forced a temporary retreat should bring little comfort because the level of misplaced bigotry seems on the rise everywhere. And, ironically, the debate over sexual harassment meant that once again African Americans probably played a lead role in affecting social change. But mostly the hearings reinforced a sense that race and African Americans remain a commodity sold and bought for the pleasure of others.

Much was made of Clarence Thomas's invocation of lynching. That it was historically inaccurate and socially reprehensible is beyond debate. In Thomas's construction Anita Hill and the civil rights establishment engineered his "high-tech" lynching. Whites were passive accomplices. You ask yourself, when was the last time a black or white man was lynched for sexually abusing a black woman? In posing the question in that manner you realize how far Thomas went to distort the historical record. Nor do you have to get on a moral high horse to be appalled by such a calculated distortion.

To single out Thomas without examining the larger social context is inappropriate, however. Black America was sold the argument that to criticize Thomas jeopardized their lock on the "Marshall" seat on the court. President Bush and his advisors turned the seat into a commodity, a thing for sale. Like any item from a bargain basement sale, the item came with a warning label: purchase advisedly because returns are not acceptable. In the language of race this meant take Thomas or nothing. Or, as a number of people who rationalized their support of Thomas argued, if we don't support this Brother and hope he finds his memory, Bush will just nominate an even more conservative white person who has never lived a day as black.

The selling of Clarence Thomas has many antecedents in American history. If one thinks of the history of advertising in this country, you realize that the techniques were perfected by selling people of African descent. Crowds gathered at public auctions to avail themselves of the most recent cargoes. A language and style of advertising developed to market those cargoes—African men, women, and children—to the highest bidder. After the abolition of slavery the selling of blacks continued, although in different form. The commodifiers no longer sold people, they sold images of groups. The message always had dual themes and minstrelsy and vaudeville expanded its audience.

We gleaned from the cultural lesson plan that blacks were docile, simple-minded, child-like creatures and sophisticated dandies and no-goods. The advent of radio technology extended the range of opportunities, although the script changed very little. The major shift—now performers sold consumer items which in turn sold the performer. Then came television. In early television blacks were nearly invisible. When they appeared, they did so as sidekicks or in traditional, comedic roles. During the 1960s more palatable but conservative images appeared—e.g., "Julia." In many respects that long-established pattern holds today, especially the performer as both product and seller of product.

For those who sell us would-be presidents, the selling of Thomas proved the ultimate marketing success. Here was a man who had known poverty, yet overcame the limits of background. A perfect Horatio Alger story some asserted; a cynical manipulation of race others muttered. Here was a man who benefited from federal legislation based on race but who assailed that policy for the benefit of the highest bidder. Here was a man who incredulously professed no prior thought on abortion or *Roe* v. *Wade*, who was poised to ascend to the highest court although many I spoke to thought he perjured himself. Yet, Thomas remained the perfect commodity, a package of symbols manipulated for a consumer-driven culture. Moreover, it was a packaging that captured the market share of blacks and whites in society, although for different reasons.

Anita Hill's charge of sexual harassment threatened the cultivated image. Lewd, offensive comments contradicted the constructed image of the proper, churchgoing, southern boy who made good in the Ivy League world at Yale. Instead of addressing the charges, the Thomas forces attacked Anita Hill, as product, as flawed commodity. She was demented, twisted, scorned, uptight and sexually constipated, we were told. In one of the ugliest scenes in post-McCarthy America, Senator Simpson implied even worse. That images of Hill contradicted one another was not important because the intent was to confuse, obfuscate, and invalidate. Therefore, the hearings about Thomas were mostly about Hill, and the need to destroy her credibility as a believable product in the minds of the public. And by and large the strategy worked.

Race as commodity remains an important theme in contemporary

America. To ignore its role in the Thomas-Hill public drama could be disastrous. Although I agree with those who viewed the event as a sophisticated example of the conflation of race and gender issues, I also think that it was one of the best examples of the manipulation of race in recent times. Of course, there are many contenders for this dubious crown. This example demonstrates anew how much we sell in this society and how we go about doing it. In the months ahead we can only hope that Thomas exercises his right to revoke his contract as performer selling a product. Otherwise, the hearings will forever be dream-like and we will remain confused, bewildered, and troubled by the selling of race in America.

EARL LEWIS, Ph.D., is director of the Center for Afroamerican and African Studies and associate professor of History at the University of Michigan, Ann Arbor. He is the author of In Their Own Interests: Race, Class, and Power in Twentieth Century Norfolk, Virginia *(1991) and several essays, articles, and reviews.*

No Peace in a Sisterly Space

Julianne Malveaux

The dress has an exciting, vivid print. Big green leaves and muted goldswirls, tan, brown, and a little yellow. Belted at the waist, it emphasized the woman's taut figure. But the print looks out of place with her lime green shoes that are a throwback to a fashion nightmare. And when the woman turns from the counter in the candle shop toward me she looks fifty, not thirty, and the dress looks like she borrowed it from one of her children.

I had been concentrating on the wild print of the small brown woman's dress because I didn't want to listen to her words. I'd finally roused myself from the hypnotic rage I felt at the Senate Judiciary Committee's treatment of Anita Hill to move out of my house, to move around streets with folks, and I made my usual Saturday stops—to the health food store, to a progressive book store, to the small, pungent smelling candle shop that a friend runs.

But everywhere I go there is the buzz buzz buzz about Supreme Court nominee Clarence Thomas, about Professor Anita Hill. In the bookstore and the health food store, support is strong for Hill. I have deliberately avoided one of the "bars in the 'hood," cause I know what to expect there from the conversations I've had with black men who combine fiction with justification to support Thomas. I have even declined to talk to my own male sibling, the fault lines of our relationship about sexism so strong that we both sense this is a conversation we cannot have without doing what may be irreparable harm.

I expected solidarity, sisterhood among my women friends, but it was not there. One of my closest friends told me that she is the mother of a teenager, that any man can stand accused. I tell her she did not raise her son to pull stunts like those Thomas was accused of, but her love for her son and her image of Hill as "treacherous" clouds her vision. And in the candle shop where the smells and sounds so often soothe, I am jarred, nearly slapped by the force of one black woman's feelings against another.

"I hate that bitch," said the woman in the lime green shoes, with such vehemence that I jump. She launches into a tirade about one black person tearing another down. All around me there are black women, a couple of whom look like they could take this woman on if they wanted to. But they sit silently, crowded onto a bench, arms folded against their chests. When I can take it no longer I offer a tentative comment. After all, I didn't come to the candle shop to fight or debate, just to buy a white candle to burn for peace in my home, for quiet thoughts, to relieve myself of the anger that grips me when I consider the way Professor Hill has been treated.

Hill's allegations had barely been made public when Arizona Senator Dennis DeConcini gave the first clue that she would be treated badly. "This lady," he described her, "Mrs. Hill, Miss Hill, or whatever." Whatever? DeConcini went on to say that the allegations were "unfortunate for Judge Thomas." He never could quite bring himself to correctly refer to Professor Anita Hill, reducing her to "some lady" both in his words and in his actions. If the allegations were unfortunate for Judge Thomas, what did DeConcini think the experience was for Professor Hill?

His October 7 comments were mild in comparison to the comments later made by Senators Specter, Hatch, and Simpson. These three stooges led the lynch mob that attacked Hill and defended Thomas, whose sudden identification with black history and culture was amazing. After days of self-effacing comments and references to his dead grandfather, I half expected Thomas to approach the Committee with a harmonica and burst into song, further establishing himself as the non-threatening handkerchief head they sought. His anger and empty threats ("I would rather be dead than go through this") suggested that there was truth to Hill's allegations.

But there was no hearing that in the candle shop, in a tiny space full of women either too weary to argue or too outraged to shut up. I am stunned by the anger and harshness some of these fiftysomething women express toward Hill. She should have known better, says one woman. If he talked dirty to her, why did she follow him from one place to another, said another woman. The woman who owns this shop is as smooth as icing on cake, she doesn't say anything, just smiles and moves her customers out of the store. But in this space there is no kind word, no empathy for Anita Hill. These women have led hard lives and know what it is to swallow pain and indignity. As far as they were concerned, the hurt had happened too long ago to matter. What Clarence Thomas had to lose was greater than her pain. She didn't have to say anything, she brought this pain on herself. These women who might have combed Anita's hair, held her between their knees when she was a girl, were now, with hard eyes and harsh hearts, condemning her.

Support for Professor Hill comes from the strangest places. Two white women friends offer $10 each to help pay for the *New York Times* ad placed by African American Women in Defense of Ourselves. Just a block down the street, at a deli where I resolve not to talk politics, an Italian man says his heart breaks for "the little professor." But too many black women say this is an indignity we are supposed to bear, that Hill should have been silent, even those who had stories to tell themselves. The most heartbreaking story I hear is from a sixtyish woman who was raped by the man of a house she worked in as a maid when she was fifteen. "I didn't tell anyone," she said. "Who could I tell? The missus would have fired me, my brothers would have fought the man and gotten into trouble. I prayed I was not pregnant, I left the job at the end of the summer. On my last day of work the man crushed up some bills, stuffed them down the front of my shirt, and patted me on the ass. I took that money, almost a hundred dollars, and put it toward my college costs. I guess you can say he bought my silence."

It seems to me that some black women's resentment against Professor Hill was resentment that she fought when they could not. Indeed, because the black women's burden is lightened by class, educational status, and generation, many black women could distance themselves from the achieving Hill, depicting her as "other" even in the community of black women. When one of the three stooge Senators mentioned her "proclivities," a weak attempt to insert the issue of sexual preference into the discussion, the gap widened even further. The women in the candle shop spoke of the accommodating that they must do to live, the juggling of pressures and personalities, the weighing of whether a nasty remark is more effective than a simple cold shoulder. "You single women don't have to follow the rules, you don't have all these burdens," one woman said gently. So in addition to everything else, some sisters held Professor Hill's independent status against her.

Black women are the targets of everyone's ire, even of an ire we turn against ourselves. Politicians scream "welfare" and our images are conjured up. They say "entitlement" and there we are again. "Illegitimate child" and can't you see some black woman, belly distended, sitting at a hospital? Black men do some of the screaming, too. In the days after the Senate Judiciary Committee hearings, brothers in suits showered black women with more contempt than most rappers. "She must have wanted it," "She was jealous," were the kindest of the statements. Dog Dogget, the egomaniac who fantasized that everyone wanted him, got his fifteen minutes of fame as an "international business consultant" (a.k.a. huckster with frequent flyer miles). Few were as harsh or as crazed as he in their assessment of Hill, but his performance set a tone for some of the other things black men said about black women.

A San Francisco State University political science professor told his class that career black women were one cause of the black family's deterioration. His remarks were timed to follow the Senate Judiciary Committee interrogation of Hill and his scapegoating of black women made local headlines. But Professor Robert Smith, like Clarence Thomas, seemed to forget where he came from and what is important. Here are the facts. Black women work because they have to, not because they are "choosing" careers over men and family. Without black women's work, about 40 percent of all two-earner families would be in poverty, not at a middle income level. True, a few black women are on the fast track—of 12 million adult black women 89,000 earned more than $50,000 in 1989 (or fewer than 1 percent of all black women). About 229,000 black men, 2 percent of all black men, earned more than $50,000, along with 1.5 million white women and 8.6 million white men. On the other hand, 7.4 million black women had incomes below $10,000, and that's 62 percent of all black women!

In many ways this is all about distance—between the sister at the bottom and the sister at the top, between the sisters at the top and the brothers at both bottom and top who resent their success, between black folk and white folk and the ways we see history. The complexity of those differences hit me where it hurt—in a place where I had only known peace, there was no peace, just tension high. On the telephone with friends, there was not always the understanding ear. Even in my family, with a brother whose sexism is in stark contrast to the feminism of his four sisters, I had to hear, just once because that was when I dropped the phone back into the vicinity of the receiver, "if she didn't like it, why did she keep working for him." *The New York Times* printed a piece by a black male scholar who said this was how black people talked to each other, and two nights later, in my role as radio talk show host, I was asked if it wasn't true that black women preferred to be called "bitch" than "baby"?

But here is the bottom line. Supreme Court Justice Clarence Thomas was confirmed because he invoked the image of a black man hanging. They don't make ropes for black women's lynchings or destroy us with high drama. Instead, it is the grind of daily life that wears us slowly down, the struggle for a dignified survival. Black women work the same endless day white women do, but when we juggle work and family, we also bear the burden of the racism that shapes the composition of our households. We are not lynched, just chipped at by the indignity swallowed, the harassment ignored, the gossamer thread of job security frayed by last hired, first fired. We have been taught silence, and Anita Hill's lifted voice is evidence that she finally found the Sojourner within her.

I finally got the candle I wanted, something white and aromatic, soothing. I brought it home and lit it, and watched the rest of the hearings against the flicker of the flame. I didn't find peace where I sought it, but I found it in myself, and was reminded that such is the definition of a true Sojourner.

JULIANNE MALVEAUX, Ph.D., is an economist, writer, and syndicated columnist whose weekly column appears nationally in some twenty newspapers through the King Features Syndicate. She is also a contributing writer at Essence *magazine, a regular contributor to* Ms. *and* USA Today, *and the* San Francisco Sun Reporter. *She coedited the book* Slipping Through the Cracks: The Status of Black Women *(Transactions Publications, 1986).*

Dismal to Abysmal

W. H. McClendon

The Du Bois position delineating the roles of the talented tenth within the Black population, as resourceful elements to forge the way for the mass of Black people to reach an equitable status in American life, has been subject to debate among many blacks for the past eighty-seven years. The same is true for the Booker T. Washington advocacy for black accommodationism. These misunderstood and unreconciled rationales are sources of conflict and confusion that cloud the thinking of numerous blacks as well as the many whites involved with maintaining influence and direction over Black life in America. For a long time the philosophies of Du Bois and Washington have been highly debatable concepts. In many circumstances these philosophies have been at the base of opinions and proposals that raised civil rights efforts and self-help ideas to levels of intense friction. Often they have slowed the developing of positive politicization and social consciousness for many Blacks and made more difficult their comprehending the legitimacy of civil rights and self-help ideas as inseparable essentials for defining, affirming and implementing equity for any oppressed people in America. It is critical for civil rights struggles and self-help structures to be perceived as complementary and not as contradictory doctrines.

The selection of Clarence Thomas as the president's nominee for the United States Supreme Court is widely perceived as a capricious act designed to cripple politically the total Black population. There are many areas of American life where there are obvious failures on the part of the people to recognize the ideological forces responsible for such selections. Even more troubling is that many of them surely miss the demoralizing implications. For example, one annoying possibility in this selection process is the belief that the nomination was a reward for the fidelity of Thomas to this nation's competitive, punitive, perverted and inhumane values held in the custody of fanatical conservative zealots. It is not unreasonable to consider this nomination as a token of special recognition for services Thomas rendered above and beyond the most grotesque racist expectations when he directed the EEOC mischief against the elderly as well as his opposition to affirmative action and civil rights. Moreover, as a Bush memorial to Atwater, Clarence Thomas on the United States Supreme Court could be used in '92 to fill a revised role of the infamous Willie Horton which played so well in the Bush presidential campaign of '88. It is possible that Thomas may be useful in obviating the likelihood of any future Supreme Court deliberations that could sustain any interests meaningful to this nation's black population.

It is common knowledge that some blacks openly display political ignorance and attribute any good fortune they have experienced to the mythical goodwill of the influential members of the dominant population with whom they have a boy- or girl-to-boss relationship. Much of the Clarence Thomas saga seems to follow this theme. It is significant to note that nothing in the Pin Point narrative reveals political aspirations geared to his wanting to make this nation a better place in which to live. Repeatedly, attention is given to docility in manner as a strategy for material acquisition only. The spirit and objectives of struggle for dignity, equity and justice are never referred to or acknowledged as basic values for black people in America. Unfortunately there has been placed before this nation the record of a nominee to the United States Supreme Court who appears satisfied with and remains passive about the status quo. Thomas is never shown to have engaged in any action to reach higher ideals common to the black struggle. Political thought from Richard Allen and Absalom Jones through Jesse Jackson asserts that the best interests of the Black population and America are never served by Blacks who think and act as accommodationists. The sojourns of Reagan and Bush in the White House have helped some Blacks understand that White racist power and its arbitrary policies are the real recurring obstructions to civil rights, human rights, and self-help for any and all oppressed peoples and classes.

For several weeks frequent media accounts mentioned the endless supernatural paternal supervision Senator Danforth exercised over his protege, Clarence Thomas. These could be taken to be clear messages stating there is never a limit to the care given to assure that Blacks are placed where white folks want them. After all is said and done, prior to the Bush announcement of the Thomas nomination at Kennebunkport, no black anywhere (conservative, radical, religious, agnostic, atheist, affluent, homeless) had proposed or suggested that Thomas be considered for anything.

Many explanations, charges and criticisms are at large now focusing on political connivances in high places that gave the Thomas nomination the flavor of a genderized contest/conflict. Blacks and others should weigh seriously whether they are acting responsibly when they avoid facing the realities of those racial and gender antipathies that are omnipresent in all three branches of the American government. Persons anywhere seeking justice and equity continually must be cause-oriented and situation conscious. Ms. Hill provided traditionally defenseless constituencies of the American population with an intelligent and graceful exercise of situation recall. In doing this she exhibited a quality of leadership that penetrated the smoke screens erected by the Senate to make inscrutable the deceptions and evasions permeating the judiciary committee hearings, and their political devastation. The testimony of Anita Hill is an important milestone in the long journey traveled by black martyrs to improve the quality of life for nondominant ethnic populations in the United States. Her responses to challenges and diatribes coming from judiciary committee members illuminated with shocking clarity that no black can be free as long as one black is making it by Tomming. For those who do not understand the dynamic historical course of uninterrupted and unrelenting white racism, the significance of this assertion may be difficult to grasp. This is why some persons actively support and defend ridiculous aberrant public policies and racist practices imposed upon the black population. Alongside them are members of the dominant population who readily exploit selected Black accommodationists to serve as primary voices of expression to bring about mass false impression among other Blacks. This influences many apolitical Blacks to dissociate themselves from the most painful indignities inflicted upon our people. Ironically, many explain their uncritical stances as acts of loyalty to skin color. They are convinced that because of pigmentation their support should override any realistic objections that may surface based upon principles of sound social thought. Regrettably this results in blacks continuing to share a common deplorable condition because of white racism, while remaining unable to weld a common consciousness for effective political resistance.

Political collusionists of the Hatch, Specter, Simpson and Brown class are responsible for making the Black existence in the United States one of life's gravest hazards. As for Thurmond, his expressions, comments and interruptions were probably inspired by his fantasies of Thomas standing firm for the South and cheering for the Confederate Army during the Civil War.

Anita Hill had the misfortune to believe that her concerns would be given maximum protection by the judiciary committee. The history of the Senate is replete with examples of conflict resolution handled to favor the Senate exclusively. Ms. Hill had only her intellect and integrity as bargaining chips. While these are prized qualities among most oppressed peoples, they have little to do with the politics that prevail in elected officials' strategies for maintaining ultimate power.

In the circumstance of conservative vs. liberal positions to assess the fitness and determine worthiness (professional and moral) of Clarence Thomas, the judiciary committee acted as the broker to market the political schemes of President Bush and his White House staff. From this performance came the appalling revelation that if and when a Black woman reports character deficiencies of anyone selected, designed or mentored by rancorous administration and senate manipulators, it is futile to expect that among the plotters there will be awakened any conscionable interest. Anita Hill's mistake may have been her misplaced confidence that she could strike an arrangement for fair play with any part of the Senate of the United States.

The Thomas and Hill testimonies offered excellent opportunities for viewers to distinguish the differences between self-esteem and self-aggrandizement. Moral issues did not affect the outcome of this drama. The Senate Judiciary Committee asserted its prerogative to act as advocate for the system of white racism. In filling this role, the antics of the Committee were described by the chairman as "the process." This process came off as a simple repetitive political ideological contest between Republican and Democratic committee members. The hearings were structured for both groups to collaborate comfortably in the vilification of a black woman. The judiciary committee turned these assemblies into a dramatic farce where the theatrics of senators titillated public opinion. They used tactics ranging from clown-like entertaining to raw political campaigning to criminal court procedures.

The judiciary committee's actions in dealing with Ms. Hill's presence were demonstrations of excessive malicious adversarial disdain, discourtesy and disrespect. Had she been a less secure person her life could have been made irreparably unstable. Racism and gender bias expressed in the Senators' admonitions, opinions and questions, along with their self-targeted compliments, filled every crevice. Despite the elaborate and profuse explanations voiced, there was a detectable noxious theme of meanness directed toward the supporters of Ms. Hill. The mentors, supporters and strategists for Clarence Thomas are suspected of advising him to assume a charade of blackness. This was accomplished by his describing the unanticipated ramifications of Ms. Hill's testimony as a high-tech lynching. Such an uncharacteristic upsurge of Black consciousness on the part of the nominee suggests that a bizarre reservoir of ambiguities, incongruities and anachronisms could fill his life. It must not be forgotten that it was Thomas who did not provide any answers to any inquiries about his political, legal or social concerns. He refused to articulate any awareness or comprehension of matters of common interest, or of serious concern, to persons and organizations throughout the nation. News accounts have repeatedly called attention to the Pin Point Clarence Thomas as a product of whites doing their missionary type things in a run-of-the-mill fashion where no checks and balances were held by the surrounding Black community. Such information now stirs conjectures that the Thomas of today may be burdened with a mendacious spirit and an intellectual shortfall.

Senate and administration contempt for the Black population has never been displayed more blatantly. The entire sequence of events is socially flawed by unreceptiveness to input expressing the interests, preferences or concerns of Black individuals and organizations. The nomination was an insult to Thomas, Hill, the Black population and the American polity. There are more than 750,000 lawyers and judges in this nation. Bush's statement that Thomas was the best choice as a United States Supreme Court nominee is incredible. Questions and challenges voiced by spokespersons representing broad professional, religious, political and social thought sectors of American life were disregarded completely. Through several media presentations Clarence Thomas was reported as a significant point man in carrying out anti-black, anti-poor and anti-labor policies for the Reagan administration. Some of these accounts were anything but flattering. To modify the effects of these reports, judiciary committee members used supercilious rhetorical abrasiveness in what seems an unprecedented hostile intent to erode professional and social compatibility among Black women and men.

In acting to preserve a psycho-social history of keeping Blacks in their place, the Senate risked trashing the United States Supreme Court. Customarily and historically Black people's lives are filled with stress, crisis and catastrophe. These are unavoidable for all peoples who live under white racist repression. The extreme racism and chauvinism manifested by Senators during the hearings shook the sensitivities of the nation. Now, from the top levels of global corporate control downward through all branches of government and on into the polity, thinking is more focused on ameliorating some of the abominable governmentally created disorders rampant throughout the country. Events so vividly reviewed in the hearings should create for some Senators unexpected problems because of their fervor to use the troubled circumstances for some Blacks as evidence that a White racist system is forever desirable and preferable.

Throughout the history of this nation Blacks seeking improvements in status were committed to achieving civil rights as a priority. Irrespective of their origins, there was dedicated use of minds, bodies, education, money, organizations, political skills, legal talent, scientific capability, intellectual proficiency, artistic genius, social thought and military propensity. These and more were applied to loosen the white racist choke-hold gripping the Black Population.

There are no records or reports showing real successes for Blacks who attempt to realize civil rights through endorsing or practicing accommodation. Concomitantly, increased elevation of status for oppressed people never occurs solely because of expressions or acts of benevolence on the part of some empathetic members of the dominant population. Struggles of the oppressed must be marked clearly by internal consciousness, social and political. There must be a decisive rejection of racist behaviors, in or out of government, that affirm a devalued human status for any citizens or inhabitants. The history of blacks in America is, in addition to other content, the chronicle of resistance to slavery, exploitation, deprivation and maltreatment.

Civil rights struggles resulted in the eventful presence of a distinguished civil rights advocate and defender, Thurgood Marshall, becoming a United States Supreme Court Justice in 1967. A turnabout in 1991 has a Black justice seated on the court through the political machinations of an administration broadly perceived as anti–civil rights. White House strategists and senatorial collaborators are not likely to understand, or care, that dissenting Blacks do not seek justice and respect as favors. As a people, we are committed to achieve these despite the continuing criminal and discriminatory actions defended and often fostered by an insensitive government and the culture to which it conforms.

W. H. McCLENDON is an author, educator, and consultant. He is presently compiling a collection of his essays called Culture and Education: Realities, Perspectives, Responses, *to be published by Black Scholar Press.*

The U.S. People/Thomas Hearing

Adam David Miller

The recent Senate Judiciary Committee hearings on Judge Clarence Thomas's elevation to the U.S. Supreme Court revealed again the lack of integrity and paucity of imagination parading as leadership in the Senate. We saw also the extraordinary ability of media gate-keepers and Thomas's handlers to control events and manipulate public opinion.

(The hearings also revealed that the nature of radio/television presentation is such that most people are bound to receive only partial information, with the result that their judgment must necessarily be flawed. For example, a poll taken of the Denver area after our Persian Gulf massacre showed that viewers who watched the most television were more ignorant of the details of the fighting than those who watched none at all.)

The Senators' shortcomings were most evident in their handling of the witness Professor Anita Hill. Professor Hill, Republican, Christian, tenured at University of Oklahoma Law School, had been asked by aides of Senator Metzenbaum, (D-OH), if she had information about nominee Thomas. She faxed statements to the Committee alleging sexual misconduct by Thomas when she worked for him at the Department of Education and later at EEOC. Hill and Thomas were then interviewed by the FBI. When Thomas denied Hill's charges, Chair Biden (D-MD), and the Committee decided to dismiss her allegations and not make them public. The Committee completed its questioning of Judge Thomas and on a 7–7 vote sent the nomination to the full Senate for confirmation.

The matter did not rest there. Hill's charges were leaked to the Press. Headlines that ensued created public pressure which forced the Senate to hold off its vote until the charges could be aired openly. Thus, Professor Anita Hill was called before the Committee to tell her story.

To make the most of what follows about the Senators' mishandling of events, we need to keep in mind that the sole purpose of the hearing was to evaluate Judge Thomas's fitness to be elevated to the Supreme Court. News leaks notwithstanding, nothing should have been permitted to divert the Committee from this purpose. If at any point during the proceedings members of the Committee had decided that they had heard enough to declare either for or against the nominee, they could have halted the hearing and taken their vote. They also could have extended the hearing as long as they felt it necessary to reach a sound determination. Senator Strom Thurmond's (R-SC) focus on qualifications, integrity, and judicial temperament was a correct one.

In remembering that what we had was a Congressional hearing and not a court trial, we should also understand that it was the Senate Committee's hearing and not Professor Anita Hill's hearing.

The rules governing what is admissible in a Congressional hearing are different from those of a court trial. A hearing requires a less rigorous standard of proof. During the hearing several Senators mentioned the burden of proving the case (against Judge Thomas) "beyond a reasonable doubt." This would hold true if they had been in a court of law having a trial. It was not and they were not. This point cannot be emphasized too strongly because it is possible that it was this kind of confusion about the difference between a court room and a hearing room that gained Judge Thomas Senator De Concini's crucial seventh vote in the Committee and the Senate votes necessary for his narrow confirmation.

Given the wrong-headed "beyond a reasonable doubt" standard, Chair Biden blundered when he, in an apparent attempt to be fair, stated that any doubt should be resolved in favor of Judge Thomas. Since we were not in a court of law, any doubt should have been resolved in favor of the People and the Supreme Court and not in favor of the nominee.

This point was made eloquently but in vain by Senator Robert Byrd (D-WV) during the Senate vote for confirmation. The air had already been poisoned by Senator Biden's blunder; several senators used this crutch for their vote to confirm. Not even Senator Bill Bradley's (D-NJ) brilliant defense of Professor Hill's credibility as a witness could sway them.

In allowing the hearing to become an adversarial rather than an uncovering proceeding, Chair Biden and the Democrats failed miserably in their duty to focus on Judge Thomas's qualifications and character so that when they called Professor Hill to testify, they let her be the object of venomous attack instead of the possible possessor of information they could utilize in evaluating Judge Thomas's character.

Professor Hill was *not* a party to the Thomas hearing, she was called as a witness. The parties were the People and Judge Thomas. Professor Hill could not call herself. She could volunteer and still not be called should the Committee not want her to be. Angela Wright, who, while not knowing Professor Hill as she worked for Judge Thomas at a later date, claimed an experience similar to Professor Hill's that she was willing to testify to. She was not called.

So when Chair Biden said, "Professor Hill has contacted us and said that in the *interest of time* she was fully prepared to forego having the Wright panel testify" (on her behalf), the senator was giving several false impressions: 1) that it was Professor Hill and not the Committee whose business it was to call witnesses, and 2) that Professor Hill suddenly took an interest in saving time when someone was to testify *for* her (emphasis added).

Time was not the most important consideration of the Committee. The uncovering process can go on as long as necessary to bring out the truth. How long did they take to confirm Justice Brandeis? (Six months) If Angela Wright and Rose Jourdain and Sakari Hardnett, all former employees of Judge Thomas in positions similar to those held by Anita Hill, had information that would have aided the Committee in evaluating Judge Thomas's character (and they said they had), then the Committee was remiss in not presenting that information in the manner other information was being presented. And no deal should have been cut with *any*one to prevent this information from being presented.

Because Chair Biden permitted the hearing to become adversarial and allowed the terms of inquiry to be *Hill* v. *Thomas*, the People and the Supreme Court and Thomas got buried under the media event that followed.

Had the Committee kept its focus on the People and Thomas, and the fitness of Thomas's character for a seat on the Supreme Court, Judge Thomas could have been required to clarify some questions left muddled during the first part of the hearing, such as, "Why should we believe you now when you told us that in *twenty years* you had never once discussed *Roe* v. *Wade* although you testified under oath that you regarded it as one of the three most important decisions of recent times?" And, "How can we accept your character when you refused to disqualify yourself from sitting on a case your friend and mentor had an interest in or your veracity when you tell you condemn sexual misconduct if you did not fire an employee who had exposed himself to women on the job?" (*Unity*, Oct. 31, 1991)

Chair Biden seemed more interested in the form rather than the substance of the hearing. He was more interested in being polite to fellow senators than calling offensive personal and irrelevant remarks out of order.

It was plain to all who wished to see that a black woman's claims had no standing in the senators' eyes, even such an exemplary woman, even against a black man.

Chair Biden wanted a neat hearing. To pursue Professor Hill's charges would have made things messy. Chair Biden and the committee had wanted to bury Professor Hill's allegations in the first place. Only the leaked story forced them to extend the hearing. When the genie began to slip out of the bottle and they were attacked by Judge Thomas, they could not tell him that he had never answered the charges lodged against him but only complained that he had been hurt by them. Not one of the senators suggested to him that he had hurt Professor Hill if her charges were true.

Instead they allowed themselves to be guilt tripped by Judge Thomas's "electronic lynching" and "uppity black," terms fed him by Sen. Orrin Hatch (R-UT) and his white handlers. No black would use lynch in that way. But his white handlers knew that Judge Thomas, a black of sorts, could play on the Committee members' collective racial guilt, not for anything they were doing or had done to him, which was precious little, but for what they and other whites had done and were doing to blacks as a group.

The Committee was derelict in its duty when they allowed the question before them to become "Should we believe her or him?" Their question should always have been "Should we recommend this nominee to the Supreme Court?" That the Democrats lost sight of this allowed the Republican misdirection play that sneaked Judge Thomas onto the Court.

ADAM DAVID MILLER is a freelance journalist, a member of National Writers Union, and lifelong supporter and contributer to The Black Scholar. *He is the president of Mina Press Publishing. S. Elise Peoples, a philosopher and his wife, assisted in the preparation of this article.*

Race, Gender and Liberal Fallacies

Orlando Patterson

Clarence Thomas's second round of confirmation hearings was one of the finest moments in the modern history of America's democratic culture, a riveting, civic drama that fully engaged the electorate in an exposure and examination of its most basic fears and contradictions concerning class, race, sex and gender.

But even as it urged us to question some of our basic values and position, it reconfirmed the strength and suppleness of our system of governance. It also revealed one of its greatest weaknesses: there are serious misperceptions of what is really going on in our society, and lamentable failure in our threadbare, predominantly liberal discourse on it.

Thanks to this drama, we have entered an important new phase in the nation's discourse on gender relations, and it goes well beyond the enhanced realization by men that the complaints of women must be taken seriously. Implicit in these hearings was an overdue questioning of the legalistic, neo-Puritan and elitist model of gender relations promoted by the dominant school of American feminists.

We must face certain stark sociological realities: in our increasingly female, work-centered world, most of our relationships, including intimate ones, are initiated in the workplace; gender relations, especially new ones, are complex and invariably ambiguous; in our heterogeneous society, the perception of what constitutes proper and effective male-female relations varies across gender, class, ethnicity and region; and in keeping with our egalitarian ideals, we take pride in the fact that the WASP boss may legitimately desire or want to marry his or her Puerto Rican aide or chauffer.

One revealing feature of these hearings is the startling realization that Judge Clarence Thomas might well have said what Professor Anita Hill alleges and yet be the extraordinarily sensitive man his persuasive female defenders claimed. American feminists have no way of explaining this. They have correctly demanded a rigorously enforced protocol of gender relations in the workplace. But they have also demanded that same intimate bonding that men of power traditionally share, the exclusion from which has kept them below the glass ceiling. There is a serious lacuna in the discourse, for we have failed to ask one fundamental question: How is nonerotic intimacy between men and women possible?

Clarence Thomas emerged in the hearings as one of those rare men who, with one or two exceptions, has achieved both: in general, he rigorously enforced the formal rules of gender relations, and he had an admirable set of intimate, nonerotic relations with his female associates.

And yet, tragically, there is his alleged failing with Professor Hill. How is this possible? While middle-class neo-Puritans ponder this question, the mass of the white working class and nearly all African Americans except their intellectually exhausted leaders have already come up with the answer. He may well have said what he is alleged to have said, but he did so as a man not unreasonably attracted to an aloof woman who is esthetically and socially very similar to himself, who had made no secret of her own deep admiration for him.

With his mainstream cultural guard down, Judge Thomas on several misjudged occasions may have done something completely out of the cultural frame of his white, upper-middle-class work world, but immediately recognizable to Professor Hill and most women of Southern working-class backgrounds, white or black, especially the latter.

Now to most American feminists, and to politicians manipulating the nation's lingering Puritan ideals, an obscenity is always an obscenity, an absolute offense against God and the moral order; to everyone else, including all professional social linguists and qualitative sociologists, an obscene expression whether in Chaucerian Britain or the American South, has to be understood in context. I am convinced that Professor Hill perfectly understood the psycho-cultural context in which Judge Thomas allegedly regaled her with his Rabelaisian humor (possibly as a way of affirming their common origins), which is precisely why she never filed a complaint against him.

Raising the issue ten years later was unfair and disingenuous: unfair because, while she may well have been offended by his coarseness, there is no evidence that she suffered any emotional or career damage, and the punishment she belatedly sought was in no way commensurate with the offense; and disingenuous because she has lifted a verbal style that carries only minor sanction in one subcultural context and thrown it in the overheated cultural arena of mainstream, neo-Puritan America, where it incurs professional extinction.

If my interpretation is correct, Judge Thomas was justified in denying making the remarks, even if he had in fact made them, not only because the deliberate displacement of his remarks made them something else but on the utilitarian moral grounds that any admission would have immediately incurred a self-destructive and grossly unfair punishment.

The hearings also brought to light the fact that the American public is way ahead of its journalistic and social-science commentators with respect to race relations. The sociological truths are that America, while still flawed in its race relations and its stubborn refusal to institute a rational, universal welfare system, is now the least racist white-majority society in the world; has a better record of legal protection of minorities than any other society, white or black; offers more opportunities to a greater number of black persons than any other society, including all those of Africa; and has gone through a dramatic change in its attitude toward miscegenation over the past twenty-five years.

Increased reports of racial and gender conflicts are actually indicative of things getting better, not worse, as commentators seem to think, since they reflect the greatly increased number of contacts between blacks and whites, and males and females, in competitive, high-powered situations as the number of Thomases and the many capable, strong-willed women we saw during the hearings rapidly increase.

One great good to come out of the hearings was the revelation to the average white American that, superstar athletes, news anchors and politicians aside, not all African Americans are underclass cocaine junkies and criminals, which is an understandable delusion in any white person whose only knowledge of African Americans comes from the press and television.

Above all, they saw in Judge Thomas and Professor Hill two very complex, highly intelligent persons who knew how to get and use power in the mainstream society, and were role models for black and white people alike.

However, perhaps the most remarkable feature of the hearings is the response of the public. Here again, liberal expectations were at odds with realities. It was thought that racism would be reinforced by these hearings—which is one simple-minded reason given for criticizing them—but in fact what has emerged is not only the indifference of the white public to the racial aspect of the proceedings but the degree to which white men and women have identified their own interests and deepest anxieties with the two African American antagonists. Indeed, the only aspect of these hearings likely to have increased racism was the journalists' shrill and self-fulfilling insistence that the nation is exploding with racism. This is one of those cases where the messengers deserved to be shot.

White men, especially those in power, are not tittering in locker rooms about black men, as the commentators all seem to think; instead, they are deeply worried about the implications for their relations with white women brought out by these hearings, as well they might. And women, white and black, are taking all kinds of positions on the issues raised. Indeed, most of Professor Hill's supporters seem to be middle-class white women.

My own daughter, Barbara, a post-feminist young woman brought up by two feminists who came of age in the sixties, believes along with her friends that Judge Thomas did say those raunchy things, should have been told at once what a "dog" he was and reported to the authorities by Professor Hill if his advances had continued to annoy her. But they cannot see the relevance of Judge Thomas's down-home style of courting to his qualifications for the Supreme Court.

African Americans must now realize that these hearings were perhaps the single most important cultural development for them since the great struggles of the civil rights years. Clarence Thomas and Anita Hill suffered inhuman and undeserved pain, tragic pain, in their public ordeal, and they will never be quite the same again. Nor will we all, for what all African Americans won from their pain, "perfected by this deed," this ritual of inclusion, is the public cultural affirmation of what had already been politically achieved: unambiguous inclusion;

unquestioned belonging. The culture of slavery is dead.

The great achievement of these hearings, then, has been, first, to bring us to a greater awareness of the progress in racial and gender relations already achieved by this country. Second, superficial liberal stereotypes of blacks as victims or bootstrap heroes are seen for what they are: a new form of racism that finds it hard to imagine African Americans not as a monolithic group but, as several of the African American panelists on TV correctly informed the nation, a diverse aggregate of perhaps 30 million individuals, with all the class differences, subcultural and regional resources, strength, flaws and ideologies we find in other large populations.

Finally, the hearings have also highlighted the need to go beyond mere legalistic protocol in gender relations at the workplace. If women are to break through the glass ceiling, they must escape the trap of neo-Puritan feminism with its reactionary sacralization of women's bodies, and along with men develop at the workplace something that America still conspicuously lacks: a civilized culture of intimate social intercourse between men and women that recognizes, and contains, the frailties of male and female passions. It's not going to be easy, but these extraordinary hearings have pushed us in the right direction.

ORLANDO PATTERSON, Ph.D., professor of Sociology at Harvard, is author of Freedom, *winner of The 1991 National Book Award for nonfiction. This essay was reprinted from* The New York Times, *October 20, 1991.*

The Clarence Thomas Confirmation: Facing Race and Gender Issues

Jacqueline Pope

Most of the drama that unfolded on national television between Anita Hill and Clarence Thomas was a study in commonalities. Hill, a family-centered, religious woman, a proponent of conservative ideas with Ivy League credentials, was brilliant, offering her story about a Supreme Court nominee who had a very similar political, religious and educational background. Yet they spoke at one another across a world of gender inequalities. Concomitantly, both spoke eloquently and under normal circumstances would make all people of African descent swell with pride. Instead we and non-African people were divided.

Thomas's proponents used every despicable tactic to shake Hill's resolve. But, so firm was her eloquence, sense of herstory and dignity that the attack on her character and mental stability failed. In fact, their methods seemed to strengthen Professor Hill. On the other hand, Thomas's mean spiritedness expanded in direct correlation to the sexual harassment allegations. Obviously any similarities between them stopped at that point. Two professional African Americans dedicated to their goals and careers did battle. It is no wonder lines were drawn and people were confused. Some folks didn't care or know that Thomas was "handled" by the White House. But that critical issue stayed in the minds of the rest of us. We watched as Hill indirectly challenged the most politically powerful man on earth, George Bush. That deed will ever be remembered and admired. Two African Americans, one spouting untruths, slandering, subjecting the other to public humiliation, yet she never faltered, never surrendered to the vicious slurs. At the other end of the spectrum was Judge Thomas, alternately bragging, whining and badgering, employing all the tactics attributed to females. The contrasts between them were as striking as the commonalities.

All people of color must pause, examine the Hill/Thomas issue and develop questions for public debate. For instance, should we

continue to accept collective guilt when individual African Americans engage in heinous behavior? No! European Americans, although outraged by mass murderers like the Milwaukee animal-man who dismembered fifteen people, take no blame for individual terrible deeds of whites. Alternatively should African Americans support the activities of all people of color? No! We must acknowledge inappropriate and harmful stances of those few African Americans. Such people can and will hurt us collectively and individually.

Justice Thomas is a prime example. Those backing his nomination mistakenly thought they were supporting a "brother." Professor Hill's opponents saw her as a divisive, vindictive woman, bent on destroying a distinguished African American male. She was portrayed as a "fatal attraction" type of person. This gentle, dignified woman received an epithet label while Thomas was given the title "brother" despite the fact that he was stooping low to play the ultimate race card, a "[political] lynching." Perhaps he does deserve the title "brother" Thomas, provided African Americans learn that, after all, a small number of people of color are hostile to both their race and those in dire economic straits. It is my hope that the Thomas debacle will clearly illustrate that informed decisions based on the issues, rather than ethnicity or gender, will empower us.

Another issue apparent during the Hill/Thomas hearings unspoken, but festering below the surface, was "presumed purity." How could Professor Hill's testimony be true, since women of color are assumed impure? Just as men are seldom convicted of rape when the victim is a person of color, sexual harassment allegations by women of African descent can hardly have any basis of truth. "Presumed purity" is reserved for women without color in the minds of most men of *all* ethnic backgrounds. Too many African American men, in almost second nature, call women "bitch" and "ho," abuse them physically, mentally and spiritually. If they refuse to respect African American women, why should people of other races do so? It is understood that the brothers unconsciously have internalized and do verbalize negative covert views of some powerful European Americans regarding African American women. But that *is* the issue. Moreover, African American men, in an attempt to control something or someone in their lives, project and echo negative images about African

American women. The brothers too often forget about the daily challenges African American women face in order to maintain self confidence and strong egos. These women struggle in a nation that renders brown and black skinned women invisible at best. African American men join the oppressors when they label and degrade their sisters. Furthermore they may erroneously seem to be in league with the would-be rapists and other attackers. In other words, labeling African American women "bitch" and "ho" could be life threatening for them.

What is in a name, you ask? Numerous African Americans have changed their names because of the connotations and connections to slavery. Degrading African American women with epithets supports the notion of impure, promiscuous women bent on debasing blackness. African American men must examine and bring their language into the twenty-first-century. Praise the efforts and beauty of African American women in public and private. We are your reflection; honor us and the best is brought out in you. To those opposing Professor Hill, did they apply the purity test to her, a test that only women of color fail? Such a standard is ludicrous, since African American males are routinely comforted and protected. Let me explain the last statement.

Witness the furor concerning "at risk" African American males. According to the powers that be, they are in a crisis. True enough, but all African Americans are in serious trouble, financially and culturally. Women and children encounter dangers equal to those that men face. To focus on the hardships of half the race is foolhardy. As a result we find ourselves rushing to protect the male while neglecting the woman or, worse, testing her purity.

Justice Thomas is the beneficiary of this lunacy. Despite his unsympathetic views of the poor and people of color, is he still a male at risk and a brother? Admittedly, concern about one another is critical to the continued vitality and survival of African Americans. However, the pain of racism and sexism must both be acknowledged and equally shared. To do so increases the capacity for strengthening our ethnic group and eliminating barriers of classism and sexism in our race. Never again should there be Anita Hills fighting powerful European American institutions, virtually alone.

JACQUELINE POPE, Ph.D., is associate professor of Political Science at Stockton State College, Pomona, New Jersey. She has published numerous articles and is the author of Biting the Hand that Feeds Them: Organizing Women on the Grassroots Level, *Greenwood Press, 1989. Dr. Pope was a signatory of "African American Women in Defense of Ourselves,"* The New York Times, *November 17, 1991.*

The Gang Rape of Anita Hill and the Assault Upon All Women of African Descent

Barbara Ransby

The events surrounding the confirmation hearings of Clarence Thomas for the U.S. Supreme Court and Professor Anita Hill's revelation that Thomas had sexually harassed her some ten years earlier raised a set of issues much larger than the two individuals at the center of the drama. The hearings highlighted two very ominous political trends confronting African Americans in this country as we approach the twenty-first century. Firstly, they reflected the increasing hostility toward and scapegoating of black women for a whole range of social problems now confronting our communities, including the oppression of black men. Secondly, they showcased the rise and increasing legitimacy, in some circles, of black neo-conservatives, a new breed of predators who pimp off of the call for racial solidarity when they can use it to their benefit, and then betray the best interests of the majority of black people at the first opportunity.

The first trend, the scapegoating of black women, is predicated upon an increasingly male-centered definition of the black experience and black oppression. In recent years we have seen the racist and sexist theory of the so-called pathological black matriarchy, initially popularized by Daniel Patrick Moynihan in 1965, resurrected and repackaged by white journalists, black and white neo-conservatives, and even spokespersons who profess to be genuine allies and defenders of the black community. Some of these theorists claim only to be concerned with the desperate plight of young African American men, yet in the process of demonstrating this concern, they effectively minimize the equally desperate plight of black women, often tacitly blaming black women for our own oppression and that of our families and children. At one end of the spectrum, black women are stereotyped as egotistical career climbers, better paid, better educated and more socially mobile than our male counterparts and thus not worthy of any special treatment as victims of oppression. At the other end of the spectrum we are portrayed as lazy, promiscuous welfare frauds, who leave our children unsupervised to roam the streets, grossly inflating the drug, crime and prison statistics.

The mainstream media has been one of the main culprits in painting this negative and demeaning portrait of African American women, often in conjunction with misleading statistics about the so-called breakdown of the black family. Numerous newspaper and magazine articles, pseudodocumentary television programs, and foundation-funded research projects have highlighted the crisis of the black male, always stressing internal factors within the black community, such as female-headed households and the lack of positive role models, as the alleged causes of the problems. With respect to the Clarence Thomas hearings, the mainstream media was extremely biased in its treatment of Anita Hill in particular, and by extension all African-American women. Most media commentators artificially juxtaposed the issues of race and gender, suggesting that those sensitive to racism were supportive of Clarence Thomas and those sensitive to sexism were supportive of Anita Hill. Such a narrow and mutually exclusive formulation wholly ignores the combined racial and gender identity of black women. It reflects an inability and unwillingness in the popular discourse to accept the dual realities and dual systems of oppression faced by African American women.

In the larger context, it is unfortunate that black as well as white voices are contributing to this negative and distorted view of African American women. Two extreme examples of this slavish collaboration is Shahrazad Ali's book, *Black Man's Guide to Understanding the Black Woman*, in which the author actually advocates the physical abuse of African American women. Similarly, the vulgar lyrics of a handful of male rappers like Two Live Crew graphically depict black women as either sex toys or punching bags. On a more subtle level, films like *Boyz N the Hood,* despite some powerful and positive messages about the humanity of young black men, nevertheless also help to reinforce many of these negative stereotypes about black women. For example, virtually every female character in the film personifies one of the stereotypes already mentioned. Likewise, Jawanza Kunjufu, in his 1985 book, *Conspiracy to Destroy Black Boys*, argues outright for the centrality of black male oppression, and in fact blames black mothers for their inability to effectively raise their sons. The recent controversy over all-male academies geared exclusively toward the needs of black male youth further reinforced the notion that the problems and dilemmas facing the African American community today are essentially male problems and male dilemmas. The proposition that black men are being targeted for special oppression because of their gender carries with it the implicit notion that African American women, conversely, have earned some type of gender privilege that exempts us from such special abuses. It is currently popular and acceptable to minimize the plight of black women either through glaring omission or by emphasizing black male oppression so heavily that black women's suffering is rendered invisible, just as Anita Hill's racial identity and her victimization as a black woman were rendered invisible during the public debate surrounding the Thomas hearings. While our brothers are clearly under siege from a racist society, and the alarming statistics about black male suffering should not be taken lightly, we nevertheless cannot regress in our political thinking to a point not so long ago when black women were told that it was our duty to assume subordinate roles so that brothers could redeem their manhood.

Black Harvard sociologist Orlando Patterson took this argument to new lows when he hurled gut-wrenching and slanderous insults at black women and the entire black community from the editorial pages of *The New York Times* in his pseudo-analysis of the Thomas/Hill case. Patterson audaciously suggested that while it is likely that Thomas did, in fact, say and do what Anita Hill alleged, that there was no harm intended because crude and sexually explicit language constitutes an acceptable style of "courting" within Southern black culture. Even worse, he condemns Hill for making the incidents public and applauds Thomas for lying in order to shelter himself from unwarranted retribution. What Patterson inexcusably fails to appreciate is the fact that Thomas's behavior constituted harassment, not simply because it was sexually graphic and, to many of us, crude and distasteful, but it was unsolicited and unwelcome by his young assistant, and he knew it. Moreover, the unequal power relations between Hill and Thomas put him at an unfair advantage to impose his verbal "affections" upon her against her will. Such behavior is not innocent flirtation, or a positive affirmation of black manhood, it is verbal intimidation and a form of sexual abuse. In 1991, any serious discussion of black liberation has to take us beyond this point to an agenda that recognizes the personhood of all African American people, and which recognizes that for more than half of the black population, liberation also means fighting against the sexist and misogynist culture which affects us as black women.

There are two reasons that such backward formulations are so malignant at this particular historical juncture. First of all, they minimize the reality of violence and suffering that African American women endure daily in both a racist and sexist culture. While our brothers are herded into concentration-like prisons, black women silently suffer a parallel imprisonment. On one level poor black women are trapped in the prisons of poverty, unemployment, homelessness and hunger, compounded by the constraints of unwanted pregnancies, premature motherhood and the ridicule, isolation and sometimes violence suffered by black lesbian women. The welfare system, too, with its bureaucratic structure, robs many African American women of their autonomy, their dignity, their privacy, and in some cases their physical mobility, and represents yet another prison for thousands of our sisters. And in terms of violence, black women are beaten, raped and killed daily with impunity. The media coverage of the Central Park rape case two years ago not only stereotyped all black and Latino men as animals, but also highlighted the double standard experienced by black and white women in the area of sexual violence. A week before the now infamous Central Park incident, a young black woman in upper Manhattan was similarly brutalized, raped and murdered, yet her case went almost unnoticed by the media, typifying the lack of value placed on the lives of African American women, and the lack of serious attention the sexual abuse of black women receives. It is important to note that Clarence Thomas's conservative philosophy, as well as that of many of his right wing colleagues, is a philosophy steeped in misogynist and victim-blaming attitudes directed largely at African American women.

African American women, especially poor and working class women, have been some of the principal targets of the Reagan/Bush assault upon progressive social reform. Poor black women are maligned and castigated as welfare dependent leeches, bleeding the beleaguered white middle class dry. Middle class black women are labeled as the undeserving recipients of compound Affirmative Action benefits, who steal jobs, scholarships, and college entrance slots from their ostensibly better qualified white counterparts. Given this national attack upon the collective character of black women, it is not surprising that the two individuals who were the most visible targets of Clarence Thomas's expressed contempt for all black people were two black women, his sister, Emma Mae Martin, and Professor Anita Hill. When speaking before a group of black Republicans, Thomas coldly berated his hard-working but impoverished sister, erroneously characterizing her as a shiftless welfare recipient. In an equally malevolent vein, Anita Hill was portrayed by Thomas's backers as a selfish, overly ambitious careerist who expected undeserved personal and professional attention and was viciously vindictive when she did not get it. The personal attacks upon these two individual black women personify the venomous and dual edged assault being waged upon all women of African descent in this country today.

This brings us to the second, but related, political trend confronting black Americans in the 1990s: the way in which black conservatives, of varying shades and styles, have managed to carve out space for their essentially racist and sexist ideas within the major arenas of black political thought and discourse. Conservative economist Thomas Sowell and his cohorts were considered marginal 'Uncle Toms' at best ten years ago, but seem to be enjoying growing influence among a small but nevertheless significant sector of the black community today. In a sense many of these conservative ideological trends are nothing new and simply represent a modernized version of the old Booker T. Washington, pull yourself up by your bootstraps (or by your toenails if you can't afford boots) philosophy. Nevertheless we must take seriously the fact that these views have the potential of receiving a larger audience today than they have received in quite some time if we continue to allow the nature of the problems confronting our communities to be distorted and misdefined. The appropriation of the rhetoric of self-help and self-determination, coupled with the forcing of ill-fitted connections between conservative agendas and the

Civil Rights Movement of the 1950s and early sixties are two factors which have helped conservatives gain a greater foothold in the black community.

Black neo-conservatives have appealed to the ethos of self-reliance among African Americans to try to justify the Reagan/Bush regime's complete abandonment of even the most basic commitment to social service programs and anti-discrimination protections. Traditions which for most African Americans represent an affirmation of pride and resourcefulness have been exploited by black conservatives as a rationale for denying much needed and much deserved resources to the poor, the unemployed and the homeless. Further, some have even tried to use Martin Luther King's calls for a color blind society as justification for the abolition of Affirmative Action programs which they argue reinforce low black self-esteem and constitute reversed discrimination against white males.

In sum, the contempt and verbal abuse heaped upon Anita Hill by the white male Judiciary Committee during the Thomas confirmation hearings was ironically quite similar to the kind of abuse she had received from Thomas himself a decade before. More importantly, her treatment symbolized the wholesale assault upon and scapegoating of all African American women by black and white conservatives alike. In fact, the degrading treatment of black women as objects of male ridicule, anger, and entertainment is what some would have us believe is and should be acceptable within the bounds of African American culture. And those women who insist upon a greater amount of respect and autonomy than that are deemed castrating betrayers of the race. In terms of the Thomas/Hill confrontation, what was termed by reactionary white conservatives as a "high-tech lynching" of Clarence Thomas was in actuality a public gang rape of Anita Hill, and by extension, a violent assault upon all women of African descent. Fortunately, there are many progressive men and women within the black community who were outraged by what transpired during the Thomas hearings, were clear on the nature of the attack, and see the need for a unified and uncompromising stand against the twin evils of racism and sexism. Some of these sentiments were expressed in a major signature ad taken out by 1,603 women of African descent which appeared in *The New York Times* on November 17 and in a half dozen black papers the following week. Significantly, a number of brothers also heartily supported this effort. If nothing else, the Thomas/Hill drama raised some important political issues that now confront us in a way that cannot be ignored. African American Women in Defense of Ourselves (317 S. Division, Suite 199, Ann Arbor, Michigan 48104, 312-918-2702), the group that initiated the newspaper ad campaign, is a loose network of African American women across the country who are working to facilitate a broader dialogue about the issues raised by the Thomas hearings and related issues of concern to women of African descent. No one will speak for us but ourselves.

BARBARA RANSBY, Ph.D., is a freelance writer and has had articles published in the Guardian, *the* Nation, Southern Exposure, Columbia Journal of Ideas, Michigan Feminist Quarterly *and* Sage: A Scholarly Journal on Black Women. *She has forthcoming articles in* Race and Class, New Directions for Women, Third Wave: An Anthology of Writings by Women of Color *(Kitchen Table Press, 1992).*

Comments on the Controversy Surrounding the Nomination and Confirmation of Judge Clarence Thomas to the Supreme Court

William W. Sales, Jr.

It would be naive to think of the Supreme Court as an agent of social change. In the American political system, while it ultimately determines what the Constitution is, the High Court enjoys no independent ability to enforce its decisions. Its membership is selected by white male members of the American elite and reflects their interests and background. The Supreme Court is enmeshed in a political system which is biased against social change and moves at a snail's pace when implementing incremental and marginal alterations in the legal, political and economic realms.[1] Nevertheless in the immediate post–World War II period and for a quarter of a century thereafter, the High Court was the branch of government most sympathetic to the rights and immunities of African Americans as citizens of this country. It became a very important platform upon which the fundamental moral claims of Black people were articulated, first in the great arguments of the pathmark civil rights cases argued by the NAACP and later in the presence on the Court of Justice Thurgood Marshall.

The willingness of the American elite to reorder aspects of American race relations was first revealed in the deliberations and decisions of the post–World War II Supreme Court. Its decisions legitimized the goals and objectives of the Civil Rights Movement in constitutional terms. These Court decisions gave to non-violent direct action part of its moral impact on decision-makers in the legislative and executive branches and in the public and corporate bureaucracies. Justice Thurgood Marshall is recognized as an extraordinary jurist, a champion of the civil rights of Black people and a bulwark of liberalism during the period of the Court's rightward swing.

The ascension of Judge Clarence Thomas to the Supreme Court completes the process of transforming the liberal Warren Court into its conservative opposite. It is the Supreme Court for the era of George Bush's New World Order. The Court will no longer have the capability of rendering the kinds of decisions to which African Americans became accustomed during the Warren years. Consequently, most African Americans have viewed this trend in the Supreme Court with consternation.

African Americans have paid particular attention to this most recent appointment since it is occasioned by the retirement of a recognized role model, spokesperson and champion of black interests. In every respect Thurgood Marshall represented the kind of "talented tenth" leadership which has historically emerged out of the African American protest tradition. African Americans rightly believe that the interests of their people can be adequately represented on the High Court only through the presence of at least one black justice. They echo the sentiment of black judge Bruce Wright when he suggested that:

> Black judges who have themselves escaped the gravitational pull of the ghetto, but who still bear the marks of their narrow escape, know the rough tensions of a two-culture existence. There is, therefore, a special insight of compassion which only a black judge can bring to the law.[2]

Black people, however, were not prepared to accept the nomination of just any Black person to the High Court. Implicitly, Thurgood Marshall set the standard against which future Black aspirants to the Supreme Court would be measured by African Americans. He possessed the compassion to which Judge Bruce Wright refers. In addition, he was a first rate legal scholar whose judicial philosophy emerged out of his nurturing within indigenous institutions of the African American community. He was further trained and tested for leadership within the indigenous protest tradition of twentieth century African American history, the Civil Rights Movement. Black people viewed Thurgood Marshall as one of their own, and they felt that he viewed himself as a son accountable to the Black community. They did not require of him that he agree with whatever was the prevailing majority opinion among African Americans as a condition of acceptance. Nevertheless, he was expected to carry himself in the tradition of African American leadership, of Du Bois's "talented tenth"; that is, as a "race man."

Judge Clarence Thomas was not able to meet this standard and therefore he did not command the respect and allegiance of the established Black protest organizations, the established Black political leadership or most African Americans in his quest for a Supreme Court seat. In addition, opposition to Thomas was widespread outside of the Black community among liberal organizations, pro-choice advocates and those concerned with the rights of women, and among those legal scholars who questioned his advocacy of the "natural law" approach to judicial decisions.

Black people recognize that Judge Thomas is no more nor less than a political hack. He has not lived up to the standard of excellence and commitment established by Thurgood Marshall. Thomas has no recognizable reputation as a legal scholar. His legal opinions are notably undistinguished. He is disingenuous, opportunistically refusing to discuss his legal and social philosophies in the nominations process. Moreover, he has a questionable record in the only significant position he held where he could have been of concrete help to Black people, the Chairperson of the EEOC. Judge Thomas rose from humble beginnings and with help from Blacks and Whites achieved an education which should be but is not the birthright of all Black people. He acknowledges that the Civil Rights Movement had a role to play in creating educational and employment opportunities for him and many thousands of Americans of all colors and both genders. Yet his professional behavior and political and social views belie that assertion.[3] As one legal scholar observed, Judge Thomas does not seem to acknowledge the role of race in his own ascension to the Supreme Court.[4] More precisely Judge Thomas does not accord respect to the African American protest tradition which created the conditions for anyone like him to be seriously considered for a position on the Supreme Court. African Americans believe that George Bush nominated Clarence Thomas out of partisan political concerns to camouflage his policy of malignant neglect for the social welfare needs of Black people. Therefore they asserted their own right to oppose Thomas out of consideration for their own partisan political concerns.

Some conservatives who are Black took issue with the African American opposition to Judge Thomas's nomination. They saw it as a particular manifestation of the sins of "political correctness," that African Americans demanded liberal views from Judge Thomas as a condition of their support. In their opinion, the Black community failed to acknowledge the bankruptcy of civil rights liberalism and the appearance of an unhealthy dependency syndrome among the black underclass.[5] Spokespersons like Shelby Steele and Glenn Loury argued that it is counterproductive to blame the plight of the Black underclass on racism and that whites cannot be seen as causing or perpetuating the contemporary plight of Blacks. These neo-conservatives indicted the present leadership for stifling discussion of alternatives to liberalism in the Black community and opposing their right to hold and speak their opinions against the African American orthodoxy. The Black neo-conservatives used the occasion of Judge Thomas's nomination and confirmation to launch an offensive to de-legitimize the prevailing African American leadership.

The Black neo-conservative response to African American opposition to Judge Thomas's nomination was erroneous. Black opposition to Thomas was not a "free speech" issue nor did it reflect a trend to suppress a segment of the Black community's right to hold and express its opinions. Rather it was a recognition that Judge Thomas was not capable of standing as a legitimate spokesperson for the African American community on the Supreme Court. Initially, Judge Thomas seemed neither knowledgeable nor sympathetic to the Black protest tradition. Actually, Judge Thomas had read Malcolm X while in college as well as having participated in demonstrations against racism on campus. His friends do not remember him in his college years as anything like a political conservative. Judge Thomas's early professional career did not move into channels of service to African American civil rights, service or cultural institutions. Rather, Judge Thomas became a protege of the monopoly capitalist class. In cold blooded fashion, Judge Thomas turned his back on the African American liberation struggle, raised the Confederate flag in his first professional office and went over to the service of racist reaction.

Blacks who supported Clarence Thomas often did so applying criteria of achievement which did not factor in specific service to

Black people and Black institutions. Judge Thomas has never had to be accountable to any Black institution as a condition of his existence or his professional or personal advancement. A history of accountability engenders trust in the mass of Black people, not merely the color of one's skin. Judge Thomas and others of this particular variety of Black neo-conservatism articulate an ideology which derives not from indigenous African American sources but from the New Right. Most African Americans recognize that the implementation of this ideological perspective in the social policies of the Reagan-Bush era has created untold misery for Black people. Most Black people recognize that many so-called Black neo-conservatives have not earned the "right to speak" in the great debate on which way toward Black liberation because they have not been able to demonstrate, either a commitment to the welfare of the Black community as a first order of allegiance or concrete accomplishments which they have garnered for Black people through membership and contributions to the African American protest movement. They are not suspect merely because they articulate positions unpopular to African American orthodoxy. They are suspect because they have concrete links to the enemies of Black people through membership or links with far right institutions, foundations and think tanks. Black neo-conservatives accept funds and sponsorship from organizations which have a record of undeservedly stigmatizing the most disadvantaged among Black people. Some like Thomas have very close links to and are proteges of the Reagan-Bush administrations whose policies have constituted a mean spirited attack on the welfare of poor Black people.

Ironically, all of the retrograde trends associated with the nomination of Judge Thomas came together in the brutal persecution of Anita Hill, a fellow Republican neo-conservative, before a nationwide TV audience. This spectacle exposed the far right perception of women and women's rights, the male dominated bipartisan consensus on this issue as demonstrated by the spineless behavior of the Democratic members of the Senate Judiciary Committee, and the opportunism of white middle class feminists who rushed to the defense of Anita Hill but who had no previous profile in issues and struggles related to poor Black women.

Many of the arguments which see rape victims as the cause of their own victimization were also used against Anita Hill. It is a measure of the strength of white ruling class male dominated ideology that many Blacks claimed that Anita Hill somehow invited Clarence Thomas to sexually harass her. The final irony is that Anita Hill herself was abandoned by those to whom she ideologically affiliated. Embedded in the ideological orientation or Republican conservatism and far right reaction is an inability to recognize the kind of victimization to which Anita Hill was exposed as a woman and a Black person.

One has to take note of the continued inroads that ruling class ideology and male supremacist notions have made in the minds of many African Americans. Many Black men and unfortunately not a few Black women showed little sympathy for Anita Hill even though they acknowledge that she probably did not lie. Dr. Barbara Omalade recently pointed out that one aspect of gender discrimination within the Black community is the expectation that the agenda of Black women as women will not be advancement.[6] Too many Black people were unsympathetic to Professor Hill not because she was lying but because she spoke out against Judge Thomas and therefore jeopardized his ability to advance to a position which brings prestige to the race. Dr. Omalade effectively argues that racial advancement has often been defined in the Black community in sexist terms, as Black women are expected to continue to suffer gender discrimination from Black males in silence. This point is reinforced in a recent *Village Voice* article by Lisa Jones, who noted the "invisible" Black women in the Clarence Thomas affair, his sister and mother and the myriad of African American women who struggle on in family and social circumstances like theirs.

The philosophy of the Reagan-Bush administrations premises that:

> Economic growth will flow from the inherent entrepreneurial spirit and enterprise of the American people; that social problems can be largely solved by church, family, and neighborhood; that freedom is our greatest national asset; and that its protection requires, above all, military strength.[7]

It is this philosophy to which Clarence Thomas subscribes. In relationship to African Americans, what have the Reagan and Bush administrations achieved? In both the economic and sociological literature, there is now considerable empirical documentation that African Americans have lost much of the ground gained economically in the immediate aftermath of the Civil Rights Movement. Two social scientists who have authored a recent major article on the economic status of African Americans concluded that:

> There is no question that one of the major, ongoing contributors to the crisis in the black economy is the discrimination blacks still suffer in virtually every aspect of their economic, political and social lives. . . . Labor market discrimination did not "collapse" with the passage of civil rights legislation; instead it underwent a metastasis, living on, one suspects, having received considerable nourishment from the past Reagan administration. . . . One of the most unfortunate effects these exaggerated claims [that labor market discrimination against Blacks has disappeared] have on public perceptions and policies is by buttressing the view that any further government efforts on behalf of blacks is undeserved special treatment and amounts to reverse discrimination against whites. They also give comfort to those who want to believe that the economic problems of blacks are now of their own making, since labor market discrimination has been all but eliminated.[8]

The economic plight of Black people has weakened family ties and neighborhood vitality, undermining the abilities of these institutions to effectively respond to a social crisis in the Black community of unprecedented proportions. The Black Church remains the African American's strongest institution but it does not stand outside of those economic and social forces that plague the community it serves. In an era of government retrenchment in social welfare and growing corporate parsimony in charity, the Black Church has access to few resources independent of those already in the possession of its increasingly impoverished constituency.

The Reaganite focus on freedom as an asset naively sees that freedom in abstraction from the concrete social conditions which prevail in U.S. society today. Freedom is not "free" but is always a function of the level of development of the productive forces and the access the individual has to society's wealth. To recognize that African Americans are in an economic crisis in which they have lost economic ground to whites is also to infer that these same African Americans are less free than they were two decades ago. On the other hand, the deregulation of the Savings and Loan industry created even greater freedom for the rich to destroy in the name of profit institutions central to the wellbeing of ordinary people. Ironically, government will now have to bail out the S and L's and perchance the commercial banks and insurance companies, with a level of public indebtedness which makes the government's expenditures on African American welfare shrink into insignificance.

This ephemeral "freedom" has been undermined by huge defense budgets, impervious to the anticipated peace dividend that was to have resulted from the end of the cold war. In fact under Reagan and Bush, United States militarism has returned to the era of intervention and gunboat diplomacy. The U.S. invasions of Grenada and Panama were widely condemned as violations of international law both in the United Nations and the Organization of American States. These incursions cost the lives of literally thousands of Black people. The brutal destruction of Iraq masked the shabby treatment accorded the all-Black army transportation unit based at Harlem's famed 369th Regiment Armory. These events reflect the mean spirited approach to race relations characteristic of the Reagan-Bush administrations. Although formally opposed to David Duke, George Bush's domestic and international policies have created a climate within which a Nazi and klansman like David Duke gets a respectable hearing from most whites.

Clarence Thomas is a scion of this New World Order. As such he has been an apologist for two Republican administrations even though they have been essentially racist in their orientation and action. That is why President Bush nominated him and the Senate confirmed that nomination. Thomas reflects the mediocrity that has been characteristic of the Reagan-Bush years.

The Black neo-conservatives like Thomas are trying to replace a politics of protest with an apolitical doctrine of self help. They are trying to disguise the true enemy of African Americans, racist United

States monopoly capitalism. But they argue against a straw man. No political tendency in the Black community ever opposed self help or independent economic initiative. That is not the issue. The question is the proper relationship of politics and economics. Black neo-conservatism is mounting an attack against Malcolm's doctrine of "by any means necessary" because they are attempting to inject into an essentially political protest tradition an essentially economist doctrine.

While lifetime membership on the court offers Thomas the possibility of establishing a stance independent of his mentors, his ideological orientation and the nature of his socialization to adulthood suggest that he may well be incapable of the kind of growth and thinking African Americans would require of him as a representative of their interests on the court. Nevertheless, he should be consistently pressured by African Americans and their legitimate organizational representatives and leadership to "do the right thing." The fact that he is Black should not mute the criticism that he rightly deserves whenever he does not address the legitimate interests of Black people.

WILLIAM SALES, Ph.D., is professor of Afro-American Studies at Seton Hall University in New Jersey, and an activist in the Harlem community.

NOTES

1. Marcus D. Pohlmann, *Black Politics in Conservative America* (White Plains, N.Y.: Longman, 1990), p. 108.
2. ibid., p. 127.
3. *The New York Times*, July 9, 1991, p. 19.
4. *The New York Times*, July 14, 1991, p. 1.
5. The following discussion follows summaries of the neo-conservative position and Judge Thomas's biography as presented in *The New York Times*, July 13, p. 1 and July 3, 1991, p. 1 respectively.
6. Presentation by Dr. Barbara Omalade at the *Second Annual Malcolm X Conference: Radical Tradition and a Legacy of Struggle*, held at Borough of Manhattan Community College, December 14, 1991. The session was entitled *Malcolm X* versus *Clarence Thomas: The Crisis of Black Unity in the 1990s.*
7. John L. Palmer and Isabel V. Sawhill, *The Reagan Record: An Assessment of America's Changing Priorities* (Cambridge, Mass.: Ballinger, 1982), p. 2.
8. J. Cotton, "Opening the Gap: The Decline in Black Economic Indicators in the 1980s," *Social Science Quarterly*, vol. 70 (December 1989), p. 818.

Ain't Gonna Let Nobody Turn Me Around

Barbara Smith

Early Friday evening, the day the Hill-Thomas hearings began, a friend called and said that she wasn't sure why she was so fascinated by the proceedings, she could barely tear herself away from the screen. I said it might be because we almost never see more than a few seconds of a real Black woman on television talking about *anything*, let alone the painful realities of racial-sexual politics. Both of us found it compelling simply to watch Anita Hill—bright, sincere, Black, and female—describe what had happened to her hour after hour. Here was someone we recognized, unlike the handful of Black women caricatures who populate the world of television sitcoms. Here was someone we believed.

I can think of no other situation which has commanded the nation's undivided attention that has so clearly illustrated the inextricable links between racism and sexism. It's difficult to conceive how the hearings could be understood from anything other than a Black feminist perspective, a perspective which doesn't require the shortchanging of any aspect of Black women's experience and which doesn't assume that racial oppression is more important than sexual oppression or vice versa. But of course Anita Hill's description of sexual harassment was responded to with anything but a Black feminist consciousness, which explains in part why this drama ended as it did.

As a Black feminist, I've known for nearly two decades that political analyses and strategies that take into account how racism, sexism, homophobia, and class oppression dovetail and interlock, provide the clearest and most revolutionary agendas for change. Unfortunately, the outcome of the Hill-Thomas confrontation seemingly illustrates that my perspective and that of most women of color simply doesn't count, because ultimately it's the white male ruling class that gets to define reality and to call the shots.

I was furious at how Anita Hill was treated by the Senate, by the media, and by the majority of the U.S. populace (if the polls are to be believed), but as a Black feminist, a socialist, and a lesbian I was not particularly disillusioned or surprised. I don't expect justice from either the Republicans or the Democrats, whose duplicity and ineffectualness stood out in bas relief during the hearings. I also don't agree with the mainstream women's movement's singular solution to run as many women for office as possible. It's obvious that no matter who fills the slots in the current system, the system remains intact. Late twentieth-century U.S. capitalism cannot be fixed by adding new faces to the ruling class. Indeed, it was the Bush administration's cynical tactic of replacing a Black progressive Supreme Court justice, Thurgood Marshall, with a Black conservative which set this whole debacle in motion in the first place.

The worst consequence of the Hill-Thomas hearings for me was not the familiar lessons they revealed about the corruption of the power elite, but what they revealed about African Americans' level of consciousness about both sexual and racial politics. It was truly demoralizing to see how the Hill-Thomas confrontation reinforced the perception that any Black woman who raises the issue of sexual oppression in the African American community is somehow a traitor to the race, which translates into being a traitor to Black men. I've always wondered how Black women (who are half the race) living free from fear and degradation and achieving their full human potential would undermine the well-being of the race as a whole.

It has always taken courage for Black and other women of color to speak out about sexism within our communities, but in this instance in which an African American woman did so more publicly and dramatically than at any time in history, who was attacked not only by white right wing misogynists, but by African Americans who felt that she had stepped out of line by accusing a Black man whom white racists had picked for a high public office.

It was not only Black men who succumbed to the Bush administration's calculated effort to divide and conquer the Black community via the nomination of Clarence Thomas. Black women also danced to the White House's tune. Those African American women who disassociated themselves from Anita Hill's revelation of sexual violence, and who gave their support to the man she accused, evidence a tragic degree of self-hatred. Instead of reacting with outrage, some actually had the attitude "I took it [sexual harassment, rape, battering] so why can't you?" Some Black women have so thoroughly internalized the message that Blackness and femaleness are inherently worthless that they think the only way to cancel out these "negatives" is to embrace the political agendas and values of whites and males. The Black feminist movement has worked very hard to offer Black women a more accurate perception of ourselves. Confronting our self-hatred has been a necessary prerequisite to organizing on our own behalf.

Ironically, there are probably a lot of Black people who believe Anita Hill's charges, but who still think it's more important to stand behind a Black man, even when he has utter contempt for the struggles of African Americans, than it is to support a Black woman's right not to be abused. The Monday morning polls that said that most Black Americans still support Thomas tell me how much work Black feminists still have to do to alert our communities to issues of sexual violence and also to get out the message that respecting Black women's freedom does not subtract from the freedom of Black men.

Unfortunately, the attitudes that were brought to the surface by the Hill-Thomas confrontation are not unique. In the last few years misogyny has become a growth industry in the African American community. As in the heyday of the Moynihan Report, Black women are once again viewed as the source of the myriad problems our people face and despite the fact that we experience sexual oppression on top of racism and class oppression, we are portrayed as being in a much better position than endangered Black men. Blaming Black women instead of capitalism, racism, and those who run the system and benefit from it is a political dead end, yet negative views of Black women abound whether in rap, in films, or on the street.

Recent films by Black men ridicule Black women, scapegoat us for all of the race's problems, and portray physical violence against us as perfectly justified. Rap music frequently defines Black women as shrews, with no value other than as sexual commodities. Last summer on the streets of Oakland I saw a Black male youth wearing a tee-shirt with the words "SHUT UP BITCH" written on it in bold letters. Friends to whom I've mentioned it have seen the same tee-shirt in other cities all over the country. I can just imagine Clarence Thomas and his cronies wearing this tee-shirt underneath their three piece suits and judicial robes.

The Hill-Thomas confrontation was incredibly depressing, but it was also politically catalytic. Although the outcome seemingly demonstrated the overarching power of the white-male ruling class, I got a very different message. The powers that be in this country are in serious trouble. This was only the latest example of their efforts to maintain their hold upon the political economy and upon an image of power by using desperate means. And as usually occurs nowadays, whether it be the S and L crisis, the war in the Gulf, or a failing domestic economy, they have to resort to ever more outrageous lies and deceptions just to stay in the same place.

Real political power, however, lies in the hands of the majority of people in this country who do not benefit from this system: people of color, women, lesbians, gays, workers, elders, and the differently abled. Inspired by the multi-issued leadership of radical women of color, oppressed groups are increasingly banding together in grassroots coalitions to fight the system and to bring about fundamental political change. Feminists of color who consistently make the links between issues are building a movement whose politics have the revolutionary potential to free us all. The Hill-Thomas case illustrated why our work is so crucial and it also helped to radicalize more women. One of them, I hope, is Anita Hill.

I see numerous signs that women of color are refusing to be silenced and are on the move. African American Women in Defense of Ourselves is a grassroots network that sprang up only days after the hearings and placed ads in *The New York Times* (November 17, 1991) and in Black newspapers all over the country. Their clear analysis of the hearings signed by 1,603 Black women marks a watershed in Black feminist organizing. Never have so many Black women publicly stated their refusal to pit racial oppression against sexual oppression. The ad has elicited an outpouring of enthusiasm and support and the women who initiated it intend to create an ongoing mechanism through which Black women can organize and speak out.

Revolutionary Sisters of Color is a one-year-old socialist feminist organization which is building a political base both nationally and internationally. Founded at the 1990 "I Am Your Sister" conference which honored Black lesbian feminist poet Audre Lorde, RSOC (P.O. Box 191021, Roxbury, MA, 02119-1021) has broken ground as the first autonomous group embracing all women of color in this country and abroad who are committed to an explicitly socialist and feminist action agenda that confronts the capitalist basis for racial, sexual and homophobic oppression.

I also find it encouraging that there were Black men who were furious about what happened to Anita Hill and who had the integrity to speak out. Many more need to do so.

I hope that white feminists have a better sense of the kinds of challenges women of color face when we make the commitment to confront sexual oppression. If white women really want to support the struggles of women of color, the best thing they can do is to clean the racism out of their own house and they can only accomplish this when they participate in political organizing that directly challenges the multiple oppressions that women of color face, oppressions which undermine their lives as well. Not only would we then have more trustworthy allies, it would also be that much harder to accuse us of being the dupes of unprincipled white women.

Of course as we already knew, it's going to be a long struggle. But in the aftermath of the Hill-Thomas episode my new tee-shirt will display the words of the old freedom song: "AIN'T GONNA LET NOBODY TURN ME AROUND!"

BARBARA SMITH is the editor of Home Girls: A Black Feminist Anthology. *She is a founding member of Revolutionary Sisters of Color and the publisher of Kitchen Table: Women of Color Press. (A shorter version of this article originally appeared in* Ms. Magazine, *January/February 1992, vol. 2, no. 4.)*

The Thomas Spectacle: Power, Impotence, and Melodrama

David Lionel Smith

Americans always prefer a grinning Negro. A grin suggests mindless pleasantry, a surface effect with no other content. Smiles, by contrast, are ambiguous, capable of expressing various feelings. Restrained and fleeting, they suggest unspoken thoughts. Thus, a smiling Negro is a suspicious Negro. He must be hiding something, and besides, subtlety is a troubling characteristic in Negroes. The ostentatious grin of Clarence Thomas virtually guaranteed that he would receive confirmation to the Supreme Court, regardless of his merits. The testimony of Anita Hill against him provided an apparent but not real impediment to his confirmation. Hill never grinned and rarely smiled. Clearly, she had to be dismissed.

Let us consider Thomas and Hill as they were presented to us, not as real people but rather as images within a television spectacle. The Thomas/Hill encounter was the most compellingly dramatic episode of its kind since the Watergate hearings. Watergate was more momentous, but Thomas/Hill more focused and intense. It galvanized our emotions and held our attention day after day. Because the encounter raised such profound issues and so profoundly stirred the public, we believed, mistakenly, that important concerns were being decided. In truth, nothing was being decided except which of George Bush's nominees would desecrate Thurgood Marshall's seat on the Supreme Court. The episode was pure spectacle: a public ritual in the most traditional sense. This is not to deny that the Thomas drama was important, but rather to specify how it was important. Its significance lies not in what it decided but rather in what it reveals.

Several factors made Thomas's confirmation inevitable. Thomas is black, he has committed no known crimes, he has an Ivy League law degree and an up from Southern poverty biography, and George Bush unequivocally supported him. In the present political climate, his obvious mediocrity was no disadvantage. Indeed, it rendered him less threatening and thus more acceptable. Only in sports do we admire excellence, and even there, we want it packaged with grins. Furthermore, the Democrats could gain nothing by defeating Thomas. The President surely would have responded by accusing them of racism, and his next nominee would likely have been a Hispanic or a white woman, to the delight of his Negrophobe constituents. He could claim either one in 1992 as evidence of his commitment to "minorities," while painting the Democrats as betrayers of "African-Americans." Democrats know a checkmate when they see one, and anyone who thinks that principle outweighs self-interest in our politics has been watching too many reruns of "Star Trek: The Next Generation."

Though the hearings began as yet another cynical affront to American intelligence, Anita Hill's testimony transformed them into a riveting participatory ritual. Aroused from our listless somnambulism, we vented our miscellaneous passions of sympathy, outrage, and contempt for the dramatis personae. Articulate, sincere, and composed, Hill represents the consummate professional woman. She is precisely the kind of woman most Americans, male and female, loathe: intelligent, independent, single, successful, a challenger of male authority and prerogative. Hill's testimony provided an opportunity for the expression of countless irrelevant opinions on various subjects, while we ignored the only pertinent issue: the fitness of Clarence Thomas to serve on the Supreme Court.

By their very nature, Hill's charges could not be proved or disproved, and given the realities of party politics, only Thomas's withdrawal could have derailed the confirmation. Bush had no reason to back down; and for Thomas to withdraw would have required courage and integrity. Perhaps he possesses those traits. We shall never know. In any case, the process produced its expected result, thus affirming the President's authority. It also incited the emotional engagement of the public, thus giving the illusion of democratic participation, while at the same time revealing the impotence and confusion of the public as spectators empowered to make noise but not to make change. This is the paradox of television. It appears to offer immediate participation, but in fact it perpetuates alienation. It appears neutral, but in fact it strictly controls what the viewer may perceive. It makes us feel active, despite our utter passivity. The real lesson of these hearings is how thoroughly mass media politics has reduced us to manipulated spectators, incapable of effective intervention or even clear self-awareness.

Some of us lament the confirmation of Thomas, but we should understand that he is no more than a manifestation of the Republicans' power. We cannot eliminate dismal conservatives from the Court except by stripping the power of conservatives to choose the nominees. The Presidential election, not the confirmation process, is where the fundamental choices are made. As for Anita Hill, she had nothing to gain from this process but pain and notoriety. Many passionate spectators mistakenly thought that she came forth to testify against Thomas, when, in fact, the process itself forced her to choose between perjury and public humiliation. Like most sexual harassment victims, she had chosen expedient silence as long as that option remained available. Most such victims never receive the phone call that thrusts their shame before the public. Only this bad luck and her extraordinary grace and strength of character distinguish her from all the rest. Perhaps other women will benefit from her example or from the discussion opened by this episode, but if so, those will be accidental benefits, rather like the emergence of Teflon from the space program. This process was in no way concerned with the welfare of Anita Hill or any other woman. Her moment in the spotlights was merely a sideshow, albeit a sideshow far more compelling than the main event. Ultimately, the purpose and inevitable result was to confirm a Supreme Court Justice of the President's choice. It just happens that we got Clarence Thomas. It might as well have been Daffy Duck.

Though this episode convulsed the black community, it has little bearing on us. After all, it was primarily an exchange between two lily-white enclaves, the White House and the Senate, who cynically used Anita Hill and Clarence Thomas to stage rhetorical gestures toward the public. Obviously, black opportunists like Thomas bring such misery upon themselves and those around them; but ultimately, in the absence of effective political movements, all of us are reduced to pawns. That we have fixated upon Bush's neo-Republican lackey and his former assistant is sad and yet apt.

Walter Benjamin has noted that fascism gives people not power but the opportunity to express themselves. Before we leap to the defense of our "democracy," we might be wise to ask ourselves what political engagement we have left once we eliminate the televised spectacles. The answer may not please us. It was depressing to witness Clarence and Anita, their failings exposed to perverse scrutiny, as routine bureaucratic opportunism betrayed them both. We must sympathize with both of them as victims of extraordinary humiliation. Nonetheless, the real tragedy is not their embarrassment but rather our own invisibility in this cold process. Thomas and Hill did not represent our interests but rather our total subordination in the political machinations of a tiny, calculating elite. In this grand American parade, we trudge closely behind the elephants without so much as a broom in our hands.

DAVID LIONEL SMITH, Ph.D., is professor of English and Afro-American Studies at Williams College.

Hand Me the Rope—I Will Hang Myself: Observations on the Clarence Thomas Hearings

Robert Staples

One can only marvel at the circumstances which brought together a black man and black woman, on national television, to reveal charges that the black male made sexually inappropriate and offensive remarks to the black woman. For three days, a national television audience, composed primarily of Euro-Americans, sat mesmerized by the sexual candor of the two protagonists. After all, it was excellent theater combining the combustible elements of politics, sex and race. This was a nation that could pretend that the most important aspect of a Supreme Court nominee's qualification was his dating style and consumption of pornography when he would be rendering judicial decisions on affirmative action, abortion and workers' rights that could result in the wasting of millions of human lives in the United States. And, it was a nation that suddenly pretended to care about a black woman's sexual sensibilities, after ignoring the most vicious and blatant transgressions against her body for 400 years.

To put into proper historical context the allegations of sexual harassment against Clarence Thomas by Anita Hill, it is necessary to know that black women have not been depicted as sexual objects as much as they have been used as sexual objects. From their first voyage on the slave ships, where they were raped by the ship's crew and male slaves, there has been little respect for or protection of a black woman's sexual integrity. As Crummell observed of the slave woman: "At the age of marriage—always prematurely anticipated under slavery—she was mated as the stock of the plantation were mated, not to be the companion of a loved and chosen husband, but to be the breeder of human cattle for the field or the auction block."[1] Some Southern states had laws that no white man could be convicted of fornication with a black woman or, in the case of rape, there had to be a white witness. Until the 1960s throughout the South, white men were able to sexually use black women in the course of the women's employment, or in the course of their seeking employment.[2] As a consequence, there failed to emerge in the black culture the rigid sexual regulations so prevalent in Euro-American culture.

Given the greater liberality and permissible limits of black sexual attitudes, why was Anita Hill charging Clarence Thomas with the "milder" form of sexual harassment? This situation can only be understood in its political context. Had Clarence Thomas been a Jesse Jackson or Thurgood Marshall, warts and all, who had paid some dues in the black community, it is highly improbable that she would have come forth with sexual harassment charges against them, even if similar cases of sexual harassment had transpired. Her actions were most likely based on who Clarence Thomas was and why he was nominated to the U.S. Supreme Court. One columnist wrote, "President Bush, who has done nothing for African Americans but use them to scare white voters, pushed Thomas in the black community's face. There, he said, fight about that for a while."[3] Another equally observant columnist noted, "The obscenity is nominating a nothing of a right wing Judge, with very little experience, to take the place of a jurist of the stature of Thurgood Marshall. The fact that Thomas is black, staunchly supported by former segregationists Strom Thurmond (Jesse Helms and David Duke), is Bush's big racial joke."[4] The political strategy was that by making the conservative a black man, in an all-white Senate, there were too many Democrats who could not afford to oppose any black nominee, though he be to the right of Genghis Khan.

In effect, Clarence Thomas became the racist nominee by proxy. He had earned the support of Thurmond, Helms, and Duke, not only by his words and deeds against civil rights laws and affirmative action regulations, he was willing to validate the right wing Republican agenda across the board. He was a threat to the rights of women, the elderly and workers too. However, his greatest use will be as a racial symbol. When he signs off on the Court's anti–civil rights rulings it gives them a legitimacy that an all-white judicial ruling does not. It also gives him a leadership role in the black community by virtue of his elite position. A racist in blackface did not deter most black organizations from opposing his nomination although some remained neutral such as the Urban League and a few endorsed him (SCLC). Among the black leaders on record, the most prominent ones supporting him, who were not known as black conservatives, were writer Maya Angelou and Niara Sudarkasa, President of Lincoln University (in Pennsylvania). Most of the other progressive groups, representing 70 percent of the American population, also opposed him. Up to the time of Anita Hill's charges, the polls showed a larger percentage of whites than blacks supported Thomas's nomination.[5]

Enter Anita Hill, whom Jesse Jackson ranks along with Rosa Parks for her contribution to the black struggle.[6] Had Thomas not been a racist by proxy, certain events were unlikely to have occurred. Would her elderly parents and members of her family have accompanied her to the judiciary hearings to deny a black man his seat on the Supreme Court? Would Hill herself have testified against a black man to an all-white male panel? Knowing black women's reluctance to testify against black men in divorce court and child support cases, I think not. Would white feminists have taken on Thomas if they knew it would pit them against black organizations? Despite Thomas's support among the grassroots, he had no visible support among black leaders except the two black women mentioned earlier, and they had to be embarrassed by the sexual allegations. Until Hill's emergence Thomas's confirmation seemed a done deal. She was the black community's last chance to prevent a black man representing racist interests from sitting on the highest court in the land.

The hearings were based on the sexual harassment charges but a great deal more was at stake. And old alliances meant nothing. The former segregationists, the current perpetrators of racial buzzwords (e.g., quotas, welfare, crime) found themselves supporting a black man, with a white wife. Anita Hill's most visible supporters were middle-class white women, who identified with her issue—if not with her. Most non-Southern white Democratic males sided with Hill and Republican white males overwhelmingly supported Thomas. Since people claimed that it was impossible to tell who was telling the truth, they came down on the side of their racial, gender or political preferences and interest—at least the whites did. Blacks were almost divided down the middle over Thomas (about 60 percent supported him after the hearings.) One person's explanation is that the black supporters of Thomas reflect the continuing significance of race in American life.

He said, "There is a lot of diversity of blacks with respect to where they fall in terms of identity. A lot also depends on where they are and what's going on in their lives."[7]

Guessing at the veracity of the protagonists is fruitless and besides the point. Still, I am inclined to believe the things she claims Thomas said and did. Besides the polygraph test she passed, she has no discernible motive for not telling the truth. And everything we know about him leads us to believe he is capable of such deeds. Any man who is capable of selling out his race is certainly capable of a crude sexual approach to women and other women, so stipulated.[8] So, why did the TV viewers believe him over her? In a racist, sexist society, it is relatively easy for white men with power to discredit and to dismiss a black woman. All she had on her side was the truth. He had a better television performance, more aggressive Republican interviewers and the willingness of white male viewers to see the attack on Thomas as an attack on themselves. Ultimately Thomas won because of his racial views, not on the basis of whether he sexually harassed Anita Hill. The Republican members of the Senate were already committed to voting for him. The key southern Democrats, who provided the votes necessary, voted for Thomas out of fear of offending white conservatives in their home state, while knowing they stood to lose few black votes for their decision.[9]

What was so startling was the high percentage of blacks who supported Thomas, as high as 67 percent in some polls.[10] And his black support appears to have come from a cross section of Afro-Americans, albeit few polls gave a detailed breakdown of the black vote. One journalist's conclusion was "For blacks, there was a solid show of support for an embattled black man, even one assailed as an enemy of civil rights, that reinforced the degree to which blacks have behaved as a unified political force."[11] A black minister claims some of Thomas's black support is a result of slavery. Reverend Amos Brown says, "You don't go and tell the white man on a member of the family. That's why many blacks are still sympathetic to him. It clouds the real issue."[12] My own reading of the situation is that many blacks supported Thomas despite his philosophy, not because of it. I also suspect that most Afro-Americans began to pay attention to Thomas's nomination only after the Hill charges were aired on television. Probably many of them, at that point, did not know what

Thomas stood for, why he was nominated, and who his supporters were. Being unaware of what was at stake, their instinctual reaction was to support a black man besieged by whites in a nationally televised hearing.

More politically sophisticated blacks, especially the leadership class, knew why Anita Hill was there and what her role was. Much has been made of the fact that she was a Republican conservative. However, her testimony before the judiciary committee showed she had philosophical differences with Thomas, and one of them was the need for affirmative action. Probably more than most, because she had worked with him, she knew what a danger Thomas was to the black community. By testifying against Thomas, she has probably ruined her political career, particularly if the Republicans continue to control the White House. And blacks who achieve a brief notoriety do not get the multimillion dollar book, movie, TV, commercial endorsement deals as do Euro-Americans. She may be asked to pose nude for *Playboy* magazine. And the greatest injury she may suffer is the knowledge that her own people turned against her and became political bedfellows with their worst enemies.

Sexual harassment was ostensibly the issue on which Clarence Thomas was to be questioned. It is an issue of grave importance, yet so vaguely and subjectively defined as to be one of the most divisive issues of our time. In part, men and women are divided because of their different sexual socialization and values. The courts have said that the more conservative sexual values of women shall be the determination of what constitutes sexual harassment. Consequently, 50 percent of American men say they have been guilty of sexual harassment in the past and 44 percent of American women say they have been subjected to sexual harassment.[13] One has to raise the question of a potential half of each gender group in litigation against half the opposite gender group.

Those implications are even greater for the black community, whose historical sexual liberality mitigates against current definitions of sexual harassment. In his study of black and white cultural styles, Kochman observed that "In black culture it is customary for black men to approach black women in a manner that openly expresses a sexual interest, while in white culture it is equally customary for 'respectable' women to be offended by an approach that presumes sexual interest and availability."[14]

While that is a more accurate observation of lower income, urban and non-southern blacks, it serves to explain Orlando Patterson's claim that "Professor Hill perfectly understood the psycho-cultural context in which Judge Thomas allegedly regaled her with his Rabelaisian humor (possibly as a way of affirming their common origins), which is precisely why she never filed a complaint against him."[15]

While she may have understood the cultural context of his courtship style, that does not mean she liked it when it came from a man who was her supervisor and held absolute authority over her hiring and firing. I suspect she was more bothered by his insistence on a personal relationship she did not desire than some of the sexually oriented conversation. Either way, it meets the prevailing definition of sexual harassment and Thomas knew that when he told her if she revealed his behavior, it would ruin his career. Yet Patterson, himself a black neo-conservative, charges Hill with "lifting a verbal style that carries only minor sanction in one subcultural context and thrown it in the overheated cultural arena of mainstream, neo-Puritan American where it incurs professional extinction."[16] That distinction is probably irrelevant to an upwardly mobile, quasi-Southern, religious woman like Anita Hill.

What are the future consequences of the Thomas hearings for the black community? Poussaint says that it will reinforce negative sexual stereotypes of black men, "it will increase their level of tension and vulnerability around charges of this type and make them tiptoe carefully because they may feel that they will be more likely targets."[17] Certainly, the white dominated media has highlighted black males accused of sexual harassment, rape and violence against women. While most black males are not in a position to harass women sexually, they may need to adjust to changing norms of male/female interaction. Trying to appeal to a woman's mind, instead of concentrating on her body, might be the first step to a more harmonious relationship between the sexes.

ROBERT STAPLES, Ph.D., is professor of Sociology at the University of California, San Francisco. He is one of the leading authorities on black family life and has written or edited nine books on that subject. Among his books are World of Black Singles *(Greenwood Press, 1981) and* The Urban Plantation *(The Black Scholar Press, 1987).*

NOTES

1. Alexander Crummell, quoted in Robert Staples, *The Black Woman in America: Sex, Marriage and the Family* (Chicago: Nelson-Hall, 1973), p. 35.
2. Calvin Hernton, *Sex and Racism in America* (New York: Doubleday, 1965), p. 128.
3. Bill Mandel, "Thomas Stars in America's Nightmare," *San Francisco Examiner*, October 14, 1991, p. A-3.
4. Rob Morse, "The Thomas Clown Affair," *San Francisco Examiner*, October 15, 1991, p. A-3.
5. "How the Poll was Taken," *The New York Times*, October 15, 1991, p. A-12.
6. Teresa Moore, "Jesse Jackson Gives Hill a Spot in History," *San Francisco Chronicle*, October 14, 1991, p. A-2.
7. Dr. Robert T. Carter, quoted in Leno Williams, "Blacks Say the Blood Spilled in the Thomas Case Stains All." *The New York Times*, October 14, 1991, p. A-1.
8. "A Moment of Truth." *Newsweek*, October 2, 1991, p. 323.
9. "Playing White Male Politics." *Newsweek*, op. cit. p. 27.
10. "New Polls Show Most Americans Favoring Thomas," *San Francisco Examiner*, October 14, 1991, p. A-9.
11. Peter Applebome, "Despite Talk of Sexual Harassment, Thomas Hearings Turned on Race Issue," *The New York Times*, October 19, 1991, p. A-7.
12. Reverend Amos Brown quoted in Gregory Lewis, "Strong Feelings Among Blacks in Bay Area," *San Francisco Examiner*, October 15, 1991, p. A-12.
13. Elizabeth Kolbert, "Sexual Harassment at Work is Pervasive, Survey Suggests," *The New York Times*. October 11, 1991, p. A-1.
14. Thomas Kochman, *Black and White Styles in Conflict*, (Chicago: University of Chicago Press, 1981), p. 75.
15. Orlando Patterson, "Race, Gender and Liberal Fallacies," *The New York Times*, October 20, 1991, p. A-15.
16. Ibid.
17. Alvin Poussaint, quoted in Williams, loc. cit.

Don't Write Off Thomas

Niara Sudarkasa

When the venerable historian John Hope Franklin speaks, I listen. When the NAACP takes a position, I usually agree. But not this time. I am not a conservative; but I, and many others like myself, are not convinced by the NAACP's and Franklin's view that Clarence Thomas's appointment to the Supreme Court would be detrimental to African-Americans. We see a greater risk in casting our lot with an unknown nominee whose record might be far worse.

What concerns me here is that Thomas might be opposed because "he does not speak for the majority of blacks." I am reminded of the time when some NAACP chapters led a campaign against the film *The Color Purple* because it did not "represent the black experience."

The movie was picketed at the box office, blasted in the press and passed over at the Academy Awards largely because some blacks decided this was not an acceptable portrayal of black life. Who were the losers? Alice Walker, who wrote the probing and compelling novel; the movie's outstanding cast, led by Danny Glover, Whoopi Goldberg, Oprah Winfrey and Margaret Avery; and Steven Spielberg, the film's producer-director.

But the biggest loser was the black community, because we denied our own the chance to be honored for their artistic achievements. And why? Because we could not allow a fictional work to be judged as fiction. We had to judge it as a historical treatise.

I wonder what would have happened to *The Godfather* if the Italian-American Civil Rights League, which had objected to some aspects of the film, had opposed its nomination for the Academy Awards because it "did not represent the Italian experience." *The Godfather,* with its three Oscars, is remembered as one of the great movies of recent decades. *The Color Purple,* with eleven nominations and no Oscars, has been pushed aside as a "controversial film."

The reaction to Clarence Thomas's nomination to the Supreme Court is analogous to what happened to *The Color Purple.* Of course, the two situations differ in substance, importance and impact. But in both cases, there is a presumption that there can be only one valid interpretation of the African-American experience. More than anyone, we should understand the potential value of a minority point of view.

Thomas may not speak for the majority of black people, but his voice, his views and his experiences are those of many African-Americans who "came up the hard way." This is not to say that everyone who grew up poor ends up a conservative. I was born in Florida to a teenage mother who picked beans, scrubbed floors and worked in a dry cleaner most of her life to send her four children to college. My grandparents' home, where we grew up, had no plumbing or electricity until the house was literally moved into town from the countryside. Before that, we used an outhouse, drew water from a well, bathed in a tin tub in the kitchen and lit the house with kerosene lamps. That was not uncommon in the rural South in the forties and fifties.

I do not share Thomas's political views, but they are the views of many people who grew up with me. Liberals need to listen and learn from conservatives, just as conservatives can learn from liberals.

Many complex experiences made Clarence Thomas a conservative. His way may not be our way, but that does not mean it cannot produce results. His ambivalence toward affirmative action, for example, could lead to a search for an alternative approach to providing equality for African-Americans and others.

Those of us who went to college in the fifties, before there was affirmative action, welcomed this federal initiative of the sixties as a means of helping deserving black students get into college. But we did not experience affirmative action from the point of view of the student—as Clarence Thomas and his peers did. I recall many of my students at The University of Michigan resenting the notion that they did not make it to college on their own merit. They suffered slurs and innuendoes from faculty as well as other students. Although they appreciated the opportunity for an education, they felt there had to be a better way of opening the door. I would guess that today many of them have mixed feelings, if not wholly negative feelings, about affirmative action.

Those of us in my generation who entered college without affirmative action should stop and think about how much pride we take in that fact that "we made it on our own" (although we too had help), and how much that affects our own sense of self-worth.

As African-Americans, we have always fought for access to America's institutions of power and influence. We demanded representation regardless of who was sitting at the table. When we raised our clenched fists in the cry for "black power," I don't think we meant power for black liberals only. Thomas should not be barred from serving on the Supreme Court because he does not speak for the liberal black leadership or what we think is the majority of black people. The fact that he speaks for many blacks, including a growing number of black leaders, should carry some weight.

We know that with or without Thomas, this conservative Supreme Court will no longer interpret civil and individual rights as the court has done over the last three and a half decades. Thomas's background and experience could make him a moderating influence and a distinctive voice among his conservative peers. His appointment would represent a personal triumph over poverty and racial discrimination. Many in our community would see his success as a victory for us. As African-Americans, we can live with Clarence Thomas on the Supreme Court. Let this not be a repeat of the *The Color Purple* episode, where we all end up losers.

Testimony

Niara Sudarkasa

Presented to the Senate Judiciary Committee Hearing on the Nomination of Judge Clarence Thomas to the Supreme Court September 17, 1991, Washington, D.C.

Mr. Chairman, Members of this Distinguished Committee of the U.S. Senate, Judge Thomas, Ladies and Gentlemen: My name is Niara Sudarkasa, and I am pleased to have the opportunity to appear before you today in my capacity as an individual scholar who supports the nomination of Judge Clarence Thomas for the U.S. Supreme Court.

In my view, Judge Thomas has the education and experience, as well as the intelligence, integrity and high ideals necessary to serve on the nation's highest court. But much of the debate over Judge Thomas's nomination has focused on his ideology rather than his qualifications.

Many who oppose Judge Thomas and some who support him seem to assume that his ideology can be pigeonholed and used to predict the positions he will take on cases that will come before the Supreme Court.

From what I have read by and about Judge Thomas and from what I have heard this week, I believe that he is an open-minded and independent thinker, not only with rigid pre-packaged views. He has been characterized as insensitive to the concerns of African Americans. But I think that because of his independence, and his keen sense of justice and fairness, Judge Thomas looks at all sides of issues when others might be content to examine only one.

For example, Judge Thomas wrestles with the issue of individual rights when considering group entitlements because he knows that fairness and justice are not one-sided concepts. He struggles with the points of conflict between the principle of equality and the practice of affirmative action. But because of his open-mindedness, I believe Judge Thomas can be persuaded to see that in order to redress past discrimination, the concept of equity, rather than strict equality, must

be applied. The Constitution speaks of equality, b
justice, and under various circumstances, the princip
be applied to insure that justice and fairness will be

Leaders must be understood in the context of t
spawn them. This is as true of Judge Thomas as it is o
African Americans, we have been fortunate in having a lo
leaders who, in retrospect, seem right for their times. These le
not always have the same ideology or agree on strategies, but
agreed that the goal was to secure freedom and justice for our pe
and thereby help to insure freedom and justice for all. Who can
that we are not the better off for having had the benefit of the
separate and distinct voices?

In the 1850s, there was Frederick Douglass fighting for the abolition of slavery, for voting rights for free blacks and for what we now call integration. But there was also Martin Delaney, an equally strong abolitionist, who sought freedom and prosperity through economic and political linkages with Africa, including the establishment of African American settlements on the African continent. The legacy of Douglass is the fight for equal rights; that of Delaney, the struggle for economic empowerment for blacks in America and in Africa.

At the turn of the twentieth century, there was Booker T. Washington speaking for vocational education for the masses, self-reliance in the black community, and co-existence with segregation. At the same time, W. E. B. Du Bois advocated a liberal education for the "talented tenth," economic interdependence and an end to segregation. Booker T. Washington left us Tuskegee University, a healthy respect for black colleges and other black institutions, and an appreciation of the value of self-help. On the other hand, Du Bois's legacy is that of the NAACP, admonition to "the talented tenth" to reach back to help the less fortunate, and the demand that America help those upon whose backs this country was built.

The decade of the 1920s saw the rise and fall of Marcus Garvey, the nationalist, who preached "Africa for Africans" and "Back to Africa" while envisioning a black-owned economic network spanning the Atlantic. In the same decade, A. Philip Randolph, the socialist, emerged as the leading spokesman for jobs and justice here in America. Both Randolph and Garvey were geniuses at mass mobilization

mass organization. Garvey left us a legacy of racial pride, and a mmitment to cooperation among Africans "at home and abroad." . Phillip Randolph, who disavowed socialism and became one of the ountry's greatest labor leaders, taught us the effectiveness of direct action and planted the seeds for fair employment practices legislation.

In more recent times, there were Martin Luther King and Malcolm X, both committed to justice, equality and empowerment, but while Dr. King chose the path of integration, Malcolm chose separation, at least until near the end of his life. Both of them were taken from us in a flash, leaving a legacy of work unfinished and a job to be done.

Different leaders have "brought us thus far on our way." Different voices have spearheaded the crusade for freedom and justice.

Now, in the judicial arena itself, we see the great legacy of Thurgood Marshall, the brilliant architect of legal desegregation and the undefeated champion of civil rights. Thurgood Marshall—a man of and for his times.

Today, as we anticipate the appointment of Clarence Thomas to the Supreme Court, we see in him a leader with a different voice, for a different time. We who have put our faith and confidence in him now come forth to challenge him to choose well the means by which he will carry on the quest for justice and equality. We ask him to be ever mindful of the words of Robert Hayden, the celebrated African American poet, who suggested that we must not rest until "it is finally ours, this freedom, this liberty . . . needful to man as air, useable as earth. . . ."

Senators, Judge Thomas: As a nation, we must not rest until Dr. King's dream becomes a reality. We cannot rest until we as a people have overcome.

NIARA SUDARKASA, Ph.D., is an anthropologist and the president of Lincoln University, Lincoln University, Pa. This article was reprinted from Newsweek, *August 19, 1991.*

Clarence Thomas and the Question of Fitness

Clyde Taylor

Whether or not Clarence Thomas said those things to Anita Hill was a spectacular but subordinate question beside that of his fitness for the Supreme Court. Sexual harassment is an important issue, but Clarence Thomas was unfit to take a seat on the Supreme Court before the question of his wolf-hounding Anita Hill came up. Feminists were right to demand that the issue be taken seriously. But black Americans were misled if they believed that this was the stake on which Thomas's confirmation should hinge.

It was disheartening that this no-win issue was the focus of most of the public outrage the hearings provoked among blacks. The greater danger to most black women is not sexual harassment *on the job.* The hearings raised an unneeded tension among some African Americans over which gender's sexual identity was more badly damaged in that trial by klieg lights. We were being asked to choose between two venomous myths. One, that black women, not being angels, must be whores, with no feelings about their sexuality that men need respect (a variation on the Dred Scott decision), subject to rage and recrimination at the hand that nature had dealt them and likely to create revenge fantasies of sexual harassment. Or two, that black men of whatever training were oversexed, animalistic rapists unable to control their impulses or check their urge to make gross, sexual advances toward women the first chance they got. Even in private one heard little recognition that the whole drama pitted black participants as surrogates in a scenario staged, controlled and orchestrated by political forces with varying agendas in mind.

The hearings formed a watershed in reasonable perspectives on the position of black Americans in the present scheme of things. They brutally rubbed in our faces the fact that right wing Republicanism has, over two decades, effectively constructed a species of black professional who owe their greatest loyalty to the retrogressive mentors who spoonfeed them offices and ideological scripts. Among the wonders yet to be understood is the aspect of Justice Bork's judicial philosophy that compelled the support of Anita Hill. The parade of highly educated black witnesses revived in nightmarish form memories of ancestral warnings about the danger of getting schooling while being separated from one's common sense.

The hearings sent the black activist community yet another painful message. The majority support for Thomas *after* the hearing from blacks as well as whites, women as well as men, indicated the success right wing Republican hegemony had achieved in driving a wedge between civil rights and women's organizations and their constituencies. The volatility of mass black political consciousness is suggested by the overwhelming support for Jesse Jackson's Presidential campaigns, followed by this contradictory support for Clarence Thomas. The source of this vertigo lies in the pain and hurt and disorientation endured by African Americans under repeated blows from several political and economic directions over the span of a generation. The trauma goes so deep as to brighten the frail hope that the arrival of *any* black leadership to levels of national prominence must be taken as a symbolic victory, a welcomed psychic Band-aid. The exposure of our condition post Thomas-Hill makes me lament the absence of a Jackson campaign in the 1992 election race, as limited and symbolic as that effort might be in the face of our new difficulties.

The political situation of African Americans in this new light is akin to the sudden shifts in political fortunes taking place in many nations around the world in the nineties, and may have related causes. I would offer one modest step toward recovery, recognizing its inadequacy to satisfy the greater need, and the difficulty of its achievement in any case. The struggle toward empowerment by African Americans might well be served if we concentrated on advancing the leadership of African American women in all our institutions, movements and campaigns for justice. It is an irony that black women are now almost routinely selected to lead national organizations such as Planned Parenthood and the National Education Association but are never seriously considered for leadership of civil rights and activist groups.

Promoting black women's leadership might open several advantage points. For one, it would speak to the issue of gender raised by the Thomas hearings and to our dilemmas in national politics at the same time. The hearings brought to the surface backward notions of male supremacy among African Americans. Within the many ill-conceived ideas of black manhood in circulation, some displayed by Lawyer Doggett, and others by the persistent chauvinism of our civil rights leadership, lies the key to many of the horrendous evils rending our social fabric. What percentage of NAACP *branch* presidents have been women, I wonder?

The time may have arrived to put aside spite politics and self-defeating separatisms in favor of addressing these and other issues on the political, not merely gender level of thought and action. As Jesse Jackson enlarged the national agenda of the black human rights struggle by including the needs of disenfranchised and disempowered white Americans, so the campaigns for leadership from African American women must widen to include a complete political agenda.

It's hard to imagine a population better ready to step up to a new level of leadership than black women in the United States. Their capacities for leadership have been proven in the past, often against surly resistance. By the count of some sociologists, black women make up 60 percent of the black professional class. While black women may already be doing more than their share in preserving and advancing black social development, the acceleration of their roles in formal leadership positions might assist their self-empowerment and that of black society at the same time. But the most important reason for reaching toward leadership from African American women is the need to enlist at a higher level of participation an under-used source of social and political reconstructive energy. Black America badly needs new political energy, new ideas, goals and agendas, new personalities, a new political posture—and black women as leaders in a new campaign for social justice is one likely place, out of a narrow field, we might find them.

The broad support of Clarence Thomas over Anita Hill in the polls taken after the hearings may shadow a slide toward a traditional acceptance of male domination, male privilege, the reflex presumption that the man is right. The trial of William Kennedy Smith for rape in Florida unearthed similar attitudes, even among women ("What was she doing going there at 3 A.M. in the first place?"). The demotion of women from possible equal social and political status is part of a return to pre–World War II perspectives that prepped the rise of fascism.

The coming African American struggle to defend the gains in human rights made since the 1960s against assaults from many directions could be fought with greater spirit and resonance by a society that counted among its strengths the capacity to take precedence in the world by enlisting and benefiting from the progressive leadership of women. No one who seriously believes African American society is in crisis will look on this as a radical proposal.

CLYDE TAYLOR *is professor of English and Afro-American Studies at Tufts University. Widely acclaimed as a film critic, Taylor's work has appeared in numerous journals and magazines.*

Becoming the Third Wave

Rebecca Walker

I am not one of the people who sat transfixed before the television, watching the Senate hearings. I had classes to go to, papers to write, and frankly, the whole thing was too painful. A black man grilled by a panel of white men about his sexual deviance. A black woman claiming harassment and being discredited by other women. . . . I could not bring myself to watch that sensationalized assault of the human spirit.

To me, the hearings were not about determining whether or not Clarence Thomas did in fact harass Anita Hill. They were about checking and redefining the extent of women's credibility and power.

Can a woman's experience undermine a man's career? Can a woman's voice, a woman's sense of self-worth and injustice, challenge a structure predicated upon the subjugation of our gender? Anita Hill's testimony threatened to do that and more. If Thomas had not been confirmed, every man in the United States would be at risk. For how many senators never told a sexist joke? How many men have not used their protected male privilege to thwart in some way the influence or ideas of a woman colleague, friend, or relative?

For those whose sense of power is so obviously connected to the health and vigor of the penis, it would have been a metaphoric castration. Of course this is too great a threat.

While some may laud the whole spectacle for the consciousness it raised around sexual harassment, its very real outcome is more informative. He was promoted. She was repudiated. Men were assured of the inviolability of their penis/power. Women were admonished to keep their experiences to themselves.

The backlash against U.S. women is real. As the misconception of equality between the sexes becomes more ubiquitous, so does the attempt to restrict the boundaries of women's personal and political power. Thomas's confirmation, the ultimate rally of support for the male paradigm of harassment, sends a clear message to women: "Shut up! Even if you speak, we will not listen."

I will not be silenced.

I acknowledge the fact that we live under siege. I intend to fight back. I have uncovered and unleashed more repressed anger than I thought possible. For the umpteenth time in my twenty-two years, I have been radicalized, politicized, shaken awake. I have come to voice again, and this time my voice is not conciliatory.

The night after Thomas's confirmation I ask the man I am intimate with what he thinks of the whole mess. His concern is primarily with Thomas's propensity to demolish civil rights and opportunities for people of color. I launch into a tirade. "When will progressive black men prioritize my rights and well-being? When will they stop talking so damn much about 'the race' as if it revolved exclusively around them?" He tells me I wear my emotions on my sleeve. I scream "I need to know, are you with me or are you going to help them try to destroy me?"

A week later I am on a train to New York. A beautiful mother and daughter, both wearing green outfits, sit across the aisle from me. The little girl has tightly plaited braids. Her brown skin is glowing and smooth, her eyes bright as she chatters happily while looking out the window. Two men get on the train and sit directly behind me, shaking my seat as they thud into place. I bury myself in *The Sound and the Fury.* Loudly they begin to talk about women. "Man, I fucked that bitch all night and then I never called her again." "Man, there's lots of girlies over there, you know that ho, live over there by Tyrone? Well, I snatched that shit up."

The mother moves closer to her now quiet daughter. Looking at her small back I can see that she is listening to the men. I am thinking of how I can transform the situation, of all the people in the car whose silence makes us complicit.

Another large man gets on the train. After exchanging loud greetings with the two men, he sits next to me. He tells them he is going to Philadelphia to visit his wife and child. I am suckered into thinking that he is different. Then, "Man, there's a ton of females in Philly, just waitin' for you to give 'em some." I turn my head and allow the fire in my eyes to burn into him. He takes up two seats and has hands with huge swollen knuckles. I imagine the gold rings on his fingers slamming into my face. He senses something. "What's your name, sweetheart?" The other men lean forward over the seat.

A torrent explodes: "I ain't your sweetheart, I ain't your bitch, I ain't your baby. How dare you have the nerve to sit up here and talk about women that way, and then try to speak to me." The woman/mother chimes in to the beat with claps of sisterhood. The men are momentarily stunned. Then the comeback: "Aw, bitch, don't play that woman shit over here 'cause that's bullshit." He slaps the back of one hand against the palm of the other. I refuse to back down. Words fly.

My instinct kicks in, telling me to get out. "Since I see you all are not going to move, I will." I move to the first car. I am so angry that thoughts of murder, of physically retaliating against them, of separatism, engulf me. I am almost out of body, just shy of being pure force. I am sick of the way women are negated, violated, devalued, ignored. I am livid, unrelenting in my anger at those who invade my space, who wish to take away my rights, who refuse to hear my voice. As the days pass, I push myself to figure out what it means to be a part of the Third Wave of feminism. I begin to realize that I owe it to myself, to my little sister on the train, to all of the daughters yet to be born, to push beyond my rage and articulate an agenda. After battling with ideas of separatism and militancy, I connect with my own feelings of powerlessness. I realize that I must undergo a transformation if I am truly committed to women's empowerment. My involvement must reach beyond my own voice in discussion, beyond voting, beyond reading feminist theory. My anger and awareness must translate into tangible action.

I am ready to decide, as my mother decided before me, to devote much of my energy to the history, health, and healing of women. Each of my choices will have to hold to my feminist standard of justice.

To be a feminist is to integrate an ideology of equality and female empowerment into the very fiber of my life. It is to search for personal clarity in the midst of systemic destruction, to join in sisterhood with women when often we are divided, to understand power structures with the intention of challenging them.

While this may sound simple, it is exactly the kind of stand that many of my peers are unwilling to take. So I write this as a plea to all women, especially the women of my generation. Let Thomas's confirmation serve to remind you, as it did me, that the fight is far from over. Let this dismissal of a woman's experience move you to anger. Turn that outrage into political power. Do not vote for them unless they work for us. Do not have sex with them, do not break bread with them, do not nurture them if they don't prioritize our freedom to control our bodies and our lives.

I am not a postfeminism feminist. I am the Third Wave.

REBECCA WALKER is a student at Yale and a contributing editor to Ms. *magazine.*

Clarence Thomas and the Meaning of Blackness

Ronald W. Walters

Among the issues surfaced by the Clarence Thomas affair, the most serious one for the future, in my opinion, was the confusion it engendered—and perhaps uncovered—about the meaning of Blackness. The confusion ran the gamut: there were those—the majority as demonstrated by the polls up to late October—Black people who were not familiar with Clarence Thomas but who supported him essentially because he was a Black man vying for the highest Court in the land. Thomas's support among Blacks increased from 57 percent to the mid-70s (depending upon the poll one uses) after the Anita Hill charges against him, suggesting that he appeared to those supporters to be a Black man in trouble, which is perennially a cause for high levels of Black mobilization. Then, there were those who knew his record and supported him in any case because they believed that a Black person of whatever ideological persuasion should be on the Court to represent the Black community and that this was our "one shot" to accomplish this. Next, there were those who likewise understood his record and supported him because he was Black, hoping that all of the spirits of his Black ancestors would rain down upon him and that this divine revelation would cause him to "do the right thing" by Blacks with respect to issues facing the Supreme Court. This group, sprinkled with some of our most celebrated artists and intellectuals, relied upon their belief that Thomas would not ultimately forget nor forsake his cultural heritage. Finally, the last group did not support him, even though he was Black, because of his undistinguished record as a lawyer among other Black lawyers and because of his proven hostility to mechanisms for racial redress which promoted group progress such as affirmative action. As such, his past positions on issues critical to Blacks ran contrary to the objectives of Black political struggle.

It should be clear that in most of the groups above, Thomas's race was the most significant factor which motivated their support. To render this support, many were prepared to overlook his professional status, his past activities, his philosophical advariance with the mainstream of the Black community and other pertinent factors. In fact, the way it seemed to work is that there was an inverse relationship between those with knowledge of Thomas's record and their support of his candidacy to be an Associate Justice. Thus, while we understand the political support of those who had little information about Thomas as normal, what are we to say about those who deliberately subordinated the role of information, containing evidence of his principles and activities, and elevated race as the principle variable?

It is most disturbing that the answer to this question by some has been that the civil rights movement and other movements for social change were launched in order to make possible the elevation of *any* Black person, espousing *any*—presumably credible—set of values. Some of these individuals who were ready to make the easy trade of the value of our tradition of struggle for Thomas's color were hired guns, Black neoconservative intellectuals, professionals, and Republican party hacks; others were young people, genuinely confused about the meaning of our struggle, or those who have figured out what unlimited personal gains may be achieved by getting in the short line of Black conservative Republicanism. The most surprising were those who had been participants in the struggle for social change at some level and who, one thought, thoroughly understood its long-term significance, but who came to support Thomas, perhaps out of the frustrations of the Democratic party's current indifference to Blacks or their calculation of what would be possible in a conservative age.

This last group is important because their defection has raised the question whether or not the lessons of our past struggle are relevant to current challenges. I believe that they are. Affirmative action is not a revolutionary tool of social change. Indeed, I would argue that its history is one which has engendered far more economic empowerment to white families than Black. One fact: In the 1991 issue of *The State of Black America*, published annually by the National Urban League, Dr. David Swinton points out that in the fifteen years between 1972 and 1987, the labor force participation rate of Blacks increased 2 percent and that of white women increased 14 percent. (Table 13, p. 52.) Presumably white women marry white men and create white families, such that they have been assisted far more than Black families to stable positions in the workforce. Again, the mechanism has been discrimination: although Title VII of the Civil Rights Act of 1964 established certain employers have discriminated within the protected class of "minorities" in a way which has skewed the benefit of even this mild corrective strategy to the benefit of their own group. Nevertheless, given the fact that affirmative action may clearly be shown to have benefited Blacks *less than* whites, do we throw it out altogether or cease to fight to maintain it?

As Director of the Office of Civil Rights in the Department of Education, Clarence Thomas failed to enforce the Adams Decision of 1970 that was an affirmative action principle for Black colleges and universities which mandated states to compensate them for past inequities in funding. Also, as Director of the EEOC, he failed to enforce group remedies of employment discrimination in favor of *documentable cases of individual discrimination*. This method of racial correcting the evils of past discrimination not only takes 1,000 years to affect social change, but runs counter to the political direction established by the movement of Black people in the 1960s. So, the current question is do we still need a group remedy and is the standard followed by Thomas acceptable: many of those currently alarmed by the stagnation in Black labor force participation, the massive private and public job layoffs beginning in 1989 and the alarming deterioration in the status of Black males, would all answer yes and no.

If the answers given to the above questions are at all valued, then one measure of our evaluating of Thomas on the evidence should have been that he has not, and would not, represent the interest of Black people fairly, according to the standard of fairness they themselves established through struggle. By what right, then, does he or others change that standard of group progress and the mechanism to attain it and easily posit others?

To be Black is to stand in a tradition of culture and to be identified with that culture insofar as one shares its basic tenets with others of that group. To that extent, Thomas shares a "Blackness" with others of his race. But to be Black also has a political content which emerges out of the way in which the group has sought to pursue its interest, often in conflict with other groups in society. Perhaps the issue here is what it means to be *politically Black* and to share the goals and methods of the

Black mainstream both in their historical importance and in their current application to problems facing the Black community. I would argue that Clarence Thomas and his supporters are not politically Black and have no right, either based on history nor, just as important, on any demonstrated validity of their ideas, to change the political standard.

It should be understood that besides the fact that the political standards and methods which accrue to us from the past were established through the inordinate sacrifice of our people, they may also be validated by the frequency with which they have arisen as answers in each age of our existence in America. Thus, Black moderate integrationists have always felt that there needed to be correctives to slavery and to the social subordination of racial discrimination and they fought as hard for land, education and civil rights in the eighteenth and nineteenth centuries as they did for "Fair employment practices" since the 1930s. Black nationalists have consistently raised the question of emigration to Africa and, for those who stayed, self-determination and reparations to the Black community as a group corrective.

What has varied over time is the shifts in the historical circumstances within which they were pursued, including the mood of whites toward them. We now appear—as we have been before—to be in a period where the mood of whites is against some of the corrective strategies established by Blacks in the past. And the choice that has been made by some Blacks is to accommodate to that mood by rejecting the corrective strategy rather than to fight for it. If this accommodationist trend continues to grow, there may well have arrived in the Black community a generation that is willing to adjust to the comparatively mild discomfort of the majority to these mild correctives, rather than to place a higher value upon the profound and continuing discomfort of their own people. At present that constituency is small, but the Thomas saga gives us a disturbing look at the direction in which they would take the Black community and the kind of people willing to give these untested strategies sanction.

RONALD WALTERS, Ph.D., is professor and chairman of the Department of Political Science at Howard University. He has published many articles on race and politics in America and abroad in The Black Scholar *and other journals, and is author of several books among which is the award winning* Black Presidential Politics in America.

The Three Ring Circus of Clarence Thomas: Race, Class and Gender

Karen P. Wanza

America, land of opportunity, land of Horatio Alger and of "pulling oneself up by one's bootstraps." A land where one in five people was unemployed during some time in 1991. A land where a sharecropper's grandson can go on to become a Supreme Court justice. How do we keep the American Dream credible? Update the dream, integrate it, let black bleed through with white and surely *no one*, not even the sharecropper's granddaughter, can vouch for the necessity of welfare programs and Affirmative Action. This is the lie we lived throughout the latter months of 1991. This is the lie that pits Black against White, Black against Black and female against male. The Clarence Thomas hearings had a little something for everyone, no matter how little that something had to do with the issue, which was the question of Thomas's qualifications and credibility. This article will review Thomas's record and personal history, explore the maladroitness of the Senate in their unwavering deference to the president and finally consider, where does Anita Hill really fit in these proceedings?

It is obvious after reviewing Thomas's record that he would never have been a nominee if he were a liberal Black (much less a conservative White). His record is lacklustre, even for one who "made it on his own." Certainly there are other Blacks on the federal bench who were not brought up in the lap of luxury. The difference between Thomas and such Black judges as Constance Baker Motley (Southern District, NY), Amalya Kearse (2nd Cir. Ct. of Appeals) and Lawrence Pierce (2nd Cir. Ct. of Appeals and Reagan appointee) is that their qualifications speak for themselves and there is no need to resort to the double edged sword of being "po and Black in Amerika." These judges also went to top law schools but unlike Thomas, their academic records put them near or at the top of their classes. Yet they support Affirmative Action programs and they have not been quoted as believing that everyone in this country has the same chance to succeed through hard work.

It is almost laughable that the one judge who appears to have benefited most from Affirmative Action now repudiates it. Thomas was born in Pin Point, Georgia, went to segregated parochial schools in Savannah, then on to a seminary (which he reportedly left due to a racial slur he heard) and then after attending Holy Cross College, his academic career culminated in his entrance to Yale Law School. Although Thomas contended that he got into Yale on his own merit, Yale had another story, and in *The New York Times,* July 14, 1991, the admissions office at Yale said that indeed the school had set up separate criteria for minorities, but that these students had to be deemed qualified enough to get through the program. In today's competition for professional degrees, even an openly Affirmative Action program would be unlikely to set such slim standards. Yet race is such a slippery slope question that two weeks later in *The New York Times*, Dean Calabresi of Yale was quoted as supporting Thomas's nomination, despite his uneven qualifications.

Race was an issue to be danced around, skirted or misconstrued, but it was never properly dealt with. Conservatives grabbed onto the idea of conjoining the image of Thomas bringing himself up from his sharecropper roots with images of Jim Crow and lynchings. Of course this all came to a head when after the testimony of Anita Hill, Thomas spate out his now-famous allegation that the Senate was guilty of a "high-tech lynching." For their part, the liberal Democrats were afraid to assert much at all, countenancing the lack of credibility that Thomas was adding to each day as he would deny ever making comments which would link his view of natural law with being anti-abortion. Blacks and other "interest groups" were afraid to oppose Thomas at first because they didn't want to be viewed as intolerant and restrictive in their views. Only women's groups such as the National Abortion Rights Action League and the National Organization for Women had the status of oppressed and the apparent consensus of their memberships to voice opposition. The slow action of the NAACP and other groups supposedly influenced liberal groups. In the meantime, Thomas was engaged in doublespeak throughout the hearings. He said natural law is not a "political ideology," yet he was quoted as favorably citing Lew Lehrman's article which states that the fetus has an inalienable right to life, and concluding that this is a good example of the use of natural law.

What is natural law? According to Black's Law Dictionary it is a term used "to denote a system of rules and principles for the guidance of human conduct, which independently of the enacted law. . . might be discovered by the rational intelligence of man and *would be found to grow out of and conform to his nature*." In other words, natural law is that ideological "higher law" that reigns supreme over mere statutes, precedents and rules. It is hardly necessary to say that this view of law has not been popular for at least seventy years, when the natural law was used to keep "inferiors," such as women and Blacks, in their place.

One group whose view was not given enough weight was the American Bar Association. The standing committee on Federal Judiciary evaluates the qualifications for nominees to the federal bench. Their ratings range from "well qualified" (reserved for those who meet the highest standard of integrity, professional competence and judicial temperament) to "qualified" (not unqualified but not the best available nominees) and finally "not qualified." Clarence Thomas received two "not qualified" votes and the rest were "qualified." The committee is quick to point out that its ratings are based upon an investigation based on interviews with those who have worked with the nominee and the process is confidential. While it is true that under the Constitution, one does not even have to be a lawyer to sit on the Supreme Court, surely questions of character and credibility should apply equally to everyone.

Thomas's outbursts during his testimony to the Senate were apparently a sign of his true temperament. As the *Wall Street Journal* noted on August 6, 1990, Thomas "scolded antitrust prosecutors as if they were ill-prepared law students" [in a major antitrust case], and in the *Almanac to the Federal Judiciary* Thomas's one noteworthy ruling while on the D.C. circuit bench was an antitrust issue involving the merger of two major competing companies. In permitting this merger, Thomas's curious rationale was that such a merger would not be anticompetitive since it was "unrealistic" to expect more than a small number of competitors in a specialized market. Needless to say, lawyers who have argued before him did not have much positive to say about his work on the D.C. bench. In fact, a further hint to the Senate as to Thomas's qualifications was the fact he received a unanimous "qualified" rating from the ABA when he was appointed to the D.C. Circuit Court. Surely the charges Anita Hill levelled against him were not the only blemish on his record. His argument for natural law threatens the concept of a balance of power between the President, Congress and the Judiciary; since he supports the idea that natural law deems that abortion is wrong, he would be very likely to refrain from upholding such a right or any other that would conflict with the natural law as he sees it. In addition, Thomas's general inexperience and lackluster career would have been fuel for the Senate to reject him. *Why didn't they?*

According to Article II Section II of the U.S. Constitution, the President shall nominate and, with the "advice and consent" of the Senate, shall appoint justices to the Supreme Court. Although it rose to the occasion during the Bork hearings in 1987, the Senate seemed to forget what the phrase "advice and consent" meant in terms of its duty to evaluate Thomas. The Senate was unduly deferential to the Executive Branch. In a short interview this writer conducted with Sylvia A. Law, Professor of Constitutional Law at New York University, she indicated that it was shocking that the Senate ever voted to affirm the Thomas nomination *before* Anita Hill's allegations. Further, she said, "the Senate should take a strong role where the president has politicized the position to be appointed." The Senate's deferential role led to snowballing events. An attack commercial on television supporting Thomas savaged senators Ted Kennedy, Joseph Biden and Alan Cranston. There was Senator Danforth's culling of a list of friends and relatives whom the media could contact for rave reviews and, finally, there were the Thomas tactics, playing the Pin Point, Georgia, card very heavily and beating around the bush when it came to giving answers on natural law or abortion. Much of the Senate's stalling appears to have been because Senators wanted to measure the temperature of their constituents. As earlier alluded, interest groups were slow to respond due to internal dissension and fear of appearing reactionary. The Senate seemed to be waiting in the wings for some indication of their positions. The "race card" was played by George Bush splendidly; while disassociating the Pin Point experience from the need for government directives that would help a person rise to the top, he at the same time wove together the lynch mob, the "self made" man and the rise from poverty. This spectrum of race and class seen through Bush's demented prism made race just a badge that went along with poverty and whose importance disappeared as one rose along the financial ladder. It is too bad that the Senate was duped by such an explanation. If race were of minor importance in comparison to class, would there be a need for a Congressional Black Caucus? The fear of being called a racist is sometimes more destructive than the risk of sounding like one. The Senate's timidity played right into Bush's hand.

As if Thomas's poor record were not enough evidence in itself to refuse to affirm Thomas's nomination, and as if the fact that there were several more qualified judges to consider (some even conservative) were not enough—Anita Hill's testimony should have at the very least damaged his credibility.

Hill's downfall was that she was Black, female and unruffled. Had she displayed the temperament of the angry, self-righteous Thomas, the hearings would have lasted approximately three hours at best. But Anita Hill was seemingly unflappable under fire and so the Republicans had to work harder to discredit her. An array of phone bills with a few calls to Thomas in years became a major weapon. Anita Hill became another character of the southern past which the Republicans were so fond of conjuring, but her character they scarcely acknowledged other than through the actions—the Black woman as castrating bitch, as available sex object for *any* male, but especially White males. The witness became the accused and Thomas's fate as the newest Supreme Court justice was sealed.

Meanwhile, the nation was in shock, divided over whether Thomas's nomination should be affirmed. By September 10, 1991, *The New York Times* reported, two-thirds of those polled said they were still undecided about Thomas. The Senate, having little guidance from their constituents, chose to go the safe way and affirm Thomas. There is little question that the result would have been different if Hill had been a White woman, since the race card would have been a disadvantage to Thomas in such a case. And perhaps we would have heard more about the actual issue of sexual harassment and less of Thomas's tantrums if the proceedings were closed. But in reality Anita Hill unwittingly occupied one ring in Bush's three ring circus (the other two rings being occupied by the Senate and Thomas) and much of the content of her testimony has become a national joke (e.g., Long Dong Silver jokes and comments about hairs in a soda can). There are many who ask why Anita chose to wait so long to speak. A better question is, How did she risk so much so calmly in the first place?

In summary, it is clear that Bush will feel even more empowered to push through any nominations requiring the advice and consent of the Senate in the future and, from what this historical episode tells us, the Senate will become increasingly a rubber stamp process. Issues that are as entangled as race, class and gender deserve more informed, intelligent discussion than what we witnessed during Thomas's nomination hearings.

KAREN P. WANZA is completing her doctorate in Sociology at the University of Michigan, Ann Arbor. She holds a J.D. from New York University. Her legal practice in New York included international law (at the United Nations) and litigation in firms and for the city of New York. Her current work is mainly in legal sociology and social stratification.

The Anti-Black Agenda

Sarah E. Wright

Professor Anita F. Hill wouldn't go to bed with Judge Clarence Thomas. As she tells it, she suffered unavoidably through two years (1981–1983) of his surreptitious and vulgar advances while she was under his supervision. Her humiliation persisted through her work under him in the Department of Education and later at the Equal Employment Opportunity Commission. But, she was prepared to ignore whatever psychological anguish she had to endure in the privacy of his office or on the infrequent occasions when they met to dine because she was driven by her belief that Thomas could be useful in helping her up the career ladder. She was even silent, except for mild protest only to him, through her hospitalization with acute stomach distress which she now relates as being caused by Thomas's behavior towards her. He was, after all, as his secretary pointed out, a rising star to whom everyone was eager to hitch their careers.

However, one can hardly refrain from noting, painful though it may be, that Anita F. Hill was more than willing to hug up to (figuratively speaking) the worst oppressors of her people. Perhaps this was naivete, but President Ronald Reagan had deliberately weakened the Department of Education and all but reversed the effective voice of the EEOC with the willing help of Clarence Thomas. Perhaps naivete might appear too generous, but it is the best we can allow. And for that she was amply rewarded. She even supported that man with the notoriously racist and sexist reputation, Judge Robert Bork, in his unsuccessful campaign for a seat on the Supreme Court. It is therefore difficult to accept her as a symbol for the women's liberation movement, as some feminist organizations have done. The fact is that Ms. Hill had no problem when she finally left the EEOC in working for a right-wing Christian fundamentalist organization, Oral Roberts University, which promotes views on women that could hardly be more backward. How dismaying is it, then, to observe the enthusiastic reception given to her by the National Coalition of 100 Black Women. She has served those who have made a career out of betraying both the African American people and women, thus making her, for black women, the most peculiar sort of friend.

We must now say that too much attention has been focused on Anita F. Hill in the Clarence Thomas nomination process. That this is so testifies to the success of the Establishment, the politicians and the media, in framing the issues according to their liking and in getting us to become diverted from the "real deal." For behind the Thomas nomination is the conspiracy of the right wing to create a layer of black collaborationists, to ensure their placement in positions of influence and to guarantee that they are conspicuously rewarded for their collaboration and are then to constitute the new "role models" for aspiring black people. The Thomas nomination, and now confirmation, sends out the message to African Americans that if they are willing to preach the virtues of rugged individualism and to oppose the aspirations of the masses of black people, their careers will be well greased.

This strategy, unfortunately, is already bearing fruit. The spineless position taken by a number of established civil rights organizations and community leaders shows that the rewards for playing ball with the Right are increasingly tempting to sections of the black middle class. Even people in our community of humble circumstances have become disoriented, which is a clear reflection of the vacuum that exists in progressive black political leadership.

This drive to recruit traitors to our people is increasingly urgent, for the powers-that-be know that our condition is rapidly deteriorating and will continue to deteriorate. They know that their global economic plans do not include us. And they know that we pose an ever-growing political threat to their control.

The use of the Thomas nomination as part of an *anti-black agenda* received little or no attention in the confirmation process. And for this the *Democrats* are responsible. They made a show of opposition to Thomas in order to placate their liberal constituencies. But at the same time they feared stirring up the racism issue. So, they hit upon the idea of fighting the Thomas nomination on safer grounds. They concentrated their fire on Thomas's position regarding *Roe* v. *Wade*. They calculated that white feminists were the strongest liberal pressure group. But Thomas would not make a target of himself, would not take a stand, to the Democrats' frustration. Then came the committee leak. Anita F. Hill was brought forward.

There can be no question of the truthfulness of her statements. But it also seems that what chiefly motivated her past reticence and her long-standing friendly relationship with Thomas were none of the motives ascribed to her by the feminists, valid as they may be in other situations. Can it be that attorney Anita F. Hill simply was driven by ambition? That she had no intention of burning any bridges to advancement? We are indeed troubled.

The Senate committee took up the issue of sexual harassment only to trivialize it. The dozen or so Senators reacted in mock horror to the relatively mild story told by Anita Hill, as if they did not know that most African American women can tell personal stories of much greater abuse, on and off the job, at the hands of those who exercise some degree of power over their lives—a husband, a boss, a foreman, landlord, merchant, policeman—she is fair game to everyone. And to resist sexual victimization has consequences far greater than throwing sand on a previously well-lubricated career path. For most black women, resistance to sexual abuse can pose a serious threat to their economic survival and that of their children.

What can we say about the spectacle of a dozen or so rich white guardians of morality feigning indignation at charges of sexual abuse, they who have raised corruption to the status of an art form in both their public and private lives? And what is that moral standard which they champion? It is one which condones the existence of millions of the homeless, which tolerates a system of health care that works only for the affluent, where the great majority don't know which to fear more, serious illness or the cost of getting well, which looks on with indifference in the face of growing unemployment and insecurity, which ignores a pattern of routine police brutality, which refuses, under the cover of words like "quota," to deal with the genocidal conditions in our community.

It is these men—pretending to sit in judgment on the credibility of Clarence Thomas and Anita Hill, they and all their political cronies, venal servitors of the rich, men who are legislating our degradation—it is they who should be in the dock, and some day will be—unless there is a god of the hypocrites!

After all is said and done, we have but to look in horror at the David Duke endorsement, enthusiastic and unqualified, of the now Supreme Court Justice Clarence Thomas and respond most vigorously to the challenge.

SARAH E. WRIGHT has published a number of poems, book reviews, and articles in various journals. Her first novel, This Child's Gonna Live, *an African-American epic, was hailed as a "masterpiece" by* The New York Times. *Ms. Wright's latest book,* A. Phillip Randolph, Integration In The Workplace, *was selected by New York Public Libraries as one of the* Best Books *for young adults for 1991. She was elected President of Pen and Brush in 1992.*

LEGAL OPINIONS AND POSITION PAPERS OF ORGANIZATIONS

These selections present critiques of Clarence Thomas's nomination from a juridical point of view; also published are the position papers of major black civil rights organizations.

IN OPPOSITION TO CLARENCE THOMAS: WHERE WE MUST STAND AND WHY

Congressional Black Caucus Foundation September 1991

INTRODUCTORY SUMMARY*

Every black Member of Congress, except one, a recently elected Republican member, opposes the nomination of Clarence Thomas to the Supreme Court. Members of the Congressional Black Caucus watched the nominee probably more carefully than most Members of either the House or Senate during his nine years of service in the Reagan and Bush Administrations—through over fifty hearings and ten GAO reports—almost all highly critical of his administration of the law. This unusual degree of oversight was made necessary by Thomas's constant refusal to carry out the laws enacted by Congress.

The decision to oppose the Thomas nomination has come because the evidence is so overwhelming that the nomination of Clarence Thomas would be universally opposed in our community if he were white and had his present record. He would almost certainly work against the Court's eventual return to its essential role in closing America's color gap using the tools painfully carved out during the last quarter of a century. Moreover, if the Senate fails us, the Supreme

*The Foundation is especially appreciative of the energetic efforts of Professor Christopher Edley, Jr., for coordinating the work that resulted in this essay.

Court will be far less legitimate and less effective as an independent third branch of government.

THE RECORD

If some African Americans have seemed to approve of this nomination, it must also be noted that few members of the public have studied Clarence Thomas's record. Instead, they have been introduced for the first time to a black man and told his life story in order to deflect attention from his record. And, they have heard and seen a public relations campaign waged by the President with all the resources of the Administration at his disposal.

Those who have carefully reviewed Judge Thomas's record, however, including the overwhelming majority of those whose principal mission for decades has been the advancement of the opportunity agenda, have strongly opposed this nomination. These include those who stand in the broad, bi-partisan mainstream of civil rights commitment. Among them are those to whom we are most indebted for the progress African Americans have achieved during this century—to name but a few, they include the NAACP, the most broadly based grassroots African American organization in this country; the NAACP Legal Defense Fund, Justice Thurgood Marshall's own original home base; and the eight million strong National Baptist Convention, the largest black organization in the world. These and other black organizations who are chiefly responsible for the advancement of civil rights and other black concerns have a long list of reasons for opposing Thomas.

THE PRESIDENT'S GESTURE TO BLACK AMERICA

From the time President George Bush presented Clarence Thomas as his choice to replace Justice Thurgood Marshall as Associate Justice of the Supreme Court, the Administration has succeeded in keeping the public's attention focused on "the story" of Judge Thomas's dramatic rise from Pin Point, Georgia, to Kennebunkport, Maine. This emphasis was made necessary by the risks of focusing where the emphasis belongs and has always been when others have been nominated—on the record of professional performance.

African Americans must be concerned with the problems of a race and of a nation. The Supreme Court has been for the last fifty years a fount of principle for the nation and a chalice of hope for African Americans. With this nomination, however, the President mocks those hopes. The nomination must be opposed:

- The nomination is a manipulation of the symbols of opportunity and racial progress rather than a promise of the substance of those ideas.
- The nomination is a calculated effort to continue the Court's dramatic swing to the far right, including both its retreat on civil rights principles and its increasing indifference to Congressional will.
- And the nomination is being used to divert attention from the Administrations' race-baiting intransigence on civil rights legislation.

By his personal campaign against the Civil Rights Act of 1991, the President has embarrassed many members of his own party. He now offers, as political salve, the Thomas diversion: a man who has the right color skin, but a zealot's hostility towards the legal rights and public policies crucial to genuine opportunity.

THREE STORIES IN THE THOMAS NOMINATION

The story of Clarence Thomas's determination must be respected in part because it is not unlike that of many black elected officials in America, many leaders of civic organizations dedicated to black advancement, and many blacks who have not enjoyed the fruits of such success. But the true import of this nomination involves three other stories as well.

The Nomination Is a False Gesture: The Supreme Court serves the nation best when it includes a range of voices and experiences. With Justice Marshall's departure it is imperative that a black join the Court—but not any black, at any cost. Judge Thomas's race is and should be a consideration, but the way in which President Bush made the choice belies his stated opposition to quotas, no matter what the President says to the contrary.

Hostility to Civil Right Policies: He has attacked Supreme Court decisions upholding voluntary affirmative action plans against constitutional and statutory challenges. He has attacked Supreme Court support for set-asides in licensing and contracting, and praised conservative Court decisions that bipartisan majorities in both houses of Congress are at this moment fighting to overturn in the face of veto threats. Invoking an incoherent "natural law" philosophy far outside mainstream constitutional theory, he has criticized basic Court decisions establishing privacy rights, and implied that the federal constitution should be interpreted to require criminal penalties for abortion—a position held by no current member of the Court.

Intolerant Independence: Thomas publicly excoriates family members to make political points. He displayed a Confederate flag (or a state flag readily mistaken for it) in his office to establish his "independence." He said that the civil rights groups had done "nothing right" and all civil right leaders ever do is "bitch, bitch, bitch, moan and whine."

Lawless Administrator: While Assistant Secretary for Civil Rights in the Department of Education, he acknowledged and attempted to justify flagrant and intentional violations of a court order compelling timely processing of discrimination complaints. He failed to enforce the laws aggressively, even those involving individual victims of discrimination. While Chairman of the Equal Employment Opportunity Commission (EEOC), Thomas consistently advocated narrow interpretations of civil rights precents, including *repeated refusals to seek the full range of remedies against discrimination* provided by statute and by case law. Thomas was so reluctant to bring class and systemic cases that Congress had to earmark EEOC funds specifically for that type of enforcement and threaten to cut the budget of the chair and members of the EEOC. Because of his mismanagement and indifference, *more than 13,000 age discrimination claims* missed the statutory deadline for action and had to be revived by a special statute.

Hostility to Congress: Thomas complained bitterly about the intrusiveness of a request by the Senate Labor and Human Resources Committee for semi-annual reports on the EEOC's accomplishments, as though congressional oversight was a threat to governance. When Rep. Augustus Hawkins (D-CA), Chairman of the House Committee on Education and Labor, requested that the Government Accounting Office audit the EEOC's investigative staff, Thomas complained that the resulting report was "a hatchet job" and referred to GAO as

Congress's "lap dog" that would "come with anything it wants."

A Rigidly Harsh Ideology: The Supreme Court overturned the conviction and jail sentence of a black grandmother who refused to evict her ten-year-old grandson. The Court invalidated the zoning ordinance's definition of "single family" household, recognizing the importance of extended families. But Clarence Thomas, raised by his grandparents, joined in a Reagan Administration attack on the Court's interference with the right of the city to "define 'family' in the traditional way."

The President did not seek a superbly qualified African American whose interpretation of personal experience and of national history are consistent with the goal of diversity on the Court. There are several such jurists and scholars of this party available. Instead, a black seat is claimed for someone whose authenticity as symbol, example and champion is based only on proclamation by Mr. Bush and the embrace of the President's more conservative supporters. *But Clarence Thomas is not our champion. He is the President's gesture.*

The Administration and Judge Thomas's supporters tell us that Thomas is our only chance for a black person on the Supreme Court. But it is simply untrue that the choice is between Clarence Thomas and a white conservative for the next forty years. The choice is between Clarence Thomas now, and some other African American later. Judge Thomas may be the only black who can meet Mr. Bush's litmus tests—someone who both is extreme in his conservatism and represents *Mr. Bush's* interpretation of the African American experience and of our aspirations. But other presidents in the years ahead will easily find more balanced and qualified blacks to serve on the Court. We must be patient, still.

The gesture of this nomination comes from a president who has vetoed civil rights legislation. The President's reward for Clarence Thomas is not justice for all, and the example of Thomas's personal success is no excuse for his demonstrated hostility toward legal tools that are vital to opportunity for others.

The Nominee's Legal Vision Is at Odds with the Black Experience: The second story is about the giants who preceded Clarence Thomas: the departing Supreme Court Justice whom Thomas would replace, and the civil rights protesters and advocates who invested their lives and dreams so that Thomas could pursue his. These African Americans were giants because they courageously dedicated their lives in service to a cause larger than themselves: the advancement of their people and other Americans.

African Americans want their experiences, aspirations and perspectives represented on the Court, and like many Americans we believe the Court and our country are better with that representation. The diversity within the African American community makes it difficult for any single individual to be truly representative, of course, and the Supreme Court is not meant to function like a political or representative body. But inherent in the diversity the court should have is legitimacy. Clarence Thomas does not bring the legitimacy necessary to inspire the confidence of the African American community.

Our hopes and Judge Thomas's promises are not enough for this vitally important seat on the Court, where his actions could affect generations of Americans—especially African Americans—so profoundly. Looking at the evidence, Clarence Thomas's recent pronouncements and judgments hold no promise of the hoped-for evolution, no matter how sympathetically one studies them. Indeed, since 1986, Thomas has gone in exactly the opposite direction—even more toward the far right. The Senate must understand its duty to make this decision based on evidence and performance, not on promises and hope.

The Court's Future Role Is at Issue: A third and final story concerns the Supreme Court itself and its role in the struggle of African Americans. Our challenge to his nomination is prompted by more than deep disagreement with Judge Thomas's idiosyncratic legal and social views, or the fact that the Thomas nomination will confuse George Bush's political opponents on the race question. We also must oppose the nomination because it is part of a continuing strategy to undermine the Supreme Court's constitutional role as the third branch of government and protector of minority rights which might otherwise be sacrificed to political expediency.

For fifty years, blacks have relied upon the Court to step in and protect their constitutional rights from the tyranny of legalized racism and hostile majority rule. The Reagan-Bush Supreme Court seems determined to assume minimal responsibility for continuing this historical role. And today's Court seems determined to erode precedents and undermine civil rights statutes. All this is clear from the court's civil rights decisions, which Congress now labors to reverse by statute over the unyielding opposition of Mr. Bush.

The Administration knows well that Thomas will be a ready participant in this trend or the President would not have nominated him. Some of the nominee's supporters suggest, however, that Thomas has fooled the President and that he will eventually become a civil rights stalwart on the Court. But who is fooling whom? Has Thomas fooled the conservative civil rights revisionists for whom he labored tirelessly for nine years, and whose agenda he zealously promoted in articles and speeches? Or has the President fooled those who support Thomas, believing that he cannot truly be the person his record reveals? The President is wrong on many things, but he is no fool. We believe Mr. Bush knows his nominee, as we certainly do.

The Thomas nomination, in view of the nominee's performance and writings, threatens to weaken further the judiciary as part of our system of checks and balances, as guardian of individual rights, and as defender of minority viewpoints and aspirations. We urge the Senate to fulfill its constitutional duty and refuse to consent to this constitutional vision.

OUR CONCLUSION

We do not believe or expect that ideological conformity or strategic agreement is required of African Americans in public service. What is required in our fight for justice, however, is a demonstrated commitment to the broad bipartisan approaches that have been adopted by Republicans and Democrats and blacks, whites, Hispanics and many others alike.

Judge Thomas has written a record which shows his firm and consistent opposition to many of those things our people need most urgently. *We will not stretch our consciences to support any nominee of whatever color who has created such a record.*

I. Although the nation is best served by a Supreme Court whose justices represent diverse experiences and perspectives, this

goal does not justify confirmation of a nominee whose record is fundamentally at odds with the very purpose of integrating the Court.

The Quota Nominee: Most observers acknowledge that it is valuable to have a black on the Supreme Court, and that the elevation of Thurgood Marshall was momentous. This reflects the facts: Given today's multicultural society, and the distinct role of blacks in American history, no national institution can long claim legitimacy without some "minority" representation.

Judge Thomas's race allegedly had nothing to do with the choice. "The fact that he is black—a minority—has nothing to do with this," the President said. "He is the best qualified." No one believes that. Indeed, two members of the American Bar Association Committee found him unqualified. No Supreme Court nominee since 1969 has been confirmed with even one vote of "unqualified" from the ABA.

Whatever the President's motives, we have never supported rigid quotas, and certainly cannot do so in the context of a Supreme Court nomination. President Bush, however, nominated Clarence Thomas precisely because Thomas is black. Perhaps he believed this would enhance the legitimacy of the Court as a quasi-representative institution; more likely, he believed that minority voters and civil rights supporters would be reluctant to criticize the nominee. We are confident, too, that the President expects that by nominating a black he will diffuse the political and moral objections to his unrelenting opposition to pending civil rights legislation.

Thomas Is Not the Last Chance: If this particular black is not confirmed, we are told, Bush's next choice may not be black, and will likely be even less sympathetic than Thomas to the statutes and legal doctrines upon which racial justice depend. However, this nomination does not present a choice between Clarence Thomas and a white conservative. The choice is between a reactionary black now, or a more representative black later. In the past when nominees have been rejected, the sitting President most often has submitted a more balanced candidate. If Clarence Thomas is not confirmed, some other African American will in fact be nominated, perhaps not by George Bush, but at some point in the not too distant future.

It is not unlikely that the next President, given a vacancy, will appoint an African American who is more representative of the views of those who have traditionally, historically, and illegally been left out of the American dream, and more respectful of the traditions and precedents of the nation's civil rights struggle.

As political realists, we believe that if confirmed, Clarence Thomas will occupy the only available black seat on the Court. His presence on the court could choke off any opportunity for any other African American, perhaps beyond the year 2030.

II. Clarence Thomas's record is not mixed; the threat to essential legal principles is clear. Evasive testimony during confirmation cannot provide adequate assurances of wise decision making in the future.

Let us examine the record in more detail.

Those who hope Clarence Thomas will return to his roots ignore the nominee's own writings and speeches, which reflect instead the pull of his more recent adult experiences and choices. As a *New York Times* story put it, those favoring confirmation cite the "symbolic importance of having a black person, particularly one of humble origins, on the High Court, however uncongenial or heretical his views"; they speak "hopefully of him as an enigma whose humaneness has so far been hidden, whose views are not yet fully framed, who could surprise sponsors and detractors alike."[1]

We acknowledge that past justices of the Supreme Court have on occasion surprised their supporters and detractors. But the abstract and theoretical possibility that Judge Thomas will be someone other than the person he has been until now is not enough to make us willingly play Russian roulette with our civil rights and liberties.

A Rigidly Harsh Ideology: Our familiarity with this record does not make us optimistic about an "evolving" Justice Thomas. For example, in December 1986, Thomas joined in a White House Working Group on the Family, which, in its report, condemned several Supreme Court cases, including *Moore* v. *City of East Cleveland.*[2] In that 1977 decision, the Court overturned the jail sentence of a sixty-three-year-old black grandmother who had been prosecuted and jailed for refusing to evict the ten-year-old grandson for whom she had cared since infancy, when his mother had died. The city insisted that because he shared his grandmother's home with a cousin, the ten-year-old was an "illegal occupant." The presence of two grandchildren in her household violated a local ordinance, which limited the definition of a family to exclude "cousins."

According to the White House Task Force in which Clarence Thomas participated, and whose report he signed, the Court was wrong to interfere with Ms. Moore's eviction and jailing by declaring the eviction unconstitutional. The Report accused the Supreme Court of improperly intruding on the right of the municipality "to define 'family' in a traditional way" in zoning for single-family occupance.[3] The Report denounces the *Moore* case as among the Supreme Court decisions that question whether "the family . . . retains any constitutional standing."[4]

We find it ironic that Clarence Thomas, raised by his grandparents, having experienced the critical role of the extended family in African American life, could join in such a report. Thomas is, after all, the man whose personal life experiences are supposed to qualify him to bring the empathy one would expect of a black person appointed to the Court. As Justice Brennan noted in his concurring opinion in the case, the local ordinance would have a devastating impact on many black families.[5] Thomas's lack of sympathy for the circumstances of Ms. Moore should give pause to those who claim that once on the Court, Thomas will remember his roots. The memory may be there, but what has he made of it? If Mr. Thomas felt no jurisprudential conversion as he studied the case of a jailed black grandmother, there is little reason to expect a conversion now.

Hostility to Civil Rights Policies: Thomas has denounced Supreme Court decisions interpreting the Voting Rights Act because the Court failed to look "at the right to vote as an individual right," instead protecting the right "when the individual's racial or ethnic group has sufficient clout."[6] It is troubling enough that he holds such a mistaken view of civil rights policy and social reality; it is even more discouraging that he seems indifferent to the hard-won bipartisan consensus, which led to reenactment of the Voting Rights Act, in part to repair damage done by overly restrictive Supreme Court decisions.

Although Thomas benefited from an affirmative action program at Yale Law School, government loans to support his education, and government employment to support his family, he would now deny the benefits of these same policies to others. He has attacked affirmative action as counterproductive and inconsistent with "truly equal opportunity."[7] He has attacked Supreme Court decisions upholding voluntary affirmative action plans against constitutional and statutory challenges.[8] He has attacked Supreme Court decisions upholding set-asides,[9] and praised regressive Court decisions which bipartisan majorities in both chambers of Congress are at this moment fighting to overturn in the face of veto threats.[10]

We have every reason to expect more of the same from Judge Thomas in the future, and we must oppose giving him the High Court as a platform from which to work his will. As Julius Chambers, current chief counsel of the NAACP Legal Defense Fund, has said, Thomas "demonstrates intemperate disdain for affirmative efforts by the government to assist those who have been victimized because of their group status."[11] The same conclusion was reached by the convention of the largest African American religious group, who, in voting to oppose this nomination, accused President Bush of "packing the bench with ideologues who would rather blame the victims of society than give them the tools that give access to the fruits of our democracy."[12]

Intolerant Independence: Thomas publicly denigrates family members to make political points.[13] He displayed a Confederate flag (or a state flag readily mistaken for it) in his office to establish his "independence" even as a state employee in the Attorney General's Office of a former border state.[14] He says for example that the civil rights groups have done "nothing right" and all civil rights leaders ever do is "bitch, bitch, bitch, moan and whine."[15] Thomas has condemned, in his words:

- "a civil rights community wallowing in self-delusion and pulling the public in with it."[16]
- "civil rights groups who are adept at the art of generating self-perpetuating social ills."[17]
- "the civil rights community['s] . . . tendency to sensationalize . . . intentionally distort and misinform . . . [and] to exploit issues rather than solve problems."[18]
- "the consistently leftist thinking of the civil rights and black leadership."[19]

• "the many blunders and follies that have occurred in the theory and practice of civil rights."[20]

Lawless Administrator: Although he may characterize the criticism as whining, the record is clear: *Mr. Thomas was lawless* when he was chairman of the EEOC and Assistant Secretary for Civil Rights in the Department of Education.[21] He did not aggressively enforce the laws, even those involving individual victims of discrimination.[22] During his tenure at the EEOC, more than 13,000 age discrimination claims missed the statutory deadline.[23] In 1985, in one of many heated clashes with Congress, over forty members wrote to Thomas expressing "their grave concern" over EEOC's failure to pursue class action cases.[24] In sworn testimony in a federal contempt of court hearing, Clarence Thomas, then head of the Office of Civil Rights, made the following admissions:[25]

> Q.) And aren't you in effect—But you're going ahead and violating those time frames. Isn't that true? You're violating them in compliance reviews on all occasions, practically, and you're violating them on complaints most of the time, or half the time. Isn't that true?
>
> A.) That's right.
>
> Q.) So aren't you, in effect, substituting your judgment as to what the policy should be for what the court order requires? The court order requires you to comply with this ninety-day period. Isn't that true?
>
> A.) That's right . . .
>
> Q.) And meanwhile, you are violating a court order rather grievously, aren't you?
>
> A.) Yes.

Mr. Thomas was reportedly unembarrassed.

The Role of Government and the Separation of Powers: If the Court needs balance, by which we mean an outsider's perspective, Thomas does not provide it. Nor does Thomas seem to share our understanding that it is critical to have forceful judicial action to protect vulnerable members of minority groups from the possibility of "majority tyranny." And the record is equally devoid of any appreciation for the role of Congress in the separation of powers scheme. Thomas's views in this sense are no different from those of other members of the far right. The Thomas nomination is absolutely consistent with an ultra conservative agenda of minimal government, dominated by the executive branch.

The constitutional role of the judiciary is to provide a check against the power of both the executive and the legislative branches; it also ensures that no majority faction will invade the rights of the minority. This means that the separation of powers in general, and judicial protection of minority rights as well as minority viewpoints in particular, are critical characteristics of our constitutional vision.

Thomas emphatically endorses Bush's vision of minimal government when it comes to protecting the rights of minorities and women. For example, Clarence Thomas claims that the problem of civil rights "is not pervasive racism," since racism is declining.[26] The problem is civil rights remedies.[27] Judge Thomas "has somehow come to the conclusion that the most important civil rights problem in America today is reverse discrimination."[28]

According to Judge Thomas, the judicial branch, the branch to which African Americans have looked for protection of their constitutional rights over the last fifty years, has too much power,[29] power which is consistently abused by "run amok judges."[30] In criticizing the judicial role, Thomas specifically aligns himself with Robert Bork on the far right, applauding "extremis[m] on behalf of the *modesty* of the judiciary."[31]

Thomas criticizes several key Supreme Court decisions upholding the authority of Congress under the Constitution to remedy the effects of past discrimination. In speeches, Judge Thomas specifically attacks Congress's oversight authority, expressing contempt for the legislative process. Thomas complained bitterly about the alleged intrusiveness of a request by the Senate Labor and Human Resources Committee for semi-annual reports on the EEOC's accomplishments, as though Congressional oversight was a threat to governance.[32] When Rep. Augustus Hawkins (D-CA), Chairman of the House Committee on Education and Labor, requested that the Government Accounting Office audit the EEOC's investigative staff, Thomas complained that the resulting report was "a hatchet job" and referred to GAO as

Congress's "lap dog" that would "come up with anything it wants."[33] In decrying Congress's role in overseeing the federal bureaucracy, Thomas claims "Congress . . . is out of control."[34]

Moreover, for Judge Thomas it seems the executive cannot have too much power, even when it exercises that power to defy Congress. In a recent case in which the Supreme Court acted to uphold a federal statute authorizing selection of a special Independent Counsel to investigate suspected criminal activity by members of the federal executive branch,[35] Thomas thought this was "the most important case" since *Brown* v. *Board of Education*, and that it was wrongly decided. According to Thomas, Justice Scalia's lone dissent, arguing that Congress had absolutely no authority to establish a mechanism for special prosecutors, no matter how serious a crime may have been committed by executive branch officials, was "remarkable." On the other hand, Justice Rehnquist, who wrote the majority opinion, "failed not only conservatives but all Americans" when he upheld the independent counsel law.[36]

Given Judge Thomas's record of executive service and his own statements of his constitutional philosophy, we can only conclude that he would continue to tilt the Court and the country in the wrong direction: toward unabashed executive power, modest judicial power, and sharply attenuated Congressional power, *especially when the issue involves remedying past discrimination or affirming the role of minorities and women in the marketplace of work, politics or ideas.* Thomas's judicial philosophy acquiesces in the destruction of a critical check in our constitutional system of checks and balances. The Senate should exercise its advice and consent role[37] to reject this nomination and to reaffirm the Supreme Court's critical contribution in protecting minority rights and monitoring the executive branch.

Natural Law & Civil Liberties: Finally, one of the more provocative of Judge Thomas's views is his belief in natural law, meaning the existence of fixed, objective truths that can trump the Constitution or other written law.[38] In his many speeches and essays since 1987, the natural law theme "is constant, the endorsement is unequivocal."[39]

We do not challenge the sincerity of his commitment to a jurisprudence of natural law. However, there is widespread consensus among distinguished scholars of constitutional theory that natural law is far outside the mainstream of contemporary jurisprudence—and has not been a respectable method of judicial decision making for perhaps seventy years, when the pre–New Deal Court used natural law reasoning to declare unconstitutional such measures as child labor laws because of their interference with private property rights. The reincarnation of this dead jurisprudence in Judge Thomas is both incoherent and, as one commentator put it, "weird."[40] Others who have researched Judge Thomas's writings and speeches in depth have found them "contradictory and vague in the extreme," mischaracterizing court decisions "to such a degree one doubts he read them."[41]

The application of natural law jurisprudence about which Clarence Thomas has been most outspoken concerns privacy and abortion rights. He has been a vigorous critic of the Supreme Court decisions preceding *Roe* v. *Wade*, which interpreted the Constitution to protect a right of personal privacy, and used that right to strike down a state statute that criminalized the private use by a married couple of contraception. But beyond that, Thomas has endorsed the view that natural law gives the fetus full rights as a human being from the moment of conception. The implication of this view is that the federal Constitution would *require* (not just permit) criminalization of abortion in virtually all circumstances. We cannot imagine any justification for appointing to the High Court anyone who holds such an extreme judicial philosophy.[42] Specifically from the perspective of African Americans, black women have abortions at approximately twice the rate of white women.[43] The devastating problem of unwanted teen pregnancies is the focus of many public and private initiatives in the black community, as yet only limited in their success. It is quite clear that here, again, Judge Thomas's view is not only indifferent to the African American experience—if adopted it would be a grievous setback.

An Opponent, Not a Critic: We will not speculate as to why Clarence Thomas has chosen to stake his professional fortune with those who are overtly hostile to the advancement of African Americans—two administrations that have vetoed civil rights legislation, undermined domestic programs designed to create opportunity, and used race as a divisive political issue in election campaigns. But we are convinced that Clarence Thomas is well-formed in his role of opponent, not just critic. Judge Thomas has come to the views he holds not lightly, but after much obvious soul searching and reflection. To the argument that Judge Thomas will not forget from whence he has come, we borrow Rep. John Lewis's response: "Look at his record. He has forgotten before."[44]

To say Thomas is a product of his roots is essentializing his blackness; it ignores the role of his intervening experiences; it fixes him in time without regard to the lessons of his more recent opportunities and the evidence of his more recent deeds. To what avail is it if the skin is black and the story is poor, but the perspectives, goals, and agenda now mirror those of the white and privileged? By his confirmation, African Americans will gain nothing but a new burden, and the Supreme Court will gain only a sham diversity.

III. Judge Thomas's personal story does not allay our serious concerns about his judicial philosophy and documented policy views.

Some who support the elevation of Judge Thomas to the Supreme Court do so on the ground that his nomination provides important symbolism for other blacks. We respect the nominee's humble origins and current success. And we wish we could be hopeful that the nominee's own respect for those origins promises to make a compassionate jurist. But we must reject the wishful thinking of some of his supporters.

First, we reject Clarence Thomas and his personal story as some ideal model or metaphor for the advancement of our race to the exclusion of other paths.

Second, we reject the notion that a black person who has no accountability to the black community and who is chosen precisely because of that fact can nevertheless "represent" our interests.

It is said that a black on the Court, no matter the ideology, brings to the Court's deliberations the perspective of those who have been called "nigger"; that a black on the Court is a role model for our young people, especially where that black has dramatically improved his lot in life by struggling up from poverty; and that a black on the Court is a welcome challenge to the African American community to show that we can redeem one of our own, and that all return eventually to our roots.[45]

There is some truth in all this, but much of it is romantic nonsense. The record demonstrates that what Clarence Thomas has drawn from his experience in order to shape his perspective and views is idiosyncratic and far outside the mainstream of African American perspectives. What he and George Bush think is good for Black America bears little relationship to what the preponderance of our community believes to be necessary. His nomination cannot be justified by the false claim that he would bring to the Court's deliberations either a typical or an acceptable African American perspective.

Clarence Thomas as Role Model and Symbol: Clarence Thomas is advertised as the embodiment of Dr. Martin Luther King's dream, a role model who walked in King's own shoes straight out of Pin Point, Georgia. We believe that Dr. King's dream is a more complicated vision than one of luck and individual success stories. That one man has lived the American dream does not make the dream come true for others; nor does the advertising which stresses Thomas's "rugged individualism" and determination accurately present the facts. Thomas's good fortune, and that of other blacks who have made it into the middle class, is difficult to emulate without the assistance of others in many forms, private and public. Indeed, Thomas himself was assisted at every step of the way by external forces, from grandparents in Georgia, to affirmative action at Yale, to political patronage here in Washington. Most important, the collective struggle for civil rights paved his way. Thurgood Marshall made Clarence Thomas possible.

In our view, Dr. King would not focus on the life of Clarence Thomas as a black version of the American dream, because the message we are told to take from Thomas's story is that we *alone* are responsible for our fate; we are all self-made human beings.[46] But Dr. King's message was in substantial part a message of community and of collective responsibility, not of self-reproaching role models.[47] Dr. King's dream is a dream in which those who are fortunate have a responsibility to help—not condemn—those who come behind them; in which we are judged by the least among us; in which all Americans can benefit from the spiritual vision of their black brothers and sisters; in which the meek but determined, not the arrogant, inherit the earth; in which the content of our character includes not only personal ambition but the determination to succeed as well.

There is a long and strong tradition of both individual and com munity self-reliance in the African American experience, which Clarence Thomas's sermons do not appear to acknowledge.[48] But for these strengths, our families, culture and very existence could scarcely have withstood hundreds of years of immoral abuse on this continent. For the least among us, these survival skills permit just that—survival. The great question for America is not whether one determined man can, with the help of luck and special advantages, rise to new heights. The question is how can the majority of others, being less fortunate, realize their dreams, too. Thomas has achieved his dream and now turns to others and preaches "no excuses" for their condition.[49]

One expects, from someone with Thomas's experiences, compassion and empathy. What we have seen for a decade, instead, is a harshly judgmental assumption that a romanticized version of his own story—stripped of the elements of luck and special advantage—is the one true path. Adding that idiosyncratic, unsympathetic perspective to the Court's deliberations will move that vital institution farther away from the struggle for racial progress.

CONCLUSION

Our careful examination of the record leads us to the conviction that we must oppose the nomination of Clarence Thomas to the Supreme Court of the United States. We regret that we find this opposition necessary, but black officials elected to national office and others from whom leadership is expected must take their responsibilities seriously—particularly to the most vulnerable among us. We also understand how much effort and sacrifice by our ancestors and our more recent predecessors was necessary for us to serve in office or otherwise to be entrusted with leadership. And we know that we owe a debt to the future; that until our people are fully free and equal, each new generation is obligated to give its best effort to the struggle.

We do not believe that ideological conformity or strategic agreement are required of African Americans in public service. What is required in our fight for justice, however, is a demonstrated commitment to the broad bipartisan approaches that, for more than twenty-five years now, have been accepted by most Republicans and Democrats and by blacks, white, Hispanics and others alike.[50]

It is our judgment that Clarence Thomas does not fall within the broad stream of this bipartisan, historic struggle. He has proven as much, time and again; whether by his reluctance to enforce vigorously laws with which he disagreed; or by his cavalier, almost careless dismissal of some of the remedies our people have found most helpful; or by his expressed disdain for leaders of our movement (even for the giant he is nominated to replace); or whether by his vocal contempt for those vulnerable members of our community who need aid, including his own sister.

Judge Thomas has written a record which shows a firm and consistent opposition to much that our people have insisted that they need most urgently. It is impossible for us to stretch our consciences to support any nominee of whatever color who has created such a record.

THE CONGRESSIONAL BLACK CAUCUS FOUNDATION has as one of its missions to undertake research to enlighten African Americans and others about important national issues which are before Congress. CPCF Board of Directors: The Honorable Alan Wheat, Chair; LeBaron Taylor, Vice Chair; Lawrence Doss, Treasurer; The Honorable William L. Clay; The Honorable Cardiss Collins; The Honorable Julian C. Dixon; Ofield Dukes; Dr. Ramona H. Edelin; Christopher F. Edley, Jr.; The Honorable Charles Hayes; Jesse Hill, Jr.; Bertram Lee; Lillian Lewis; The Honorable Kweisi Mfume; Albert L. Nellum; The Honorable Major Owens; The Honorable Charles Rangel; Barbara J. Skinner; Wayman Smith, III; The Honorable Louis Stokes; Gwen Towns; Carl Ware; The Honorable Edolphus Towns, Ex-Officio.

NOTES

1. Margolick, "Thomas Issue Pains Black Lawyers," *The New York Times*, Aug. 12, 1991.
2. 431 U.S. 494 (1977).
3. *The Family: Preserving America's Future* 12 (1986); "Defense Fund Opposes Thomas," *The Washington Times*, August 14, 1991.
4. *The Family: Preserving America's Future* at 11.
5. *See* 431 U.S. at 508–10 (Brennan J. concurring).
6. Speech at the Tocqueville Forum, at 17 (April 18, 1988).
7. *Yale Law and Policy and Review*, at 411 (1987).
8. In "Civil Rights as a Principle Versus Civil Rights as an Interest," a chapter he wrote for D. Boaz, *Assessing the Reagan Years* (1988), Thomas criticized *United Steel Workers* v. *Weber*, 443 U.S. 193 (1979), and *Johnson* v. *Transportation*

Agency, Santa Clara County, Cal. 480 U.S. 616 (1987), which upheld voluntary affirmative action programs, as "egregious" misinterpretations of the equal protection clause and legislative intent. "Principle Versus Interest" at 395.

9. Specifically, Judge Thomas wrote that the Supreme Court's decision in *Fullilove* v. *Klutznick*, 448 U.S. 448 (1980) and, by inference, cases like *Metro Broadcasting, Inc.* v. *F.C.C.*, 110 St. Ct. 2997, 58 USLW 5053 (1990) are invalid inventions of "schemes of racial preference where none was ever contemplated." "Principle Versus Interest" at 396.

10. Thomas has frequently taken issue with the unanimously decided *Griggs* v. *Duke Power Co.*, 401 U.S. 424 (1971), arguing bitterly against the holding that statistically demonstrable disparate impact by race or sex is generally impermissible. See *New York Times*, December 3, 1984. He would presumably applaud, then, decisions such as *Wards Cove Packing Co.* v. *Atonio*, 490 U.S. 642 (1989) that eroded the *Griggs* holding. Congress has been fighting a difficult battle against a veto threat to include language in the Civil Rights Bill that would reinstate the *Griggs* standards Thomas has opposed.

11. Julius Chambers, as quoted by Taylor, "Legal Defense Fund Opposes Thomas," *The Washington Times*, August 14, 1991 (also citing 23-page report which concludes "What is apparent . . . is an antipathy and hostility toward legal principles that benefit and protect the most disadvantaged of our society.").

12. *The New York Times*, Sep. 5, 1991, p. A-21, col. 1 (meeting of the National Baptist Convention USA).

13. Williams, "A Question of Fairness," *The Atlantic Monthly* 71, 75 (February 1987) (quoting Thomas explaining at a San Francisco conference for black conservatives that his opposition to public assistance was an outgrowth of his sister's experience on welfare in Georgia: "She gets mad when the mailman is late with her welfare check. That is how dependent she is. What's worse is that now her kids feel entitled to the check too. They have no motivation for doing better or getting out of that situation.").

14. Clymer, "About that Flag on the Judge's Desk," *The New York Times*, July 19, 1991 (according to Senator Orrin Hatch, Judge Thomas's recollection of whether he displayed a Confederate flag on his desk was "fuzzy" but when he checked with colleagues from the Attorney General's office they recalled a state flag of Georgia, which resembles the Confederate flag); *But cf.* Lewis, *The New York Times*, July 8, 1991 (Thomas prizes ability to resist being categorized, sometimes going out of his way to make that point, including displaying a confederate flag on his wall as if to say no one should presume to know his beliefs.).

15. Quoted in "Where Does He Stand?" *Newsweek*, July 15, 1991, p. 16.

16. Speech to EEO Coordinator's Association, July 10, 1985, p. 20.

17. Speech at the Georgetown Law Center, Feb. 20, 1986, p. 22.

18. Speech at the University of Tulsa, Nov. 21, 1986, p. 15.

19. Speech to the Heritage Foundation, June 18, 1987, p. 5.

20. Speech to the Pacific Research Institute, August 4, 1988, p. 3.

21. See *A Report on the Nomination of Judge Clarence Thomas as Associate Justice of the United States Supreme Court*, National Association for the Advancement of Colored People, Introduction, at 5, Section IV, p. 1 (August 1, 1991) (Judge

Thomas's handling of age discrimination cases at the EEOC criticized; his record of enforcement at the EEOC especially troubling; at both Education Office of Civil Rights and at EEOC, Thomas "ignore[d] his responsibilities; complain[ed] about the law he was required to enforce and allow[ed] complaints to go unattended.").

22. See *EEOC and State Agencies Did Not Fully Investigate Discrimination Cases*, GAO Report/HRO-89-11, at 17 (October 1988) (average benefit to discrimination victim dropped by one-half during first part of Thomas's EEOC tenure; length of time to process charge doubled, as did backlog of complaints); see also letter from Reps. Edwards, Roybal, Collins, Frank, Williams, Sikorski, Martinez, Schroeder, Hayes, Lantos, Clay, Hawkins, Kildee, and Conyers to President George Bush (July 17, 1989) (Thomas "has demonstrated an overall disdain for the rule of law"; he "reportedly retaliated against an employee critical of EEOC's enforcement of ADEA shortly after she presented testimony under subpoena from the Senate Committee"; Thomas's actions "as chair of the Equal Employment Opportunity Commission raise serious questions about his judgment . . ."). Also at the Education Department, Thomas ignored a Justice Department letter warning that Thomas's procedure known as Early Complaint Resolution might be illegal and would undermine enforcement and litigation efforts. Letter from Stewart B. Oneglia, Civil Rights Division, Department of Justice, to Kristine M. Marcy, Office of Civil Rights, Nov. 13, 1991; *W.E.A.L. and Adams* v. *Bell*, transcript, Mar. 12, 1982, p. 20. In 1985, a Committee of the House of Representatives investigated his agency and found that Judge Thomas had left the procedure intact despite the Justice Department's protestations. H. Rep. 99-458 at 27 and 29.

23. See letter from Rep. Edward Roybal, Chair, House Select Committee on Aging to Senators Joseph Biden and Strom Thurmond (July 16, 1991).

24. "Despite Class Action Doubts, EEOC Presses Bias Case," *The Washington Post*, July 9, 1985, p. A-1; see *A Report on the Nomination of Judge Clarence Thomas as Associate Justice of the United States Supreme Court*, National Association for the Advancement of Colored People, Aug. 1, 1991, Section IV, pp. 16–17.

25. Transcript of hearing in *W.E.A.L. and Adams* v. *Bell*, Civil Action 3095-70 (D.D.C. March 12, 1982) at 48, 51.

26. Remarks at California State University, at 3 (April 25, 1988).

27. See Thomas, *Affirmative Action Goals and Timetables: Too Tough? Not Tough Enough!*, 5 Yale L. & Pol. Rev. 402, 407, n. 2 (1987) (expressing his "personal disagreement" with the "Court's approval of numerical remedies" for discrimination because "distributing opportunities on the basis of race or gender . . . turns the law against employment discrimination on its head . . . I think that preferential hiring on the basis of race or gender will increase racial divisiveness, disempower women and minorities by fostering the notion that they are . . . in need of handouts, and delay the day when skin color and gender are truly the least important thing about a person in the employment context."). Addressing employment discrimination lawyers, Thomas says goals and timetables "make your jobs easy and neat, but it's wrong, insulting, and sometimes outright racist." Speech to the EEO Committee of the ABA's Labor and Employment Law Section, Palm Beach Gardens, Florida (March 8, 1985).

28. See *Analysis of the Views of Judge Clarence Thomas*, NAACP Legal Defense Fund, Inc., at 20 (Aug. 13, 1991) (hereinafter, LDF Report).

29. Address to the ABA Business Law Section at 13 (Aug. 11, 1987).

30. Speech to the Federalist Society, University of Virginia School of Law, at 2 (March 5, 1988); Thomas, *The Higher Law Background of the Privileges and Immunities Clause of the Fourteenth Amendment*, 12 Harv. J. of L. & Publ. Pol. 63, 64 (1989).

31. See LDF Report at 17, 19.

32. See Thomas, speech to the Gordon Public Policy Center, Brandeis University, Waltham, Massachusetts, at 5 (April 8, 1988); Thomas, speech before the Cato Institute, Washington, D.C. at 13 (Oct. 2, 1987).

33. The *Los Angeles Times*, Oct. 11, 1988; See also NAACP, *A Report on the Nomination of Judge Clarence Thomas as Associate Justice of the United States Supreme Court*, August 1, 1991, Section IV, p. 6.

34. Thomas, Speech to the Federalist Society, University of Virginia at 13 (March 5, 1988) (emphasis in original).

35. *Morrison v. Olson*, 108 S. Ct. 2597 (1988) (upholding independent counsel appointed by special judicial panel rather than the president).

36. Barnes, "Weirdo Alert," *The New Republic* at 7 (Aug. 5, 1991).

37. "A Justice Until 2030?" *The New York Times*, July 2, 1991 (Presidential presumption in favor of nominees for transitory appointments to executive branch does not apply to the coordinate judicial branch; nor is nominee entitled to a presumption in his favor because of his race; questions concern not his talent but his character); see also "Judge Clarence Thomas's Record on the Fundamental Right to Privacy," *NARAL Report* at 5 (July 17, 1991).

38. See Thomas, speech before the Heritage Foundation, Washington, D.C., at 22 (June 18, 1987); Thomas, *The Higher Law Background of the Privileges or Immunities Clause*, 12 Harv. J. of L. & Pub. Pol. 63 (1989).

39. See *Judge Clarence Thomas: 'An Overall Disdain for the Rule of Law,'* People for the American Way Action Fund at 22 (July 30, 1991) (natural law theme "pervades Mr. Thomas's speeches and writings" since the beginning of 1987; between January 1987 and April 1988, Thomas gave at least 11 speeches in which he discussed natural law and published at least eight articles that argue for natural law analysis).

40. See Fred Barnes, "Weirdo Alert," *The New Republic* 7 (Aug. 5, 1991) describing July 11, 1991 conversation with Senator Metzenbaum. Senator Metzenbaum asked Thomas to explain natural law. Thomas replied, "Well Senator, do you think it's proper for a human being to own another human being?" Metzenbaum said no. "The reason you think that's wrong is because we all have natural rights," Thomas explained. "What about," Metzenbaum continued, "a human being owning an animal? Is that part of natural law?" Thomas hesitated and then said, "I'll have to check on an answer for you. I'll consult my writings and those of some others."

41. LDF Report, at 1.

42. Constitutional interpretation based on natural law has long been seen as unacceptable by the judicial mainstream. Professor John Hart Ely noted that

"[t]he concept of [natural law] has . . . all but disappeared in American discourse." J. H. Ely, *Democracy and Distrust* 52 (1980). See also Tribe, " 'Natural Law' and the Nominee" *The New York Times*, July 15, 1991. ("[Thomas] is the first Supreme Court nominee in 50 years to maintain that natural law should be readily consulted in constitutional interpretation" and raises the possibility of a Court that would "hold that Congress and the states may not respond with measures contrary to natural law, as construed by the justices on the basis of the rights 'given to man by his Creator.' ").

43. The most recent available data (1985) show that women in the category of "Black and Other" had 55.5 legal abortions per 1,000 women. White women in the same year had 22.6 abortions per 1,000 women. U.S. Department of Commerce, *Statistical Abstract of the United States*, 1990, 110th Edition, p. 71.

44. See John Lewis, *Why I Oppose the Thomas Nomination*, July 16, 1991 ("My response to the argument" that Clarence Thomas cannot "forget" where he has come from and, therefore, he will be sensitive to the plight of the disadvantaged is: "Look at his record. He has forgotten before.").

45. See Angelou, "I Dare To Hope," *The New York Times*, Aug. 25, 1991 at E 15 col. 2: "Black youngsters of today must ask black leaders: If you can't make an effort to reach, reconstruct and save a black man who has graduated from Yale, how can you reach down here in this drug-filled, hate-filled cesspool where I live and save me? Supporting Thomas's nomination tells young blacks that they come from a people with the courage to hope." Ms. Angelou is an accomplished artist. With respect, we doubt she has studied the judicial philosophy of Judge Thomas or analyzed the probable impact of his vote on the development of legal doctrine.

46. "From reading Clarence Thomas one would never gather that a civil rights struggle ever took place in this country." *A Report on the Nomination of Judge Clarence Thomas as Associate Justice of the United States Supreme Court*, National Association for the Advancement of Colored People, at Section V, 3 n.1 (Aug. 1, 1991).

47. See, *e.g.*, Sennett, "A Role Model Unto Himself," *The New York Times*, Aug. 12, 1991 (American dream of individual achievement has little to say about the issues that hold together a community; big jump Clarence Thomas made to Yale provides no model; his career does not offer a prescription for ordinary people.).

48. See *A Report on the Nomination of Judge Clarence Thomas as Associate Justice of the United States Supreme Court*, National Association for the Advancement of Colored People, at Section V, 2–4 (Aug. 1, 1991) (Thomas's embrace of the self-made man myth does not include appreciation for self-help African American community groups.).

49. Speech to Savannah State College (June 9, 1985), excerpted in "Climb the Jagged Mountain," *The New York Times*, July 17, 1991 (arguing blacks now face a double bind, complicated by the "lure of excuses" offered by their role models). See also *A Report on the Nomination of Clarence Thomas as Associate Justice of the United States Supreme Court*, National Association for the Advancement of Colored People at 5–6 (August 1, 1991); "Administration Asks Blacks to Fend for Themselves," *The Washington Post*, p. A1 (Dec. 5, 1983) (Thomas said, "It is just as 'insane' for blacks to expect relief from the federal government for years of discrimination as

it is to expect a mugger to nurse his victim back to health. . . . Ultimately, the burden of your being mugged falls on you.").

50. See *A Report on the Nomination of Judge Clarence Thomas as Associate Justice of the United States Supreme Court*, National Association for the Advancement of Colored People, at 7 (August 1, 1991) (when Thurgood Marshall was nominated to become an Associate Justice of the Supreme Court, he enjoyed the overwhelming support of African Americans); Associate Justice Thurgood Marshall, 74, *The Crisis* 282 (July 1967) (Thurgood Marshall's nomination represents "historic breakthrough of transcendent significance," Marshall achieved national eminence as "the No. 1 civil rights lawyer of our times.").

JUDGE CLARENCE THOMAS'S VIEWS ON THE FUNDAMENTAL RIGHT TO PRIVACY

A Report to the United States Senate Judiciary Committee

Barbara Allen Babcock, Ernest W. McFarland, Professor, Stanford Law School; Christopher F. Edley, Jr., Professor, Harvard Law School; Thomas C. Grey, Nelson Bowman Sweitzer and Marie B. Sweitzer, Professor, Stanford Law School; Sylvia A. Law, Professor, New York University Law School; Frank I. Michelman, Professor, Harvard Law School; Robert C. Post, Professor, University of California at Berkeley; Norman Redlich, Dean Emeritus, New York University School of Law; Judith Resnik, Orin B. Evans, Professor, University of Southern California School of Law; Steven H. Shiffrin, Professor, Cornell Law School.

As teachers and scholars of constitutional law committed to the protection of constitutional liberty, we submit this report to convey our grave concerns regarding the nomination of Judge Clarence Thomas to be an Associate Justice of the United States Supreme Court. Careful examination of Judge Thomas's writings and speeches strongly suggests that his views of the Constitution, and in particular his use of natural law to constrict individual liberty, depart from the mainstream of American constitutional thought and endangers Americans' most fundamental constitutional rights, including the right to privacy.

Among the most alarming aspects of his record, and the primary focus of this report, are the numerous instances in which Judge Thomas has indicated that he would deny the fundamental right to privacy, including the right of all Americans, married or single, to use contraception and the right of a woman to choose to have an abortion. Judge Thomas has criticized the Supreme Court's decisions in the landmark privacy cases protecting the fundamental right to use contraception. He has endorsed an approach to overruling *Roe* v. *Wade*[1] that is so extreme it would create a constitutional requirement that abortion be outlawed in all states throughout the Nation, regardless of the will of the people and their elected representatives. Recent Supreme Court decisions in *Webster* v. *Reproductive Health Services*[2] and *Rust* v. *Sullivan*[3] have seriously diminished protection for the right to choose. Replacing Justice Thurgood Marshall with Judge Clarence Thomas would likely result in far more devastating encroachments of women's rights, perhaps providing the fifth vote to uphold statutes criminalizing virtually all abortions. Such laws have recently been adopted in Louisiana, Guam and Utah and challenges to them are now pending in the federal courts.

We submit this report prior to Judge Thomas's testimony before the Judiciary Committee in the hope that it will assist the committee, and the Nation, in formulating questions to discern Judge Thomas's views on fundamental rights to individual privacy and liberty. We urge the committee to question Judge Thomas on these matters and to decline to confirm his nomination unless he clearly refutes the strong evidence that he is a nominee whose special concept of the Constitution "calls for the reversal of decisions dealing with human rights and individual liberties."[4]

I. THE SENATE'S ROLE IN THE CONFIRMATION PROCESS

A basic element of our constitutional system of checks and balances is the joint responsibility the Constitution confers upon the President and the Senate for the selection of Supreme Court Justices. In the words of Senator Patrick Leahy:

> When the Framers of the Constitution met in Philadelphia two centuries ago, they decided that the appointment of the leaders of the judicial branch of government was too important to leave to the unchecked discretion of either of the other two branches. They decided that the President and the Senate must be equal partners in this decision, playing roles of equal importance. The 100 members of the United States Senate, like the Chief Executive, are elected by all the people.[5]

The Senate's equal role in selecting Supreme Court Justices is widely accepted by Senators of both parties. For example, Senator Arlen Specter has stated that the "Constitutional separation of powers is at its apex when the President nominates and the Senate consents or not for Supreme Court appointees who have the final word. The Constitution mandates that a senator's judgment be separate and independent."[6]

Although the precise wording has varied, a majority of the members of the Senate Judiciary Committee have indicated that to be confirmed a nominee must, at a minimum, demonstrate a commitment to protect individual rights that have been established as fundamental under the U.S. Constitution. For example, Senator Patrick Leahy described the standard as follows:

> The Senate should confirm [a nominee] only if we are persuaded that the nominee has both the commitment and the capacity to protect freedoms the American people have fought hard to win and to preserve over the last 200 years. . . . I cannot vote for [a nominee] unless I can tell the People of Vermont that I am confident that if he were to become [a Justice], he would be an effective guardian of their fundamental rights.[7]

Senators have often identified the right to privacy as among the fundamental rights that a nominee must recognize to meet the standard for confirmation. As Chairman Joseph Biden stated:

> A nominee who criticizes the notion of unenumerated rights, or the right to privacy, would be unacceptable in my view. A nominee whose view of the Fourteenth Amendment's Equal Protection Clause has led him or her to have a cramped vision of the court's role in creating a more just society would be unacceptable in my view. And a nominee whose vision of the First Amendment's guarantees of freedom of speech and religion would constrain those provisions' historic scope would be unacceptable in my view.[8]

Senator Herbert Kohl similarly stated:

> [A] Supreme Court Justice must, at a minimum, be dedicated to equality for all Americans, determined to preserve the right to privacy, the right to be left alone by the Government, committed to civil rights and civil liberties, devoted to ensuring the separation of Church and State, willing to defend the Bill of Rights and its applications to the States against all efforts to weaken it, and able to read the Constitution as a living, breathing document.[9]

Although Senator Howell Heflin indicated that he "would favor a conservative appointment on the Court," for him the question was "whether this nominee would be a conservative justice who would safeguard the living Constitution and prevent judicial activism or whether, on the other hand, he would be an extremist who would use his position on the Court to advance a far-right, radical judicial agenda."[10] As Senator Heflin noted, if a nominee's "concept of the Constitution calls for the reversal of decisions dealing with human rights and individual liberties, then people's rights will be threatened."[11]

Judge Thomas's writings, speeches and professional activities do not satisfy this standard. They strongly suggest that, if confirmed, he would interpret the Constitution in a manner that would dangerously restrict constitutional protection for civil rights and civil liberties.

The threat Judge Thomas poses to our basic constitutional freedoms is well exemplified by his views regarding the fundamental right to privacy and the protection it affords reproductive rights, including the right to use contraception and the right to choose to have an abortion. The remainder of this report focuses on these alarming aspects of Judge Thomas's record.

II. THOMAS ENDORSES A NATURAL LAW "RIGHT TO LIFE" FROM CONCEPTION

At the core of Thomas's claims to constitutional authority and a dominant theme throughout his writings and speeches is a belief that the Constitution should be interpreted in light of "natural law" or "higher law." "Natural rights and higher law arguments are the best defense of liberty and of limited government."[12] "Natural law" is a slippery concept. It has been invoked in noble causes, for example, in opposition to slavery, genocide and torture. But it has also been used in invidious ways, for example, to defend slavery and to deny women the right to vote or participate in public life. The key questions that must be posed to a proponent of natural law are: What principles are dictated by natural justice? How do we know that these answers are correct?

Despite the central role natural law plays in his professional writings, Judge Thomas has said surprisingly little about the specific content of his natural law philosophy. His discussions of natural law, though numerous, tend to be abstract and repetitive, often confusing, and sometimes contradictory. Thomas routinely cites the Declaration of Independence as the primary source of the natural law values that should be promoted through constitutional interpretation, and he frequently refers to a religious basis for those values.[13] Beyond these general references, he has been remarkably vague about the content of those values.

One striking exception to Judge Thomas's general failure to provide specific examples of how natural law should be applied is his frequent criticism of the right to privacy. One specific application of Thomas's view of natural law is his enthusiastic endorsement of the assertion that the fetus enjoys a constitutionally protected right to life from the moment of conception. In a 1987 speech to the Heritage Foundation, he stated:

> We must start by articulating principles of government and standards of goodness. I suggest that we begin the search for standards and principles with the self-evident truths of the Declaration of Independence. . . . Lewis Lehrman's recent essay in *The American Spectator* on the Declaration of Independence and the meaning of the right to life is a splendid example of applying natural law.[14]

The Lehrman article that Judge Thomas invokes as exemplary of his approach to natural law argues but one point: interpreting the Constitution, in light of natural law, as derived from the Declaration of Independence, requires that the fetus be protected as a full human being from the moment of conception. Lehrman states that the privacy right protected by the Court in *Roe* was "a spurious right born exclusively of judicial supremacy with not a single trace of lawful authority," and that even if such a right existed, it would be overridden by the natural, inalienable right-to-life of the fetus from the moment of conception.[15]

This view is far more extreme than that of any current Supreme Court Justice. The Declaration of Independence says nothing about abortion or the fetus. Abortion was then legal. An overturning of *Roe* premised on the supposed natural right of the fetus not only would strip women of constitutional protection of their reproductive autonomy, it would prohibit individual states or the Congress from allowing the legal abortion option even in extreme cases. It would *require* that the abortion be defined as murder. It would prohibit states from allowing abortion even where pregnancy resulted from rape or incest or posed grave risk to a woman's health. It would deny to women as responsible individuals the ability to exercise their own religious and moral beliefs concerning abortion.

The Lehrman article does little more than assert that it is a "self-evident" truth that the fetus possesses an "inalienable right to life."[16] We fear that Judge Thomas's strong praise of this application of natural law endorses this radical view on the critical issue of abortion, on the basis of an approach to natural law that relies on fixed and unquestionable moral "truth" rather than reasoned debate over the application of American constitutional principles to the circumstances of our times.

Natural law protection of the right to life from the moment of conception has been cited in recent years by opponents of legal abortion, such as members of the group "Operation Rescue," in defense of their actions in violation of laws against trespass, destruction of property and assault and battery while attempting to obstruct women's access to reproductive health care facilities.[17] Natural law has further provided a basis for opposition not only to abortion, but to contraception by any means viewed as an interference with "natural" human reproduction.

III. THOMAS REJECTS UNENUMERATED RIGHTS AS ARTICULATED IN *GRISWOLD, EISENSTADT* AND *ROE*

The specific content of Judge Thomas's view of natural law can be seen, not only in the applications he praises, such as the "God-given" and "inalienable right to life"[18] of a fetus, but also in the rights and values he rejects. Although Thomas advocates constitutional protection for natural rights not specifically enumerated in the Constitution, he repeatedly attacks the recognition of unenumerated rights under the Ninth Amendment and the Due Process Clause of the Fourteenth Amendment by what he dismisses as "liberal activist"[19] and "run-amok"[20] judges. Most prominent among the judicial opinions that Thomas has thus criticized are those in which the Supreme Court has protected the fundamental right to privacy.

For example, in a law review article he published in 1989, Thomas again selected opposition to the right to privacy to illustrate "the willfulness of both run-amok majorities and run-amok judges."[21] Thomas writes that the judicial decisions that "make conservatives nervous" are *Roe* v. *Wade* and *Griswold* v. *Connecticut*.[22] After describing *Roe* as "the current case provoking the most protest from conservatives," Thomas affirms his "misgivings about activist judicial use of the Ninth Amendment and the right to reproductive privacy."[23] But, he asserts, his proposed concept of "higher law" would restrain both legislative majorities and judges, and should hence appeal to those he calls "my conservative allies."

Thomas has described the protection afforded the right to privacy under the Ninth Amendment as an "invention" in an opinion in *Griswold* v. *Connecticut*, authored by Justice Arthur Goldberg and joined by Chief Justice Earl Warren and Justice William Brennan. Thomas further criticizes Justice Goldberg's opinion and rejects the Ninth Amendment as a source of constitutional protection for rights that are unenumerated in the Constitution, stating:

> A major question remains: Does the Ninth Amendment, as Justice Goldberg contended, give to the Supreme Court certain powers to strike down legislation? That would seem to be a blank check. . . Unbounded by notions of obligation and justice, the desire to protect rights simply plays into the hands of those who advocate a total state. . . . Far from being a protection, the Ninth Amendment will likely become an additional weapon for the enemies of freedom.[24]

Judge Thomas offers no real explanation in these writings of how protecting the rights of individuals promotes a "total state" or how defining unenumerated rights by reference to "natural law" is either more determinate or less a "blank check" to judges than more traditional means of constitutional interpretation.

Elsewhere, Thomas described the views on the right to privacy of Judge Bork and other proponents of original intents as follows: "restricting birth control devices or information, and allowing, restricting, or (as Senator Kennedy put it) requiring abortions are all matters for a legislature to decide; judges should refrain from 'imposing their values' on public policy."[25] Thomas then criticized this view as leading to an "indifference toward or even contempt of 'values.' Far from being an alternative to leftist activism, it readily complements it, as long as a majority approves."[26]

Although Thomas's discussion of this point is confusing, there is reason to fear it may be another endorsement of the view set out in the article by Lewis Lehrman in support of a natural right to life for the fetus. Thomas's discussion of the right to privacy in the context of arguing that the Constitution must be interpreted consistent with a particular moral view, and his expression that his moral view must be employed to constrain majorities that might otherwise engage in "leftist activism," may be a further indication that under Thomas's theory of natural law, the Constitution would not permit states to allow citizens to have access to abortion or use contraception if these activities are deemed to violate the natural order of things.

In 1986, Thomas participated as a member of a White House Working Group on the Family that produced a report on the family that severely criticized landmark constitutional decisions protecting the right to privacy. The Report went so far as to excoriate a decision protecting a grandmother's freedom to open her home to her orphaned grandchildren, without government restriction.[27] It particularly targeted cases in the area of reproductive freedom, and called for them to be overruled.[28]

In addition to *Roe* v. *Wade*, the working group singled out as wrongly decided the Supreme Court's decision in *Planned Parenthood* v. *Danforth*, in which the Court struck down a Missouri law that required a woman to obtain the consent of her husband before she could obtain an abortion and a minor to obtain the consent of a parent. The report also criticized the Court's reasoning in *Eisenstadt* v. *Baird*, which protects the right of unmarried individuals to use contraception, and in particular the Court's statement that "the marital couple is not an independent entity with a mind and heart of its own."[29] The working group described these, and other cases protecting the fundamental right to privacy, as a "fatally flawed line of court decisions" and indicated that they "can be corrected, directly or indirectly, through . . . the appointment of new judges and their confirmation by the Senate . . . a . . . amendment of the Constitution itself."[30]

IV. THOMAS'S NATURAL LAW THEORY

As we have noted above, Thomas's approach to constitutional interpretation is highly unusual in its invocation of a body of natural law.[31] Appeals to natural law in constitutional interpretation do not necessarily portend decisions that would restrict the rights of individuals and overturn core constitutional values. Depending on how its methodology and content are specifically understood, natural law might point in various directions. But Thomas's approach to natural law is disturbing, both as a matter of methodology and as a matter of content.

As a matter of constitutional method natural law is disturbing when invoked to allow supposedly self-evident moral "truth" to substitute for the hard work of developing principles drawn from the

American constitutional text and precedent. As we have noted, Judge Thomas has not sought to explain the social and historical reasons supporting the conclusions to which "natural law" leads him. The more traditional common law and constitutional method of open-ended, case-by-case development is a core strength of the American judicial approach to justice for a diverse and ever-evolving country. Natural law norms are not necessarily antithetical to a reasoned, case-by-case approach. But Judge Thomas seems to invoke "higher law" as a substitute for explanation. His concept of natural law appears to mean strict adherence to a perceived set of fixed and undoubtable normative truths. As such, it does not accommodate the principle and precedent exemplified in the work of conservative Justices such as John Harlan and Lewis Powell.

When natural law was last in vogue some eighty years ago, it was employed by the Supreme Court to strike down state laws providing basic health and safety protection to working people. The Court asserted a natural law right of employers to be free of minimum wage laws and health and safety regulations.[32] Natural law has been particularly disabling for women. In 1873, the Court upheld the exclusion of women from the practice of law.[33] Justice Bradley wrote that the "civil law, as well as nature herself, has always recognized a wide difference in the respective spheres and destinies of man and woman. . . . The paramount destiny and mission of woman are to fulfill the noble and benign offices of wife and mother. This is the law of the Creator."[34]

The impact that the application of natural law would have on core constitutional principles thus depends on the particular proponent's personal views of the content and source of the natural law principles to be applied. It is therefore imperative that the Senate Judiciary Committee determine with specificity which fixed principles Judge Thomas has in mind when he advocates the use of natural law in constitutional interpretation and how they will affect the Court's role as guardian of Americans' fundamental rights. As the preceding analysis indicates, Thomas's record contains compelling evidence that the substantive content of his natural law theory is incompatible with continued protection for the fundamental right of privacy, including the right to choose.[35]

V. CONCLUSION

Particularly given the critical moment in the history of the Supreme Court at which this nomination has occurred, the Senate should reject any nominee who is not committed to protecting fundamental individual liberties. We urge the Senate to shoulder its responsibility to determine whether the nominee "has both the commitment and the capacity to protect freedoms the American people have fought hard to win and to preserve over the last 200 years."[36] Our analysis of Judge Thomas's writings and speeches raises serious questions whether he meets this standard. We exhort the Committee to probe these questions and to approve the nomination only if satisfied that Judge Thomas has the commitment and ability to contribute to the wise elaboration of our Constitution.

September 5, 1991

NOTES

1. 410 U.S. 113 (1973).
2. 492 U.S. 490 (1989).
3. 111 S.Ct. 1759 (1991).
4. Senate Committee on the Judiciary, Nomination of Robert H. Bork to be an Associate Justice of the United States Supreme Court, S. Exec. Rep. No. 100-7, 100th Cong., 1st Sess., Additional Views of Senator Heflin, 210 (1987).
5. S. Exec. Rep. No. 100-7, 100th Cong., 1st Sess., Additional Views of Senator Leahy, 193–94 (1987).
6. S. Exec. Rep. No. 100-7, 100th Cong., 1st Sess., Additional Views of Senator Specter, 213 (1987).
7. S. Exec. Rep. No. 100-7, 100th Cong., 1st Sess., Additional Views of Senator Leahy, 193–94 (1987).
8. Statement of Senator Joseph Biden, Chairman, Senate Judiciary Committee on Nomination of David Souter to be Associate Justice of the U.S. Supreme Court (Sept. 27, 1990).
9. *Hearings of the Senate Judiciary Committee on the Nomination of Judge David Souter* (Sept. 13, 1990) (Statement of Senator Kohl).
10. S. Exec. Rep. No. 100-7, 100th Cong., 1st Sess., Additional Views of Senator Heflin, 211 (1987).
11. *Id.* at 210.
12. Thomas, *The Higher Law Background of the Privileges and Immunities Clause*, 12 Harv. J. L. Pub. Pol'y 63, 64 (1989).
13. *See, e.g.*, Thomas, *Why Black Americans Should Look to Conservative Policies*, 119 Heritage Lectures (June 18, 1987); Thomas, *Toward a "Plain Reading" of the Constitution—The Declaration of Independence in Constitutional Interpretation*, 30 Howard

L. J. 983 (1987); Thomas, *Civil Rights as a Principle Versus Civil Rights as an Interest* in *Assessing the Reagan Years* (D. Boaz ed.), 391, 198 (1989); Thomas, *Notes on Original Intent.*

14. Thomas, *Why Black Americans Should Look to Conservative Policies, supra* note 13, at 8.

15. Lehrman, *The Declaration of Independence and the Right to Life*, The American Spectator 21, 23 (April 1987).

16. Id. at 22.

17. See, *e.g.*, Senftle, *The Necessity Defense in Abortion Clinic Trespass Cases*, 32 St. Louis U. L. J. 523, 546 (1987); *City of Kettering v. Berry*, 57 Ohio App. 3d 66, 70 (1990) ("The law does not recognize political, religious, moral convictions or some higher law as justification for the commission of a crime"); brief for Operation Rescue at 7, *Roe* v. *Operation Rescue*, No. 88-5157 (E. D. Pa., filed June 29, 1988); brief for the Catholic Lawyers Guild of the Archdiocese of Boston, Inc., as *Amicus Curiae* supporting Appellants, *Webster* v. *Reproductive Health Services*, 492 U.S. 490 (1989) (arguing that *Roe* v. *Wade* should be overruled).

18. Lehrman, *supra* note 15, at 23.

19. Thomas, *Notes on Original Intent, supra* note 13.

20. Thomas, *Higher Law Background, supra* note 12, at 64.

21. *Id.*

22. *Id.* at 63 n.2.

23. *Id.*

24. Thomas, *Civil Rights as Principle, supra* note 13, at 398–99.

25. Thomas, *Notes on Original Intent, supra* note 13.

26. *Id.*

27. *Moore* v. *City of East Cleveland*, 431 U.S. 494 (1971). *The Family: Preserving America's Future, A Report to the President from the White House Working Group on the Family* 11 (1986).

28. *Id.* at 11.

29. *Id.*, at 12. *Quoting, Eisenstadt* v. *Baird*, 405 U.S. 438, 453 (1972).

30. *Id.* at 12. The Republican Party platforms for 1980, 1984, and 1988 contained strikingly similar language, pledging to work for "the appointment of judges at all levels of the judiciary who respect traditional family values and the sanctity of innocent human life." Thomas listed the Republican Party's position on abortion as the first in a list of conservative positions that he believed should attract African Americans to the Republican Party. Thomas, "Hows Republicans Can Win Blacks," *Chicago Defender,* February 21, 1987.

31. For at least the last fifty years, constitutional interpretation on the basis of natural law has been conspicuously absent from American legal philosophy and judicial opinions. Professor Laurence Tribe commented that Clarence Thomas "is the first Supreme Court nominee in 50 years to maintain that natural law should be readily consulted in constitutional interpretation." Tribe, "Natural Law" and the Nominee, *The New York Times,* July 15, 1991. As Professor John Hart Ely noted "[t]he concept of [natural law] has . . . all but disappeared in American discourse." J. H. Ely, *Democracy and Distrust* 52 (1980).

32. See, *elg.*, Lochner v. New York, 198 U.S. 45 (1905).

33. *Bradwell* v. *Illinois*, 83 U.S. 130 (1872).

34. *Id.* at 141–42 (Bradley, J., concurring).

35. In addition to Thomas's writings and speeches discussed above, Thomas has disparaged those who have used natural law arguments in support of unenumerated rights, including the fundamental right to privacy. Thomas, "How to Talk About Civil Rights: Keep it Principled and Positive," keynote address celebrating the Formation of the Pacific Research Institute's Civil Rights Task Force, August 4, 1988; speech of Clarence Thomas at Harvard University Federalist Society Meeting, April 7, 1988. (This speech was prepared but apparently not delivered.)

36. Statement of Senator Patrick Leahy, *supra* n. 7.

THE NAACP POSITION ON CLARENCE THOMAS

The NAACP Announces Opposition to Judge Thomas's Nomination

The NAACP has announced that "with regret" it will oppose the nomination of Judge Clarence Thomas to the U.S. Supreme Court as a replacement for retiring Associate Justice Thurgood Marshall.

The announcement was made in Washington, D.C., on July 31st, following a special meeting of the NAACP National Board of Directors. It was based on an extensive background report prepared by the NAACP's Washington Bureau, and the details of a private meeting between Judge Thomas and several members of the NAACP board and staff.

Earlier, at its annual convention in Houston, the NAACP had announced on July 8th that it would delay reaching a decision on Judge Thomas, an African-American, until after the report had been prepared and a meeting sought with the nominee.

"Both of these steps have now been accomplished . . . it was the judgment of the board to oppose the confirmation of Judge Clarence Thomas to the United States Supreme Court. We have concluded that Judge Thomas's confirmation would be inimical to the best interests of African Americans," the NAACP stated.

With a vote of 49–1 opposing the nomination, Dr. William F. Gibson, Chairman of the Board, presented the Association's position in a statement read before a packed press conference, thus ending weeks of speculating on how the NAACP would deal with the nomination. In the statement, Dr. Gibson said:

> The nomination of Judge Clarence Thomas . . . brought with it a special set of problems related to his record in several government positions—most notably as Chairman of the Equal Employment Opportunity Commission, and his reactionary philosophical approach to a number of critical issues, not the least of which is affirmative action. . . .
>
> Mr. Thomas is an African-American and that fact was not ignored in our deliberations. While we feel strongly the seat should go to an African-American, we looked beyond that factor and focused our attention on whether Judge Clarence Thomas, based on the criteria we have described, should, in our opinion, sit on the Supreme Court.
>
> In the final analysis, Judge Clarence Thomas's judicial philosophy is simply inconsistent with the historical positions taken by the NAACP.

Dr. Gibson cited a number of specifics leading to the decision, including the following:

- The inconsistent views of Judge Thomas on civil rights policy make him an unpredictable element in an increasingly radically conservative court.
- While he once acknowledged the benefits of affirmative action, after his confirmation to a second term at EEOC, his position shifted so dramatically that the NAACP called for his resignation.
- While Judge Thomas's rise from poverty is to be commended, it is particularly disturbing that one who has himself benefited from affirmative action now denigrates it and would deny these opportunities to other blacks.
- While heading EEOC, he constantly complained about the laws and policies he was required to enforce, and was particularly strong in his opposition to established federal policy requiring affirmative action remedies.
- During his tenure at EEOC, the agency failed to process over 13,000 age discrimination cases.

• As Assistant Secretary for Civil Rights at the Department of Education, he did little to further the cause of higher education for African-Americans and failed to implement provisions that would have funneled millions of dollars into the historically black colleges.

The statement concludes:

"We were very troubled by having to confront the possible opposition of Judge Clarence Thomas. We believe the importance of an African-American as a replacement for Judge Thurgood Marshall should not be underestimated.

"Diversity on the Supreme Court is absolutely essential and failure to confirm another African-American sends a dreadful signal to our community about where we stand in the body politic.

"It is, therefore, with regret that we are compelled to oppose the confirmation of Judge Thomas. The NAACP and the black community must and will continue to fight until an appropriate replacement who embodies the view of the majority of black Americans is nominated and confirmed."

August 7, 1991

In the Matter of Clarence Thomas

Benjamin L. Hooks

Neither joy nor haste characterized the decision of the NAACP National Board of Directors to urge the Senate to reject the nomination of Judge Clarence Thomas as an Associate Justice of the Supreme Court of the United States.

The decision to oppose Judge Thomas's nomination to succeed Justice Thurgood Marshall came after mature and agonizing deliberation by the NAACP Board, which acted after receiving an exhaustive report on Judge Thomas's philosophical and legal views as reflected in speeches and writings. Judge Thomas's nomination to the High Court is but the second occasion in the nation's history of an African American having been chosen for such a post.

In 1967, when the nominee was Justice Marshall, the NAACP, cognizant of his outstanding record and achievements as the Association's Special Counsel, as a Judge of the United States Circuit Court of Appeals for the Second Circuit, and as Solicitor General of the United States, was able to give an enthusiastic and unqualified endorsement to the Marshall confirmation.

Upon Justice Marshall's announcement of his intention to retire, we urged the President to name a well-qualified African-American as his successor. We believe that there is great value in having diversity on the Court.

The President chose Judge Thomas, a member of the bench of the Circuit Court of Appeals for the District of Columbia. Judge Thomas, who was appointed to the Court of Appeals by President Bush, previously held appointments in the Administration of President Ronald Reagan, serving as an Assistant Secretary of Education for Civil Rights, and as Chairman of the Equal Employment Opportunity Commission.

Clarence Thomas's judicial career is of such limited duration as to offer little guidance as to how he might perform as a member of the high tribunal. We must look to his work in the Reagan Administration and to his writings and speeches for clues. Unfortunately, there is little in his record to offer hope and comfort to the devotees of civil rights.

We have found Judge Thomas to hold inconsistent views on civil rights policies. We are not willing to risk his going on the Court as a member of the increasingly radically conservative right.

In his first term as Chair of the EEOC, Judge Thomas appeared to acknowledge the benefits of traditional affirmative action remedies, including goals and timetables.

After his confirmation for a second term, there was a dramatic shift in his position. Indeed, the NAACP found his position so hostile to the interests of black Americans that we called for his resignation.

During his tenure at the EEOC, Judge Thomas complained repeatedly about the laws and policies that he was required to enforce. He was particularly forceful in opposing established federal policy on affirmative action remedies.

Thousands of complaints languished in the files of the EEOC, including approximately 13,000 complaints of age discrimination. Eventually, Congress was forced to pass special legislation to restore workers' rights.

Judge Thomas has been intemperately critical of civil rights leaders, having said they "bitch, whine and moan."

The story of Judge Thomas's rise from the poverty of his youth to his present eminence is captivating and inspiring. His homilies on self-help are well taken. Judge Thomas is not, however, alone in holding such a view.

The values and virtues of discipline, restraint, hard work and diligent study are commonly held and honored in the black community. Judge Thomas is but one of a number of black Americans who have risen from adverse early circumstances.

His story, while impressive, is not more impressive than is that of Jesse Jackson or John H. Johnson. It is not more impressive than that of the late Roy Wilkins, whose mother died when he was four years of age, who was raised by an aunt and uncle, and who earned money for his college education by working in a packing house and as a waiter on a dining car. That was how bright black boys paid for their education in Wilkins's day, before liberal whites created scholarships for promising black students—as was done for Clarence Thomas at Holy Cross College.

Judge Thomas has worked hard to achieve his present professional and social standing. He has had, however, help along the way, from the nuns who educated him; from Holy Cross, which set out to enroll promising black students, and from Yale University, where he studied law, having been admitted under affirmative action policies.

Yet, despite having so benefited, Judge Thomas denigrates affirmative action and would withhold its benefits from others. How much better it would be if Judge Thomas would take the view of General Colin Powell, who acknowledged in his speech accepting the NAACP's Spingarn Award that he had climbed on the backs of others.

We have no basic quarrel with Judge Thomas's devotion to self-reliance and self-help. Indeed, we share it. What is overlooked in the emphasis on self-reliance is any concern for what government and other sectors of society ought to do to alleviate many problems in the minority community. It is not wrong to point to the historical record of abuse and denial of minority rights and concerns—and to demand redress.

The issues in the confirmation battle are larger than the personal fate of Judge Thomas. The issues are larger than the important question of an African-American on the High Court.

We believe that Judge Thomas is part of the announced intention of the Reagan-Bush political establishment to "pack" the Supreme Court—indeed, the federal judiciary—with persons sympathetic to the political and social views of the far right.

We earnestly desire the appointment of an African-American to the supreme bench. But if there is reason to believe the African-American nominee would join in the further and continued erosion of threatened civil rights gains, we don't need that appointee.

We hear it said that if Judge Thomas is rejected, President Bush is likely to appoint a person, perhaps a Hispanic, who would be equally as conservative if not more so.

That is a bridge to be crossed when it is reached. We are quite prepared to fight and to keep on fighting—until hell freezes over, as I once said—to prevent the confirmation of any person hostile to our interests.

We think Carl Rowan has put it well: Do not take arsenic today because you may be confronted with strychnine tomorrow.

August 21, 1991

Questions and Answers on the NAACP's Position on Judge Clarence Thomas

Prepared by the NAACP

Q. *Why is the National Association for the Advancement of Colored People opposing an African-American nominee for the Supreme Court?*

A. The NAACP looked beyond the matter of race and into Judge Clarence Thomas's extensive background, as spelled out in his official actions in several governmental posts, his statements and his writings. In addition, several members of the NAACP national board and staff met with Judge Thomas to explore his views in depth.

On the basis of this, the National Board of Directors of the NAACP reluctantly concluded that Judge Thomas's confirmation would not be in the best interest of African-Americans and should be opposed.

Q. How do you reconcile your opposition to the fact that Judge Thomas is an African-American, and only the second one to be nominated to the Court?

A. In our judgment, Judge Thomas represents such a reactionary approach to the law that despite our eagerness to have an African-American on the court, the negative aspects of his views are much greater than the positive aspect of his race.

Q. Are you holding Judge Thomas to some higher standard than you would apply to a white nominee?

A. No. The same standards apply. Had the nominee been anyone else, with the record of Judge Thomas, we would have opposed confirmation.

Q. If the Thomas nomination is defeated, can you reasonably expect that President Bush will nominate an African-American? If he fails to do so, will this not be a step backward?

A. We recognize this as a real possibility. However, not to oppose this particular nomination would require that we close our eyes to Judge Thomas's record and abandon our long standing principle of placing the welfare of the many above any individual interest.

We have consistently urged that an African-American be nominated to replace Justice Thurgood Marshall. This would insure a diversity on the Court that for most of its more than 200 years of existence has been restricted to white males.

Q. Why did the NAACP decide to oppose the confirmation of Judge Thomas?

A. This was not a decision reached in haste, or without considering every possible parameter. At our annual convention in July, we consciously reserved our decision pending the completion of our study into Judge Thomas's record and a personal meeting with him.

What emerged from the process was a disturbing pattern of insensitivity toward a number of critical areas affecting African-Americans; and the total embracing of a philosophy that argues all individuals are capable of lifting themselves up by their bootstraps, even when there are no bootstraps available.

Q. What are some of your principle reservations about Judge Thomas?

1. Judge Thomas's inconsistent views on civil rights policy make him an unpredictable element on an increasingly radically conservative court.

2. Prior to 1986, Judge Thomas's comments and writings acknowledged the benefits of traditional affirmative action remedies, including goals and timetables. After his confirmation for a second term at EEOC, his position on affirmative action shifted dramatically. This position was so hostile against the best interest of black people that the NAACP called for Judge Thomas's resignation at that time.

3. While we appreciate the fact that Judge Thomas came up in the school of hard knocks and pulled himself up by his own bootstraps—as many other black Americans have—our concern is for the millions of blacks who have no access to bootstraps, theirs or others'. It is particularly disturbing that one who has himself so benefited from affirmative action now denigrates it and would deny these opportunities to other blacks.

4. While heading EEOC, Judge Thomas consistently complained

about the laws and policies he was required to enforce. He was particularly strong in his opposition to established federal policy requiring affirmative action remedies. The results of this caused economic hardships on thousands of black Americans whose complaints went unaddressed.

5. Also during Judge Thomas's tenure at EEOC, the agency failed to process over 13,000 age-discrimination complaints on behalf of older workers under the Age Discrimination in Employment Act. Ultimately, this failure to act required Congress to intervene by passing special legislation to restore the rights of the workers, black and white, under the Act.

6. When Judge Thomas was Assistant Secretary for Civil Rights at the Department of Education from May 1981 until May 1982, he did little to further the cause of higher education for African-Americans and he failed to implement provisions that would have funneled millions of dollars into the historically black colleges. In sworn testimony in a federal contempt of court proceeding, Judge Thomas conceded his failure to implement the order. This had a devastating effect on the educational opportunities for young blacks.

Q. Are there any examples of Judge Thomas's views, as expressed in his own words, that specifically concern the NAACP?

A. There are many. Judge Thomas has repeatedly expressed his views through public statements, interviews, articles and testimony. A sampling follows:

Observed that a Supreme Court decision endorsing voluntary affirmative action plans was an "egregious example" of the "creative interpretation" of federal civil rights law.

On quotas, he said: "Federal enforcement agencies . . . turned the statutes on their heads by requiring discrimination in the form of hiring and promotion quotas, so-called goals and timetables."

On affirmative action, he referred to it as "social engineering . . . We're standing the principle of nondiscrimination on its head."

August 21, 1991

The NAACP Judged Thomas by His Character, Not by the Color of His Skin

Julian Bond

The NAACP's decisive vote to oppose the nomination of Clarence Thomas to the United States Supreme Court surprised many who thought the organization's decision would be influenced by Thomas's race. If confirmed, he would be the second black justice in Supreme Court history, replacing civil rights champion Thurgood Marshall.

But the NAACP's deliberations, which led to Thomas's rejection, were exactly what Thomas himself would have wanted.

One constant theme in Clarence Thomas's life has been his insistence on avoiding any special treatment because of his race.

He relaxed that important principle once when he accepted admission through an affirmative action program to Yale's law school.

But, from his earliest years, forty-three-year-old Clarence Thomas has been a crusader against being pigeonholed ideologically or professionally because he is black.

When he left law school, Thomas accepted a position on the staff of Missouri Attorney General John Danforth with the stipulation that he would not be assigned to civil rights work.

He accepted a brief stay in the law department of a large corporation with the same demand—no civil rights work for Clarence Thomas.

"If I ever went to work for the EEOC or did anything connected with blacks," Thomas told an interviewer, "my career would be irreparably ruined. The monkey would be on my back again to prove that I didn't have the job because I am black. People meeting me for the first time would automatically dismiss my thinking as second-rate."

It was surprising then when, after successfully avoiding the suggestion that his race should dictate his professional interests, and with no previous experience in civil rights, Thomas took a job as civil rights enforcer in the Department of Education in the first Reagan Administration. A year later he became chairman of the EEOC.

But even as Assistant Secretary for Civil Rights, Thomas's actions demonstrated that fighting racial discrimination was the least of his concerns.

In a federal district court case in 1982, Thomas testified that he deliberately disobeyed a court order requiring the Department of Education to conduct speedy reviews of discrimination complaints.

And at the Equal Employment Opportunity Commission, where Thomas was named Chair in 1982, he continued his policy of disobeying court orders. He reduced the number of settled cases and brought the discrimination complaint process to a slow crawl.

Before Thomas took office, 43 percent of complaints to the EEOC resulted in a settlement. The average benefit to complainants was at least $4,600. Within months after Thomas took over, the number of settled cases dropped to only one-third, and the average benefit was reduced to $2,589. The length of time to process individual charges had increased from five months to nine months—almost twice as long as the year before.

A study by the General Accounting Office found that under Thomas's direction a large percentage of the cases closed by the EEOC had not been fully investigated.

A Congressional investigation found that the Agency changed its method of operations to make it more difficult for the victims of discrimination to win relief.

Finally, while Thomas was EEOC Chair, the Agency failed to process 13,873 age discrimination complaints filed by older workers within the legal time period. As a result, the claims were dismissed, leaving the workers powerless to pursue their complaints. Congress had to pass legislation reinstating their claims.

Throughout his career, Thomas has tried to avoid being labeled because of his race. He has asked the world to judge him, like Martin Luther King, not on the basis of the color of his skin, but on the content of his character.

The NAACP gave Thomas what he wanted. On the basis of his record, the nation's oldest and largest civil rights organization voted to oppose Clarence Thomas's nomination to the Supreme Court.

Thomas's supporters had argued that he represented Black America's only chance to keep a black judge in Thurgood Marshall's seat.

"That's not our job," an NAACP member said. "George Bush can nominate another black candidate if Clarence Thomas loses. He nominated another white man after the Senate rejected Robert Bork. He can nominate another black to take Thomas's place."

August 23, 1991

Statement by Dr. Benjamin L. Hooks, Executive Director

Now that the Senate has voted to confirm Judge Thomas as an Associate Justice of the Supreme Court, the NAACP expresses the hope that the weight and consciousness of his new responsibilities will lead him to revisit his views on a number of important issues.

Our opposition to the nomination is well known and was made public in late July and was based solely on Judge Thomas's public record.

The raising of questions about his personal conduct by Professor Anita Hill did not involve the NAACP. However, once raised, our position was that in fairness to both Judge Thomas and Professor Hill, the charges should be addressed by the Judiciary Committee.

Those hearings produced much heat and very little light. This was an imperfect process that might have been avoided had the Committee dealt with the charges earlier on, and in a different forum.

Our searching analysis of the long paper trail of Judge Thomas convinced us we could not support an individual who, by words and deed, had so strongly indicated an aversion to the basic principles of fair play and equity espoused for so long by the NAACP.

We found several "smoking guns."

1. His apathy toward affirmative action for others, while he is a direct beneficiary.

2. His opposition to class actions as a way of correcting inequities and his preference for individual actions. Under his philosophy, the gain African Americans have made in moving into positions previously denied them would not have been possible.

3. His failure to stand up to the attempts to the Reagan Administration to demolish Executive Order 11246 mandating affirmative action on the part of government contractors. That the order survived was not because of him, but in spite of him.

4. His failed record as Assistant Secretary for Civil Rights at the Department of Education and as Chair of the Equal Employment Opportunity Commission which made it patently clear that his incon-

sistent views on civil rights would make him an unpredictable element on an increasingly radically conservative court.

Like so many of our fellow Americans, we are impressed with Judge Thomas's odyssey from poverty to prominence. At the same time, we are ever mindful that Judge Thomas is not unique in his accomplishments—his story is a common occurrence in the black community.

Once seated on the High Court, we hope Justice Thomas will recall the people and the community that nurtured him, that he will recall his own struggle to overcome poverty and racism and, in so doing, will exhibit a sensitivity and understanding he has not previously shown for the poor and the powerless.

October 15, 1991

THE SCLC POSITION: CONFIRM CLARENCE THOMAS

Rev. Joseph E. Lowery

In my opinion, Clarence Thomas should be confirmed. While I share concerns of many of my associates in the civil rights and religious communities, I am thoroughly convinced that the long view perspective compels us to support Thomas's confirmation. A realistic and careful study of the whole picture clearly indicates that Clarence Thomas represents our best (probably only) hope for a sensitive independent voice on the Supreme Court for a long, long time to come.

To be sure, I deplore the fact that President Bush's campaign used Willie Horton to turn whites against Blacks and the nomination of Clarence Thomas is probably designed to turn us against each other within the African-American community. A rejection of Clarence Thomas by the Senate would play into the hands of such manipulative methodology. The basic question for us, it seems to me, is how do we work to maximize the possibility of a sensitive, independent voice on the Court?

I do not believe that Clarence Thomas will sit in the ideological corner some have prescribed for him, nor will he march robotically to the beat of the right-wing drum corps. That's why right-wingers launched a vicious attack on Democrat members of the Judiciary Committee . . . hoping to invoke their wrath against Thomas . . . then hoping they could persuade the President to appoint a real right-winger of their liking!

They realize, as I do now, that Clarence Thomas, the judge, is not the Clarence Thomas of earlier date and that "it doth not yet appear what he shall be." That was clear when several of us met with him following his nomination. We all sensed that his brief but meaningful experience as a judge had stimulated growth and cleared his perspective on justice, fairness and his role as a Black American who had come out of the jungle of racist oppression and poverty. Free from administrative response to Reagan policies, was the real Clarence Thomas emerging? At the close of the meeting, we urged him to let the emerging Clarence Thomas be heard during the Senate hearings. He did just that! Senator Heflin (R. AL) commented that Thomas may very well be a "closet" liberal! The distinguished dean of the law school of Yale University in his testimony supporting Thomas—advised the committee that he saw great potential in Judge Thomas for a sensitive voice for justice on the Court. Chairman Biden called Dean Calebresi's testimony the "most compelling."

I urge thoughtful advocates of justice to take the long view. It's no time to listen to short views and knee jerk reactions of would-be militants and purists who want to "prove" something about how balanced and impartial they are when they can oppose a man regardless of his color or race. The truth of the matter is that some of them have never actually opposed any nominee until a Black person was named! Hasn't it always been easier to beat up on Black folks . . . ? Many of those now leading the assault on Thomas were noticeably silent when the archconservatives now on the Court were being confirmed. As a matter of fact, some of the women's leadership (for whom I have great respect) now vehemently opposed to Thomas because he won't commit himself on abortion . . . supported, yes, supported the woman now on the court even though she defiantly advised them that she opposed abortion, period! Isn't that a double standard? How can *we* urge the Senate to now vote *against* Thomas because he appears on some issues to be right of center when they voted *for* Scalia, and others who are indisputably *far* right of center? . . . and where were these aggressive voices when these opponents of civil rights were being confirmed? How can we urge a vote against Thomas because he didn't give clear direct answers to some questions when the Senate approved Scalia and others who refused to answer all questions? Are we supporting double standards?

I would like to respectfully ask those who are so fair and pure that they can oppose a Black person without any problem do they also oppose race conscious remedies to eliminate racial inequities or achieve affirmative action goals?

I support Judge Thomas's nomination—not solely because he is Black—but because being Black has subjected him to the "Black experience" that will help him continue to grow more and more sensitive to the responsibility of the Supreme Court to insure justice for all. I have sensed that growth when I read that he said no matter how far you go or high you rise . . . you can't escape the trials of Blackness; I sensed that growth when he testified that he was troubled by racism and classism in the administration of the death penalty; I sensed that growth when I heard him testify that he believed that the Constitution respected rights of privacy for married and non-married persons!

Our choice is not between Clarence Thomas and some proven, sensitive judge that we would name. The choice is between Clarence Thomas—our best hope—and someone from the ranks of the right like those already there who gave us the second Dred Scott decision when they admitted there was racial discrimination in administration of the death penalty but that it need not be taken into account! I choose Clarence Thomas before them, everyday!

Furthermore and finally, our reliance has always been more on the Supreme Being than the Supreme Court. Let's get this matter behind us and direct our energies toward a collapsing economy that is crashing down on those already on the bottom.

Let's call our people back from the far country where legitimate need has driven many to illegitimate greed. Let's direct our energies toward driving drugs out of our community and ushering economic alternatives into the community. Let's direct our energies toward the democratization of capitalism, the elimination of poverty, the achievement of full employment with adequate wages, affordable health care, decent housing and quality education. Let's come together in a new and vigorous movement to let justice roll down as waters and call the nation home to a new birth of justice and spirituality!

REVEREND JOSEPH E. LOWERY is president of the Southern Christian Leadership Conference (SCLC), a position he has held since 1977. SCLC was founded in 1957 by Martin Luther King, Jr., and other black ministers.

THE URBAN LEAGUE POSITION

On the Nomination of Judge Clarence Thomas

John E. Jacob

We welcome the appointment of an African American jurist to fill the vacant seat left by Justice Marshall.

Obviously, Judge Thomas is no Justice Marshall. But if he were, this Administration would not have appointed him.

We are hopeful that Judge Thomas's background of poverty and minority status will lead him to greater identification with those in America who today are victimized by poverty and discrimination. And we expect the Senate, in its confirmation hearings, to fully explore whether he is indeed likely to do so.

July 1, 1991

Clarence Thomas: Affirmative Actions and Merit*

John E. Jacob

The consensus on civil rights has been replaced by racial fears and stereotypes. The consensus against discrimination has been replaced by winking at it and hoping the issue will disappear.

It won't. That's why Congress has to pass a civil rights bill that effectively reverses Supreme Court decisions that encourage job discrimination.

Those decisions—and others that restrict basic civil liberties and limit constitutional rights—tell us that the Supreme Court no longer stands by our side. It is now on our back. It is removing gains of the past and building new barriers to our future.

While I am gratified that the President has nominated an African American to the seat held by Justice Marshall, it is clear that Clarence Thomas is no Thurgood Marshall.

I share the alarm caused by the addition of yet another Justice likely to overturn *Roe* v. *Wade* and affirmative action rulings.

But I would hope that Judge Thomas's life experiences will lead him to closer identification with those in America who are today victimized by poverty and discrimination.

And I would hope that he sees the irony in opposing affirmative action while at the same time being an affirmative action appointee.

Yes, he has the qualifications for the job of Supreme Court justice. So do literally hundreds of other people.

But there are only nine positions—and only one was vacant. So additional criteria were applied—criteria like racial and ethnic diversity . . . life experiences . . . experience in government . . . and political considerations.

**This passage was extracted from Mr. Jacob's keynote address to the National Urban League Annual Conference, Atlanta, Georgia, July 21, 1991.*

Judge Thomas's nomination should tell the Administration, and Judge Thomas himself, that affirmative action and merit are not mutually exclusive.

Without affirmative action, merit will always be equated with whiteness. And without strong anti-discrimination laws, African Americans, women, and other minorities will continue to be economically vulnerable.

That is why we so strongly urge the Senate to pass a strong civil rights bill, and why we urge the President to sign it.

Statement On the Confirmation of Judge Clarence Thomas

John E. Jacob

We congratulate Clarence Thomas on his confirmation as an Associate Justice of the U.S. Supreme Court.

We neither supported nor opposed his nomination, believing that his public positions on issues of concern to us were questionable, but also believing that as an African American who has suffered from poverty and from America's racial inequities, he might bring a fresh viewpoint to this Court.

All along, our concern was that he might simply add yet another ultra-conservative vote to those of a Court majority disdainful of civil rights. But now, having weathered the agony of nationally televised hearings that damaged his reputation and questioned his integrity, we are hopeful that Justice Thomas's service on the Court will reflect some hard-won lessons about the nature of racism, the invasion of privacy, and the rights of individuals.

The bitterness of those hearings exposed the fault lines of a society that routinely practices discrimination and ignores the rights of women and minorities. They demonstrated the explosive nature of society's racial divisions in a way that should serve as a warning to politicians of both parties who may be tempted to further manipulate racial issues in the upcoming presidential campaign.

Justice Thomas is right when he says that this is now a "time for healing" and we urge the President to begin the healing process by withdrawing his objections to passage of a strong civil rights act, and to order his political advisors to keep race out of the campaign.

October 16, 1991

JOHN E. JACOB is president and chief executive officer of the National Urban League, Inc.

Poetic Justice Thomas

—D. L. Crockett-Smith

Marshall steps down, and Love Child
auditions for the Supremes.
Don't you know what's going on?

A White House black man, civil,
right, black justice for black times:
who is this doubtful Thomas?

He licks out his grandpa's tongue.
Judge gets high on civil rights.
Let a bitch bark, Judge gets down.

Reborn, he tries his jury.
He shakes his prickly pinpoint
crown, bloody in their faces.

Bleeding, the women's bodies.
How these Pilates wash their hands.
Boss Bush cries: "Here come d Judge!"

African American Women
In Defense of Ourselves

As women of African descent, we are deeply troubled by the recent nomination, confirmation and seating of Clarence Thomas as an Associate Justice of the U.S. Supreme Court. We know that the presence of Clarence Thomas on the Court will be continually used to divert attention from historic struggles for social justice through suggestions that the presence of a Black man on the Supreme Court constitutes an assurance that the rights of African Americans will be protected. Clarence Thomas' public record is ample evidence this will not be true. Further, the consolidation of a conservative majority on the Supreme Court seriously endangers the rights of all women, poor and working class people and the elderly. The seating of Clarence Thomas is an affront not only to African American women and men, but to all people concerned with social justice.

We are particularly outraged by the racist and sexist treatment of Professor Anita Hill, an African American woman who was maligned and castigated for daring to speak publicly of her own experience of sexual abuse. The malicious defamation of Professor Hill insulted all women of African descent and sent a dangerous message to any woman who might contemplate a sexual harassment complaint.

We speak here because we recognize that the media are now portraying the Black community as prepared to tolerate both the dismantling of affirmative action and the evil of sexual harassment in order to have any Black man on the Supreme Court. We want to make clear that the media have ignored or distorted many African American voices. We will not be silenced.

Many have erroneously portrayed the allegations against Clarence Thomas as an issue of either gender or race. As women of African descent, we understand sexual harassment as both. We further understand that Clarence Thomas outrageously manipulated the legacy of lynching in order to shelter himself from Anita Hill's allegations. To deflect attention away from the reality of sexual abuse in African American women's lives, he trivialized and misrepresented this painful part of African American people's history. This country, which has a long legacy of racism and sexism, has never taken the sexual abuse of Black women seriously. Throughout U.S. history Black women have been sexually stereotyped as immoral, insatiable, perverse; the initiators in all sexual contacts—abusive or otherwise. The common assumption in legal proceedings as well as in the larger society has been that Black women cannot be raped or otherwise sexually abused. As Anita Hill's experience demonstrates, Black women who speak of these matters are not likely to be believed.

In 1991, we cannot tolerate this type of dismissal of any one Black woman's experience or this attack upon our collective character without protest, outrage, and resistance.

As women of African descent, we express our vehement opposition to the policies represented by the placement of Clarence Thomas on the Supreme Court. The Bush administration, having obstructed the passage of civil rights legislation, impeded the extension of unemployment compensation, cut student aid and dismantled social welfare programs, has continually demonstrated that it is not operating in our best interests. Nor is this appointee. We pledge ourselves to continue to speak out in defense of one another, in defense of the African American community and against those who are hostile to social justice no matter what color they are. No one will speak for us but ourselves.

**The complete text of this essay with the names of all signers is available from Kitchen Table: Women of Color Press, P.O. Box 908, Lutham, NY 12110.*